Songs of the Pintupi

Richard M. Moyle

Songs of the Pintupi
Musical life in a central Australian society

**AUSTRALIAN
INSTITUTE OF
ABORIGINAL
STUDIES**

CANBERRA
1979

Published in Australia by the Australian Institute of Aboriginal
Studies
P.O. Box 553, Canberra City, ACT 2601

Sold and distributed in North and South America by
Humanities Press Inc.
171 First Avenue, Atlantic Highlands, N.J. 07716

The views expressed in this publication are those of the author
and are not necessarily those of the Australian Institute of
Aboriginal Studies

AIAS new series no. 7

National Library of Australia card number and ISBN
0 85575 086 3 (hard cover)
0 85575 087 1 (soft cover)
USA edition ISBN
0 391 00995 8 (hard cover)
0 391 00996 6 (soft cover)

Printed in Australia by Wilke and Company Limited, Clayton,
Victoria

1000 10 79

Contents

Preface

The research for this volume was carried out under a Research Fellowship from the Australian Institute of Aboriginal Studies, the two-year tenure being extended for a further nine months to cope with the sheer size of the undertaking.

From the large number of Pintupi people without whose patient co-operation the research would have been impossible, I should like to mention individually Nosepeg Tjupurrula, George Tjangala, Mikiti Tjapaltjarri and Tjungkuya Napaltjarri from Kungkayunti, and Donkeyman Luuku, Brandy Kunymangara and Muntja Nungurayi from Balgo. At Balgo, Father R. Hevern kindly gave hospitality, and Father A. R. Peile assisted with Gugadja terminology.

Dr R. A. Gould kindly allowed a copy of his recordings of initiation ceremonies, made in 1966, to be used for musical analysis, and Mrs D. M. Thomson made available copies of Donald Thomson's tapes of Pintupi singing recorded in 1957 and 1963, for comparative purposes.

Sections of the original manuscript were discussed with Alice Moyle, Grace Koch, Cynthia Shannon, Trevor Jones, Cath Ellis, Ken Hansen, Fred Myers, Noel Wallace and Dick Kimber.

To all of these, and to numerous others known only through their voices on tape, I am most grateful.

The owners of ceremonies and song series recorded at Kungkayunti and Balgo gave verbal permission (recorded on tape) for the musical material to be included in this volume. In addition, they gave written approval for a selection of non-secret songs to be included in a radio program of Pintupi music, broadcast on the Australian Broadcasting Commission's national network, in August 1976.

All the original fieldtapes and films, together with songtexts, descriptions of ceremonies and other supportive documentation, have been lodged in the AIAS Resource Centre with appropriate restrictions governing access and use according to the wishes of the owners and performers.

Orthography

Musical orthography

Intervals

Minor intervals are prefixed with a lower case m, thus m2 = minor 2nd; major intervals are prefixed with an upper case M, thus M6 = Major 6th. Perfect 4ths and 5ths are indicated as P4 and P5 respectively.

Pitch

Specific pitches are referred to using the system of upper and lower case letters, and primes, thus:

Example 1   Pitch identification chart.

Accentuation

In the *ngalungku* series, vocal accents feature prominently, and individual notes thus treated are indicated by the sign >.

Intensity changes

Such changes occur only in the *ngalungku* series, and are indicated by the signs ⟨ and ⟩ .

Accidentals

Accidentals at the start of each stave, in the manner of a key signature, are in descending order, and apply only to those single pitches (i.e. not to octave duplications). In the transcriptions, an accidental over a note applies only to that note, whereas an accidental placed before a note continues to apply to that pitch until indicated otherwise. Slight sharpening and flattening are indicated by the signs ⫪ and ⃓ respectively, in the same manner as for normal accidental signs.

Transpositions

In order to facilitate comparison of the individual songs, the transcriptions have been transposed so that their tonics are identical, and an overall pitch selected which reduced accidentals to a minimum. Above the stave, at the start of each song, the pitch of the original is given, the figures referring to semitones, e.g. +3 indicates the original was 3 semitones higher, and −5 indicates the original was 5 semitones lower.

Abbreviations

In the transcriptions, the type of musical accompaniment is written in abbreviated form, thus:

bcl   pairs of boomerangs
sts   two sticks beaten together
hcl   handclapping
st/g   single sticks beaten on the ground

Notation

To facilitate reading, instrumental notation is used throughout this work. In cases where rhythmic grouping is clear, consecutive notes with a duration of a quaver or less are grouped together, thus

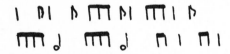

Example 2   Method of indicating rhythmic grouping.

Heterophony

Where the singers are approximately evenly divided between two simultaneously sounded notes, the two noteheads are of the same size; but where a single individual breaks away from the rest of the group, his/her part is indicated in notes with smaller heads. Where possible, heterophony continuing for several consecutive notes is written with stems up and down to differentiate the parts, thus

Underpinning

Underpinning of the text is not maintained for the duration of each song, to avoid cluttering the transcription; instead, from the first complete word sung, only the first whole wordgroup (a group of words repeated several times in the course of a song) is presented, and for reasons of economy of space, the words are not syllabified in full page presentations. In transcriptions of individual songs, each section of the wordgroup is placed in vertical alignment to facilitate reading, the sections separated by bar lines. Likewise, accompaniment patterns are not indicated for the whole of each song; only the point of commencement is given, together with sufficient repetitions to establish the rhythm. Any changes to the accompaniment rhythm are indicated at the points of change.

Pitch uncertainty

Notes appearing within parentheses are of uncertain pitch in the original recordings. In the *ngalungku* series, the periods of strong accentuation are delivered in a style approximating controlled shouting, and although general contours are followed in each song, precise pitches are lacking; in such cases, only note stems appear in the transcriptions. Where the final note in any song is of uncertain pitch and duration this note is written ⌇.

Glissands

In these same parts of the *ngalungku* series, vocal glissands occur; these are indicated by straight lines between notes whose pitch can be approximated. In other series, glissands may occur between notes of greater pitch certainty. The period of the glissand may be taken as starting from the note where the straight line begins, and continuing for the duration of the same note. Elsewhere, a pitch from which a falling glissand occurs may be followed by a note of higher pitch, e.g.

In such cases, the terminal point of the glissand is considered to be in the area of the end of the straight line.

Tempo

Purely to give the reader an idea of the speed of the songs in the published sample, each contains a metronome figure at the head of the transcription. However, for the purpose of analysing the tempi in the whole of the transcribed sample, the more objective system devised by Kolinski (1959) has been used in the Conclusions section of this volume.

Linguistic orthography

Palatals are represented as
tj (as in the English *ch*urch and *Ge*orge)
ny (as in the English ca*ny*on)
ly (as in the English mi*lli*on)
y (as in the English *y*es)

Retroflexes, with the exception of r, are represented by underlining the letter, e.g. *ma_lu*, Tjapanga_ti. There is no English equivalent, but the tip of the tongue is further back than for the non-retroflexed sounds. The velar nasal is represented as ng (as in the English si*ng*ing, but not as in fi*ng*er, where the ng is represented as ngk). The trilled r is represented as rr. The p is sounded as in the English *p*it or *b*it, the k as in *k*ing or *g*ong, the t as in *t*ick or *D*ick.
Vowels: the a is sounded as in the English *a*fter, the i as in *e*qual, and the u as in b*oo*t.

Illustrative material

The illustrative material in this work is both copious and varied. Diagrammatic and map work appears as Figures, halftone photographs are incorporated as Plates, all types of musical material in notational form over one stave in depth are called Examples, and the full page transcriptions of songs from the various song series are labelled as Musical notations.

Introduction

Who are the Pintupi? And where is their traditional territory? Two questions that are fundamental indeed to even the most generalised study of the people, and yet questions for which no unequivocal answers are currently available. The names of those who, at some time or other, have provided information on these matters reads like a miniature *Who's Who* of Australian Aboriginal anthropology and include Abbie, Berndt, Birdsell, Long, Strehlow, Thomson, and Tindale—and thus it is all the more surprising that much of their data should not be in agreement. In this present study, no attempt is made to provide a definitive answer to either question, although the earlier published information is summarised.

Who are the Pintupi?

While not agreeing about the spelling of the name, linguists appear to agree that the word Pintupi refers to a group of people who speak a dialect (of the same name) classified by O'Grady, Voegelin and Voegelin (1966:39) as belonging to the Wati subgroup of the southwest group of the Pama-Nyungan family. Tindale (1974:138-39, 235) considers the name a tribal one, also on the basis of language.

Long (1962:1) on the other hand, observed two distinct dialects spoken among the Pintupi living at Papunya:

> A southern group from the sandhill country west of Lake Macdonald across towards Mt Rennie and Ilbili and south towards Lake Hopkins is sometimes called WINANBA. Many of the earlier 'Pintupi' migrants . . . speak (spoke) this dialect. . . . The groups seen on the 1957 Lake Mackay patrol and subsequently who are now mainly at Yuendumu belong to the PINTUPI groups and were then living out of their 'Tribal country'. The northern neighbours of the Pintupi . . . are said to have gone, with many of the Pintupi, to Balgo Hills Mission. (There they are apparently all collectively known as KUKATA.)

Tindale (1974:235) offers a contrasting view:

> The Wenamba or Wenamba [sic] Pintubi who live to the south are given the status of another tribe since they regard themselves as a distinct people and say they speak a different dialect. . . . The northwestern hordes of the true Pintubi call themselves Kolo . . .

Hansen and Hansen (1969:133) also refer to minor speech variation, but claim it as the result of nomadic life in small family units, 'for this reason, small speech differences have developed from family to family'. Later, they note

> From a linguistic point of view Mayutjarra spoken east of Lakes Mackay and Hopkins can generally be termed Eastern Pintupi. There are a number of vocabulary differences between Mayutjarra and other Pintupi dialects, but very little grammatical differences.
>
> Speakers of the Western dialect of Pintupi are sometimes called *Mulyati Ngurrara.* (Those belonging to the *Mulyati* spear country.) Many of these people now live at Yayayi and at Balgo Mission. They are often referred to as the 'real Pintupi' by other Aborigines at Papunya. This is the dialect which is described in this grammar.
>
> South Pintupi dialect speakers were situated closer to Warburton Ranges but had much social contact with the Western dialect group. South Pintupi dialect speakers are now living at Yayayi, Warburton Ranges and Docker River.
>
> North Pintupi dialect speakers are sometimes called *Kanti Wangkatjarra.* They had a lot of social interaction with the Western dialect group. Many of these people live at Balgo Mission, Yuendumu and Yayayi. The above-mentioned dialects of Pintupi are mutually intelligible with no major grammatical differences. Some vocabulary differences exist, but these are minimal.
>
> The dialect of the Kukatja people at Balgo comes from both Western and Northern dialects of Pintupi. (1978:25)

In areas where Pintupi speakers are in a minority, the term is often used now to refer in a derogatory sense to individuals considered less sophisticated than the others, or who deviate peculiarly from some stated standard.[1] Among the Pintupi themselves, such individuals are sometimes called by the English 'wild Pintupi'.

Numerous written variations of the name appear in print, Tindale (1974:235) alone listing fifteen; in addition, there are the names used by non-Pintupi speakers when referring to these people, a few of which incorporate the base *pintu*, but most of which do not; Tindale lists seventeen of these. The name itself stems from *pintu*, meaning foreskin, and possibly derives from the practice of newly circumcised initiates being required to eat their own foreskins, a tradition apparently unique to the area. In this present work, the form Pintupi is used, and orthography follows that of Hansen and Hansen (1974). For the purposes of this present work, Pintupi music is defined as that body of material which the people who call themselves Pintupi sing, and which they acknowledge as belonging to them.

Where is Pintupi traditional territory?

Those who have published material on this matter may be divided broadly into linguists, and others, these 'others' including social anthropologists, explorers, journalists, and a wide variety of academics. Some of the information is in the form of boundaries expressed in both verbal description and maps, while other writers give individual locations where the Pintupi were found, or say they once lived. Tindale (1974) and the Oates (1970) have maps outlining Pintupi territory, although all include dotted lines indicating uncertainty, which is further emphasised in subsequent verbal descriptions (Tindale 1974: 235; Oates 1975, I:123). Maps of a less specific nature, in which the name Pintupi appears but without localisation beyond that of the general position of the name, are found in Abbie (1958:29) and Berndt (1959:87, 88; 1974: Fascicle One).

There are numerous accounts of people writing, mostly from firsthand experience, of isolated groups of Pintupi. By piecing these together, and by referring back to those portions of the maps where the boundaries are considered more precise, it is possible to draw up an outline of the area claimed to be traditional territory.[2] This is bounded on the north by Lake Hazlett; on the east by Mt Stanley, the

---

1. Rose (1965:175) observes, for example, that Angas Downs people said he was hitting the ground 'like a Pintupi' when he had difficulty keeping time during the singing of a *malu* series.
2. Using information from a selection of such sources, including Thomson (1962:Fig. 2; 1973:Frontispiece), Evans and Long (1965:Fig. 2, 324), Tindale and Lindsay (1963:Plate 70), Terry (1974:40), Strehlow (1970:108, 109), Long (1971:266), Johnson (1963:74).

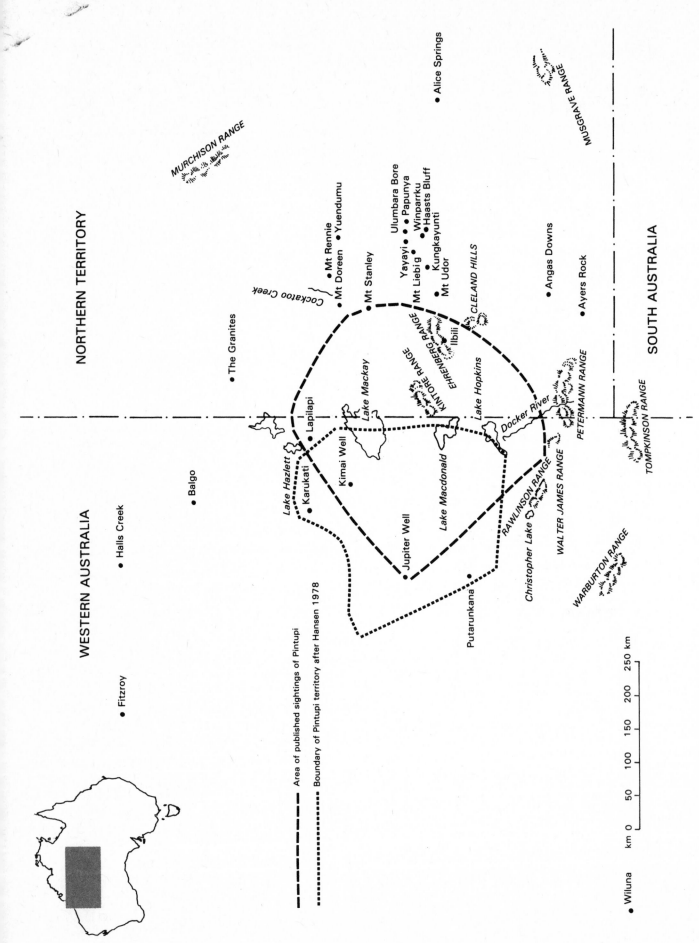

Figure 1 Estimated boundaries of traditional Pintupi territory and location of place names referred to in this book.

Ehrenberg Range and the Cleland Hills; on the south by the north side of the Petermann and Rawlinson Ranges; and on the west by Jupiter Well. The area encompassed by these points is shown on Fig. 1.

The Hansens' reconstruction of traditional pre-contact territory is also founded on personal travel (by Mark de Graaf), but differs from that above by placing the area further to the west (1978:21, see Fig. 1).

The earliest European contact with the Pintupi is not positively documented, but it may have been the explorer Giles, who observed Aborigines in the region of Mt Udor and the Ehrenberg Range in late 1872; however, Giles' guides could not make any speech communication with these people, and their identity is thus clouded. In the following year, the explorer Warburton was in the vicinity of Lake Mackay, and also made fleeting contact with the (unnamed) inhabitants. Over the next 50 years, a number of expeditions entered the Central Desert region, most of them making brief contact with Aborigines. In 1926, the MacKay expedition met a group of old men and 'sullen' boys 'about to undergo a certain initiation rite' in the Petermanns (1929:263), and four years later, contact with Aborigines was made by another expedition, led by this same man, in the Ehrenberg Range area where they had established a base camp for their aerial mapping project. In a report to the *Sydney Morning Herald* of 23 June of that year, the expedition correspondent noted, 'One of the most interesting subsidiary activities of the expedition has been a study of the Pinto and Yumo tribes of Aborigines, little-known tribes living in the Ehrenberg area.'

It seems likely that the Pinto were the Pintupi in which case this report constitutes the earliest published mention of their name.[3] The name Pinto along with early photographs of the people recurs in Clune's biography of MacKay (1942: facing p. 118).

In 1932 an expedition to Mt Liebig was organised by the Board for Anthropological Research of the University of Adelaide, and led by Norman B. Tindale. During their stay at Mt Liebig, a group of Pintupi arrived from the Mt Kintore region, and as a result, further photographs of Pintupi people were obtained.[4]

Two months later, in search of gold, Michael Terry came across a group of Pintupi further to the north and claimed discovery of the tribe as a whole (1974:40).[5]

Published references indicate a gradual move over the next 25 years by small groups of Pintupi east and north out of their traditional territory—for example, to Mt Liebig, Mt Doreen, Haasts Bluff, Yuendumu and Balgo.[6]

It was not until 1957, however, that official interest was shown specifically in the Pintupi. In that year, the first of a series of patrols was made into the area west of Papunya, to determine the numbers and condition of the Aborigines living there, with a view to planning for the future development of the Haasts Bluff Reserve and the welfare of its inhabitants. Accounts by the members of these patrols (which continued until 1964) give the first extended picture of Pintupi territory, campsites, and demography, although they contain relatively little ethnographic material.[7]

The establishment in the 1940s of a ration depot at Haasts Bluff, together with the contacts made by these patrols, resulted in numbers of Pintupi moving east to live there. In 1959, the Aboriginal population of Haasts Bluff was almost 500 (Central Reserves Committee? 1965:8), and the main settlement was transferred to Papunya, where better drinking water was available. Today, the Pintupi are established at Haasts Bluff, Papunya, Yuendumu and Balgo; in 1973, a group from Papunya moved to Yayayi, followed by a similar breakaway move to Kungkayunti a year later. There are reports from time to time, however, of sightings of small groups of Aborigines in the Gibson Desert area, from which it would appear that there are still a few people, possibly Pintupi, still living there.

On the demographic side, Birdsell (1970:118) claims a precontact population of 500, while Long

3. It is somewhat intriguing to note that in Letters to the Editor following as a result of this report, the writers (including the anthropologist A. P. Elkin, who had just completed fieldwork in the Musgrave Ranges) accept entirely the names the MacKay party give for the Aborigines, suggesting possibly that they may have already been in circulation among non-Aborigines at that time.
4. Tindale and Lindsay (1963:Plate 70) include an enlarged frame from the dance sequence of a 16 mm documentary film made by the expedition; the caption reads 'Pintupi women of Mt Kintore shuffling in a forward-moving dance in their only style of dancing'.
5. The exact date of the contact was 6 October 1932 (personal communication); there is little doubt, however, that this particular group had not seen White men before.
6. See, e.g. Abbie (1969:Figs. 2F, 2G), Thomson (1962:11, 146), Evans and Long (1965:318), Evans (1960a:21).
7. They include Long (1962, 1963a, b, c, 1964a, b, c, d, 1969, 1970), Evans and Long (1965), Evans (1960a, b) and Lockwood (1964).

(1971:264) suggests the smaller figure of 200-300, both estimates referring to the entire Pintupi territory. Post-contact population figures, however, relate to specific settlements, and reflect the movement in the '50s and '60s out of the traditional territory of most of the then known Pintupi (principally as a result of an abnormally long drought). A Department of Aboriginal Affairs tribal population map produced in 1964 gives a total of 476 Pintupi from the Northern Territory alone, most of whom were then living at Haasts Bluff, Papunya and Yuendumu, while ten years later the Hansens (1974:i) claim approximately 800 Pintupi speakers at Papunya, Yuendumu, Docker River and Balgo and enlarge this to 'approximately 1000 speakers of Pintupi living at Yayayi, Papunya, Haasts Bluff, Docker River and Yuendumu settlements in the Northern Territory, and at Wiluna and Balgo Hills in Western Australia' (1978:16). Milliken (1976:242) meanwhile claims a total of 613 Pintupi speakers in the Northern Territory on 31 December, 1972.

There has been no ethnography specifically of the Pintupi, apart from the popular narratives of Lockwood (1964) and Thomson (1975), and no attempt to synthesize the numerous isolated articles and accounts of traditional life and customs. For this reason, and because of the relative shortness of the period of fieldwork, it has not been possible to place musical activities into their social framework with as much detail and precision as one might have liked. There is no indication, however, that traditional life differed radically from that of neighbouring Western Desert groups, e.g. the Walbiri (Meggitt 1962), Ngadjadjara (de Graaf 1968), Mandjildjara and Gadudjara (Tonkinson 1974).

Specifically, this work deals with the music sung at Kungkayunti and Balgo during the periods of fieldwork.[8] During these periods, however, no initiation was carried out, and there was a general reluctance to allow recording of the various initiation series because of their highly restricted nature. Accordingly, recordings of such series made by R. A. Gould in the Warburton Range area in 1966 were used in the Analysis, having first checked with the men at Kungkayunti and Balgo that they were identical with the series they themselves sang.[9]

The Kungkayunti camp started in 1974 with a population of more than 100, comprising Luridja, Walbiri and Pintupi people, despite some opposition from those who feared their presence would frighten the cattle from the nearby bore, and from others who considered the bore water unfit for human consumption. The camp lay some 70 kilometres by road west of Haasts Bluff and consisted of shelters made from canvas, corrugated iron and brush. At the start of fieldwork the people numbered around 70, although there was considerable movement to and from Haasts Bluff, Papunya and Yayayi. During the bushfire season in January 1975, the numbers dropped to as few as 21 as the fires moved closer and eventually surrounded the camp on three sides. The purchase of two trucks for the community engendered a new population boost which lasted, however, little longer than the trucks themselves. In March 1976, only about 40 people were still there, and the numbers continued to drop, apparently because of the economic hardship of having no vehicles, and by March 1977 there were only four families remaining. Morice (1976) gives a useful summary of the life of this community.

After a month's residence at Kungkayunti in 1974, Nosepeg Tjupurrula, the acknowledged leader of the community, announced in an informal conversation that I had been given the subsection name Tjapangati. Although he did not say how or by whom this particular name had been chosen, it seems likely that it was by himself since, in selecting the name which would put himself in an avuncular relationship to me, he could then exercise the greatest control over my activities—at least in terms of Pintupi kinship expectations—if he so desired. Thereafter, most people in the camp referred to me either as Tjapangati or in terms of a kinship relationship.

Of the total population, most of the adult men and two women had at least a smattering of English; all were illiterate, although a few could write their names. Travel was by vehicle, when one could be obtained or borrowed, otherwise by foot. The men's hunting of larger animals—kangaroos, emus, wallabies—was carried out from a vehicle, as the weight of these animals prevented them from being carried back to camp from any great distance. Daily foraging on foot for smaller game, honeyants, wit-

---

8. At Kungkayunti, from November 1974 to February 1975, June 1975, March 1976, March 1977; at Balgo from March to June 1975, March 1976, March 1977. The total time spent in the field was slightly less than 10 months.

9. Throughout this work use of Pintupi terminology for, and photographs and diagrams of, a variety of objects and material considered secret and available only to certain parts of the community have been omitted, in accordance with the people's wishes. Where possible, reference is made to other publications which do include identical or similar material.

chetty grubs, yams and edible seeds and fruit was usually a women's activity. Under the Labor Government administration, several of the men were paid 'wages' but the various work programs—cutting fence posts, clearing an airstrip, removal of domestic rubbish from the camp area—were short-lived due to an apparent lack of interest. One man, a traditional doctor, was placed on the payroll of the Health Department, at least three women received widow's pensions, and two men and two women were on old-age pensions. One man was recognised as an artist, and, using canvasses supplied by an artists' agency based at Papunya, painted designs representing mythological figures and scenes, for which he was paid upwards of $50 per canvas when the agent called; other men fashioned spears, boomerangs, clubs and flat stones for sale in Alice Springs. The camp was visited fortnightly by the Government Community Adviser, who brought 'wages' and pension monies, and, when the people had no transport of their own, a truckload of food for sale. Occasionally, a District Nurse paid a routine call.

Balgo is a Roman Catholic Pallotine Mission established in the '30s, and in addition to the dozen or so people who call themselves Pintupi, there are large numbers of Gugadja, Wanmadjiri and Ngadi, amounting to a total population of more than 600 by 1976. Balgo is regarded as something of a haven for those dissatisfied with living standards elsewhere, and numbers continue to arrive from Papunya, Yuendumu and Halls Creek.[10]

Of the Pintupi adults, Brandy Kunymangara, Donkeyman Luuku and Muntja Nungurayi worked from time to time for the Mission or the Education Department, but difficulties of funding or personality apparently prevented their full-time employment. The other Pintupi adults had old-age pensions or subsisted from the earnings of employed adults, Pintupi and non-Pintupi, who were related to them by subsection or marriage. Hunting prospects for anything other than small game were poor due to sparse vegetation, and those not employed by the Mission or engaged on a government-financed housing project spent their days in the immediate vicinity of the camp living area. Most ceremonies of a restricted nature took place within a radius of two kilometres from the Mission complex. During fieldwork at Balgo, my subsection name eased considerably my entry into both everyday and ceremonial life, in that I could be fitted neatly, along with any Aborigine with the Tjapangati name, into

situations in which particular subsections performed specific roles or had close, or avoidance, subservient or protective relationships with other subsections. By contrast, my European name was never used by the Aboriginal population during the whole of fieldwork.

The present Superintendent of the Mission, while encouraging behaviour based on Christian principles and providing programs of Christian education, is not actively repressing traditional Aboriginal activities or ceremonies; on the contrary, the general attitude of the permanent staff as a whole is one of offering, rather than imposing, an alternative lifestyle. Under such conditions, ceremonial life flourishes, and at least during the three periods of fieldwork, scarcely a day went by without either preparation for or enactment of singing and dancing.

Non-Pintupi material is included in the overall repertoires at both Kungkayunti and Balgo; this includes individual examples of *tulku, yilpintji* and *wantapi*, and the *tjatiwanpa*. Of these individual series, all but the *tjatiwanpa* are excluded from detailed attention, as research was concerned primarily with those series of Pintupi origin. The *tjatiwanpa*, despite its being ascribed a Luridja origin (the precise reference was not investigated) by most people at Kungkayunti and Papunya, is included, for two main reasons. Firstly, ownership was formally extended to the Pintupi people at Balgo during the course of fieldwork, thus providing first-hand information of the nature of song ownership; secondly, the women's dance calls during performance give information on the nature of music sound. However, as the structural organisation of the music is not of the type appearing in exclusively Pintupi series, it is not included in the Analysis.

The basic unit for Pintupi music, and indeed for all Desert music, is the song series (sometimes referred to in the literature as a 'song cycle' or 'song line'), in which a number of songs (from 30 to over 300 in the recorded sample) are sung in a prescribed order. Informants were adamant that this order was never changed, and that if a particular song could not be remembered readily, songs previously sung would be repeated until the problem one was recalled, whereupon the series could continue. Of the neighbouring

10. Berndt (1976:141), writing that 'the total population of Balgo . . . is currently about 276', is thus in error. Mission censuses indicate that the total population has been above 300 since 1974.

groups on which information is available, the Walbiri do not appear to adhere strictly to this same principle.[11]

For the Pintupi, music and music-making have connotations which cause them to be regarded almost in the same way as material objects. The song series and the ceremonies of which they are a part are held to belong to certain individuals within the community; such people are considered the owners, and the songs and ceremonies are their property. As property, ownership of the music is not only established but also transferable (*see* Song origins and ownership).

Without exception, Pintupi song series have narrative texts which relate the mythological events associated with particular ancestral beings. Because, in the myths, these beings often moved from place to place (the specific locations of which are identifiable even today), the songs and sometimes also the ceremonies themselves, which refer to or portray the various geographical locations visited, are also said to 'travel'. By this synecdotal means, it is thus possible to talk of a 'song route', or to enquire a song's (or series') geographical origin. In some cases, these song routes are said to cross the traditional territory of more than one Aboriginal group; here, just as in geography so too in the mythology, there are limitations or boundaries for that part of the myth which any one group may enact in ritual and musical form.

The Pintupi have no concept of song composition; rather, they believe that their song series have always existed in the spirit realm. Through the activities of human spirits, the series are 'found' and 'grabbed' (to use the Pintupi terms); in such an act of musical discovery, man is merely the recipient (*see* Song origins and ownership).

The whole question of whether or not to include song texts is a complex one. From observations in the field it is evident that the secrecy surrounding the performance of certain Pintupi series extends to the knowledge of the associated song texts; even in cases such as *yilpintji* and *yawulyu*, members of the opposite sex should not be allowed to approach close enough to overhear the actual words of the songs, although they are permitted to be within general earshot of performances. On several occasions while eliciting song texts from singers, the information was given in whispers lest passers-by accidentally hear. In publishing texts as part of the musical transcriptions, the possibility thus exists that a Pintupi reader might gain knowledge of song material to which he or she had no right; the ongoing educational programs in bilingualism make such a possibility an ever-increasing one. Only the texts of *tulku* and *wantapi*, as well as two healing series, are freely available to the whole community, and these alone are presented here.

On the other hand, an understanding of the way the texts are fitted to the melodic contours is fundamental to performance of Pintupi music, and necessary to any non-Pintupi's comprehension of the underlying structural concepts. To omit entirely the texts from a study of Pintupi music is possibly to jeopardise such a comprehension, and also to result in an approach providing something less than a comprehensive account of the performance situation.

As an illustration of the use of strong accentuation in initiation series, I have included the text of one single *ngintaka* song; I see no way of illustrating the phenomenon without the use of a text, and I believe the appearance of this one case, in isolation and without translation or other explanation, is inoffensive. Likewise, in discussing text-reversal in the Analytical Method section, I have included the text of one song from the series in which this phenomenon is most prevalent, Restricted (a). It would seem impossible to illustrate the connection between similarity of textual material in individual songs and ease of learning without the aid of the texts themselves; in the Song Origins section, 12 texts from the *yilpintji* called *wati kutjarra* are included, again without explanation or translation. As these texts were originally written down as the singers were singing them, rather than in the controlled isolation of an elicitation session, their orthographic accuracy cannot be guaranteed, thus further minimising any possible risk.

I can understand the resultant possible disappointment of those especially interested in song texts from a linguistic or anthropological point of view, or by those wishing to make a different or closer study of the melody-text relationships. The final decision to

---

11. 'If a misplaced song "breaks the line", the singers should start the cycle again. In fact, although I heard some lines [i.e. series] dozens of times, I did not hear one sung twice in exactly the same order, and I rarely saw the singers begin anew after an error'. (Meggitt 1962:222). Munn, speaking of Walbiri women's *yawulyu* series, also notes 'There are no rules of sequence in terms of which songs can be ordered; an ideal, sequential ordering of songs associated with an ancestor characterises the masculine but not the feminine subculture' (1973:95).

omit the texts was made after consultation with the Pintupi (*see* Preface); if such material were to be included, it is ultimately they who stand to lose more than others might gain. By contrast, the Pintupi definition of music sound (discussed in detail later) is such that a song without words is not a song; there appears to be no notion of ownership or restrictions over what Europeans know as a melody. To hum or whistle or otherwise perform the melodies in this present work is not in the same class as singing them (i.e. using the words); while texts without songs are considered sufficiently potent for them to be omitted here, melodies without texts are not, and thus their inclusion will not offend.

Music sound

To the Pintupi, music is singing produced by the human voice; animals and birds may 'speak' (*wangkanyi*) and 'cry' (*yulani*), and the sounds of nature (e.g. wind and thunder) also 'speak', but the act of singing is essentially human. Within human vocal production also, quite apart from normal conversational speech, there are some phenomena associated with song performance which, while they may satisfy the technical requirements of music sound in a European sense, are nonetheless not considered 'singing' by the Pintupi. The following are four examples of this.

Solo speaking

During performance of the *wangata* series, one particular song was sung twice, followed each time by one singer's sung commentary on the situation described in the song text. His melody, however, bore no resemblance to that of the song (*see* Example 3).

The singer claimed, and the others confirmed, that this was 'speaking' and that it was not part of the performance proper.

Text rehearsal

When remembering the words of a particular song in a series, singers often hummed through the melody, or sang it to themselves until the complete text was known, whereupon they would start at normal singing volume. This phenomenon is not considered part of the song proper, nor is it described as 'singing', but as 'try and remember im' in English, and by *mayu yatjininpa* or *mayu yakuntjininpa* (tasting the melody), *mayu ngumananyi* (humming the melody), or *mulya wangkanyi* (nose-speaking) in local terminology. The distinction is clear in the Pintupi mind, 'You gotta sing im words, properly!'

♩ = 178

first time

tjamiti kulinunala kurrunparu miramira mununya mununyanila walkunu

second time

kurrunparu miramira mununala kulikulinu palyalingkula tjamiti wiruna kulinu

Example 3   Wangata song, and solo speaking.

'Speaking' or 'crying'

By contrast, it appears that song as such does not necessarily have to consist entirely of lexically meaningful sounds. A number of songs from the beginning of the *yarritjiti* series (associated with the final stage of initiation) conclude with all the men singing 'aaaa' over a melodic contour which represents a diminution of the melody of the song just completed (*see* Example 4).

This, according to the singer, is singing, but only in the context of the song which precedes it. When performed separately, the phenomenon becomes 'speaking' or 'crying' (the men were in some doubt as to what exactly to call it, but they were all in agreement that it was not singing).

Dance calls

The fourth phenomenon occurs within the context of dance, and in order to establish this context, some descriptive commentary is given. The women's dancing performed during all recorded performances of the *tjatiwanpa* ceremony was carried out principally inside area B (*see* Fig. 2) behind the men's sitting area.[1] The dancing consisted of two types of actions, the point of change coinciding in most cases with the change in boomerang beating rate.

The first, called *ngatangnatangpa* by a few of the women, but *nyanpinypa* by the others and all the men, consists of a series of forward shuffling jumps, the legs bent only slightly; the arms are bent at the elbow, held close to the body. In the course of the part of the singing using the faster boomerang speed, perhaps 10 seconds, the women dancers covered 4-6 metres, halting in one line across the width of the dance area, just behind the back row of men singers. During this forward movement, they call 'aaah', each jump causing the sound to be jerky. The men's term for this call is *tjamaru*[2] (or *tjamaru ngarinpa*), a word which the women should not (but do) know; women use the onomatopoeic term *karrara wangkapayi* — ('to utter *karrara*, with the trilled 'r' coinciding with each forward jump.

The *tjamaru* call is uttered only while the women are in forward motion; on reaching the edge of the dance area, or at the change in boomerang rate (whichever comes first), they start the second type of actions, called *yurutjinganinpa*. Holding a short stick or length of wool or strip of cloth about 30-40cm long, they stand and move the stick/wool/cloth in a series

Example 4 *Yarritjiti* song with final 'aaa' singing.

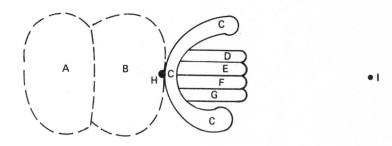

A women's sitting area
B women's dancing area
C standing men of Tjapangati, Tjungurayi, Tjakamarra and Tjapaltjarri subsections
D seated Tjampitjinpa men

E seated Tjangala men
F seated Tjupurrula men
G seated Tjapanangka men
H tall decorated pole (tjampali)
I small decorated bullroarer suspended from stake

Figure 2 Ground plan of sitting and dancing areas during *tjatiwanpa* ceremony.

of movements from shoulder height on the left side to waist height on the right side and back up again; this is done from two to as many as six times before reversing the direction of the movements. With each downward action the thighs are quivered as quickly as possible. This, technically, is *nyanpinyi*, but because it is limited to women's dancing, the term is also used in a wider sense to refer to any female dancing.[3]

---

1. No photographs were permitted during performance.
2. The Hansens (1974:208) give the word as also referring to the type of male ululation commonly known as the fluttered howl; since this is a secret male sound, women may well be reluctant to use the word *tjamaru*.
3. The quivering wing movements of the sparrowhawk, as it hovers over the ground looking for prey, is called *nyanpinyanpi*.

On completion of the singing, the women walk back to their sitting area, and depending on their mood, either sit down and regain their strength, or continue standing, awaiting the next song.[4]

The terminology used by women for the utterances occurring during the forward dance shuffles—*karrarra wangkapayi* (to repeat *karrarra*), and that used by the men—*tjamaru*—to refer to the same sound, suggest that the practice is not considered to be music (i.e. singing).

However, it would be wrong to suppose that as a result the sounds were not related to the singing which is occurring concurrently with the women's dancing. It can be shown that the pitch of these dance calls, which remain constant throughout each woman's individual performance,[5] is directly related to the tonic of the singing. In these graphs the tonic for the women is considered to be that pitch an octave above the men's tonic. Moreover, when the men's tonic changes in pitch, as a result of gradual flattening over a period of one or more hours, or at the start of a further period of singing and dancing immediately following a break for rest or food, the women's pitch faithfully follows the changes.

Analysis of the performances at Balgo shows that for the first two evenings, the women's pitches were grouped as shown in Fig. 3 in relation to the men's tonic.

In both of these, only the Balgo women danced. On the third night, when the Yuendumu women performed with the Balgo women, pitches above the tonic figured for the first time. Up until midnight, the Yuendumu women outnumbered local women, and the dance pitches tended to be higher than before (i.e. from the tonic up to m6 above the tonic), but from midnight until dawn, there was a reversal, with Balgo women being more audible; this is reflected in the pitches below the tonic. Similarly, in the final night's performance, the voices of the local women were louder than those of the visitors, and this is reflected in the preponderance of pitches lower than the tonic.

Five weeks after all but three of the Yuendumu visitors returned home, the Balgo people staged their own first full-scale performances, spread over two nights. I did not observe the first of these but the second was fully recorded. During conversations with Balgo women soon after the Yuendumu people left, one point emerged. They had noted that the Yuendumu women had pitched their dance calls higher and louder than themselves, but claimed that they preferred lower pitches, without specifying any reason beyond saying that calls which were pitched low (*purrka*) were better.

The second (and final) night of Balgo's first unassisted performance was notable musically for a rise in overall pitch occurring during uninterrupted performance. Previously, such rises had occurred immediately after breaks in performance, but on this occasion performance at the lower pitch was interrupted by one man singing at a higher pitch; within

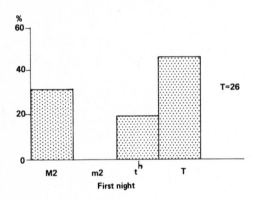

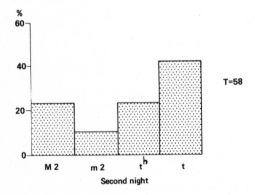

Figure 3 Pitches of women's dance calls during *tjatiwanpa* ceremony; first and second nights.

Note T is the total number of times the women's calls appeared on each occasion. In the horizontal axis, t represents the tonic of the song, and intervals to the left and right of this tonic represent pitch below and above it, respectively. Pitches slightly lower and higher than the tonic are indicated by the signs ♭ and ♯. The vertical axis indicates the percentage of T occurring at each pitch.

4. At certain parts of the ceremony, however, (but only at the command of the men), selected women would dance to the area north of I, to be part of a larger group re-enacting the death by fire of characters in the myth. They returned to area A immediately on completion of these re-enactments.

5. The word 'performance' is used in a general way in this work to refer to the singing of a song series with or without the associated ceremonies, or to those ceremonies by themselves; no notion of formality is implied.

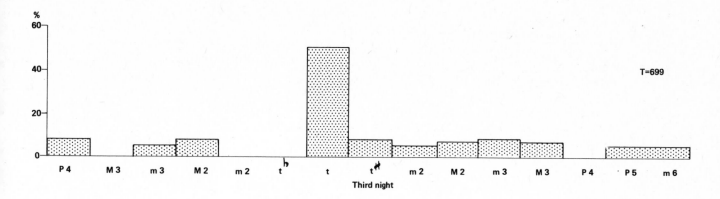

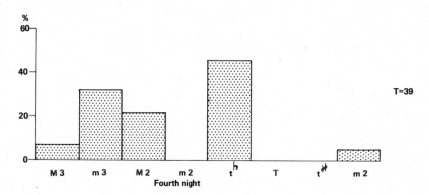

Figure 4 Pitches of women's dance calls during *tjatiwanpa* ceremony; third and (fourth) final nights. *See* note to Fig. 3.

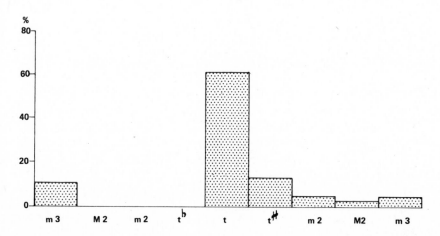

Figure 5 Pitches of the Yuendumu women's dance calls during *tjatiwanpa* ceremony. *See* note to Fig. 3.

15

a few seconds all the singers had changed to this new pitch, which they maintained until the end of the ceremony. Up until that point, the three Yuendumu women who had stayed behind were prominent dancers, and the pitches of their dance calls reflect this (*see* Fig. 5).

After the pitch rise, however, coincidentally or not, these three women were less active, and although still dancing, did so silently. The pitches of the calls indicate the lowering favoured by the Balgo women (*see* Fig. 6).

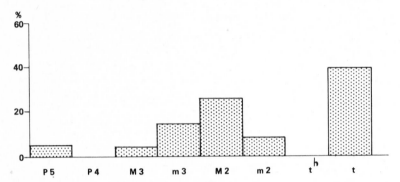

Figure 6   Pitch of the Balgo women's dance calls during *tjatiwanpa* ceremony. *See* note to Fig. 3

The Balgo women denied that they listened to the men's singing as they danced, but they did pay attention to the rate of beating on the boomerangs,[6] in particular to the point of change, which signalled a change in their own dancing. The high degree of coincidence of the singing tonic and the women's dance-call pitch, as indicated in the graphs above, suggests strongly that the women are listening to the singing and adjusting their own pitch to it, even if they themselves are unaware of this. The persistence of this practice, despite both rapid and gradual changes of the overall pitch of the singing, further highlights the connection.

However, the Pintupi concept of music sound is such that these women's dance calls are considered 'speaking' (*wangkantja*) rather than 'singing' (*yinkantja*).

---

6. There did not appear to be any attempt at synchronisation between the boomerang rate and that of dancers' forward movements.

Categories of song

The Pintupi group their ceremonies, which invariably include song series, into a number of named categories; those for which more than one example is known are as follows: *tulku*, *yilpintji*, *yawulya*, *ngalungku*, *tingarri*, *tuyutu* and possibly *wantapi*. Ceremonies for which single examples exist include: *kutitji*, *yarritjiti*, *kutatji* (*wanapa*), *pukalkarra* and a number of restricted women's ceremonies whose names cannot be revealed.[1] The term 'example' is used here to refer to any discrete song series or ceremony, regardless of whether or not this is normally performed continuously from start to finish or is spread over several days or nights.

Nomenclature for both these two groupings is such that the same word may apply variously to some (but not necessarily all) associated ceremonial objects, each individual song in the series, the singing as a whole, and the entire ceremony. For example, during the performance of the *tjatiwanpa*, which is of the *tulku* category, individuals who were ignorant of the specific names for the ceremonial objects (or who did

---

1. Of the above, however, an *exclusive* Pintupi origin is not claimed for *ngalungku* and *kutitji* (*see* below). A breakdown of the musical material from Balgo is not given here, as the Pintupi there represent a minority who freely participate in ceremonies and songs of non-Pintupi origin which are performed by the Gugadja and Wanmadjiri people there; the statistics would thus not be comparable. Non-Pintupi song series currently known at Kungkayunti, however, included the following:

genre and name	claimed language
pulapa: wantanturu	Nyining (Walbiri)
wantapi (un-named)	Pitjantjatjara
tulku: tarrkalpa	Pitjantjatjara-Pintupi 'mix-up'
yilpintji: wami	Yanmatjirri
yilpintji: kalatjiti	Walbiri
yilpintji: kalaya	,,
yilpintji: kungkaku	,,
tulku: wankara	Aranda
yilpintji: urrumpula	,,
tulku: tjatiwanpa	Luridja (although at Balgo this is claimed of ultimate Pintupi origin)
ngalungku	'mix-up'
kutitji	Pintupi-Luridja-Aranda-Walbiri 'mix-up'
yukurukuru	Walbiri

not want nearby women to overhear their secret names) referred to them simply as '*tulku*'; in the informal singing practices prior to the ceremony, men would occasionally request that they all move on to another song in the series, saying, '*Tulku kutjupala yinka*' (Let's sing another *tulku*), or the like, or when trying to remember the next song in the series, ask, '*Nyaa tulku pala?*' (What's that next *tulku*?). When recordings of the *tjatiwanpa* ceremony were played back to people who had not been present, they confirmed that the performers were singing the *tulku*; and finally, in general conversation before, during and after the ceremony, context made it clear that the references to the *tulku* or to *tjatiwanpa* were to the ceremony as a whole. Similar nomenclature was observed for other *tulku* and for the other categories in the first list above. Where only single examples of categories existed I did not observe individual songs being referred to by the same name as for the ceremony as a whole. Instead, such songs were described as *kutjupalingku* (another fine one) or *kutjulingku* (a fine one), or the like. There is evidence that the word *tulku* is also the approximate equivalent of 'song', insofar as it was heard to refer to single songs in the *tingarri*, *wantapi* and *yilpintji* categories, as well as to songs in the *tulku* series.

In cases where more than one example within a given category existed, such individual examples are distinguished by reference to the chief character(s) in the associated myths, e.g. *mungamunga* (a *yawulyu*), *malu* (a *ngalungku*) or the general subject-matter, e.g. *tjiwiri* (rain—a *tulku*). In the case of two *yilpintji*, two names, one commonly known and another known only to the performers, were in use; this situation is discussed later, when dealing specifically with *yilpintji*. The nomenclature for the *tarrkalpa* is somewhat unclear; this also is discussed later.

A summary in tabular form of these categories of song series (and associated ceremonies) for which more than one example is known by the Pintupi is presented below.

Among some, but not all, Pintupi the word *yinma* is used in such a way as to cut across the above classifications and refer to ceremonies and singing of a social nature, i.e. *tulku* and *wantapi*. Such a meaning is identical with that for the Pitjantjatjara cognate form *inma*, and the present close contact with those people may be suspected as the origin of the Pintupi use of the term in this sense. What may be regarded as the true Pintupi meaning of the same word also cuts across the above categories, but in a diame-

CATEGORY	EXAMPLES
tulku	*yikuluku* (eaglehawk)
	tjiwiri (rain)
	tarrkalpa (meaning unknown to me)
	yununtju (meaning unknown to me)
	wantjiwantji (meaning unknown to me)
	yunpu (a man's name)
yilpintji	*marali* (meaning unknown to me)
	kungka kutjarra (two girls)
	wangata (echidna)
	maanytja (moon)
yawulyu	*mungamunga* (a woman's name)
	kungkayunti (a place name, cf. note 14, p. 23)
	Restricted (a)
	Restricted (b)
ngalungku	*malu* (kangaroo)
	wayuta (possum)
	kipara (turkey)
	ngintaka (perentie)
tingarri	*Tingarri* ceremonies and song series appear to be distinguished individually not so much on the basis of a name, as for the examples above, but rather by a spoken description of, or reference to, the associated myth (*see* pp. 26-27)
tuyutu	*yawarra* (spear wound)
	kirrpinpa (meaning unknown to me)
	paniya (meaning unknown to me)
	kuniya (snake)
	tuyutu (a)
	tuyutu (b)

trically opposite way, as it refers to any men's ceremony which may not be seen or heard by women and children, i.e. *ngalungku*, *yilpintji*, *tingarri*, and *wanapa*. The secrecy involved in these ceremonies is emphasised, and the meaning of the word differentiated from that described above, by the frequent habit of enunciating it in a whisper.

Tulku

Both men and women may sing at *tulku*, the men accompanying themselves with boomerangs and the women by clapping hands or (more often) slapping the crotch area. Children may also be present, but none was seen to join in the singing. In most observed performances, all participants were seated, and usually the men would sit in a tight circle facing inwards, the women grouping themselves in a larger circle around them. Any dancing which took place occurred on a cleared space outside the women's circle, and when a particular time for dancing occurred, most of the singers, with the exception of a few old men, would turn around to watch. The principal function of the *tulku* seems to be one of entertainment, and possibly for this reason there are more examples known locally only than for other song categories.

Two particular *tulku* recorded at Kungkayunti deserve individual attention at this point; by name at least the first is linked with areas as far away as Eucla on the south coast.

There are references in Daisy Bates' notebooks[2] to a '*wanji-wanji*' ceremony observed in Eucla (South Australia) in 1913, a portion of which was subsequently published (Bates 1938: 123-26), which may be related to the Pintupi *wantjiwantji* recorded at Kungkayunti in 1975. McCarthy (1939:84) has published a map based on Bates' information, on which the route of this *wanji-wanji* (travel dance) is traced; according to the map, part of the route lies close to the western boundary of Pintupi territory. Bates also observes (1938:125) that 'neither those who brought the dance, nor those who watched it, could interpret the words or the actions', and observes that one elderly man had seen a performance of it at Ayers Rock (some 700 kilometres north of Eucla and inside Pitjantjatjara territory) in his youth. From all this one might reasonably admit the possibility that the Kungkayunti and Eucla performances were of the same ceremony. There is, however, evidence to support a contrary view.

The recorded *wantjiwantji* was said to be simply a *tulku*, that is, an informal song series with occasional dancing, and thus lacking the connotations of Bates' 'travel dance'. There is certainly nothing apparent on the surface to tie it in with Bates' notebook descriptions of Eucla men taking 'temporary wives' following the performance. She describes it as 'an ancient dream dance, a dramatic rendering of the arrival of the second horde into Australia' (1938:125), whereas the Kungkayunti song series concerns a single woman. Bates contends that the *wanji-wanji* accompanied Aborigines along a con-

tinental trade-route and was performed whenever a trading group arrived at a permanently inhabited point on that route. The Kungkayunti *wantjiwantji* was described as follows by one of the singers:

Tulku from Alice Springs, down south, bin come up. *Tulku* this one bin come up, *wantjiwantji*, go that way [pointing] Petermann Range. (RMM: field tape 76)

This would seem to imply that the *wantjiwantji* was of specific duration and number of songs, rather than constituting a long myth shared among several tribal and language groups. It would also seem to indicate a northwesterly movement into Pintupi territory, in contrast to Bates' and McCarthy's claims of a southeasterly spread from a point in the southern Kimberleys to another point on the Great Australian Bight.

Bates herself includes texts for 30 *wanji-wanji* songs in her notebooks, none of which was sung at Kungkayunti, but some of which appear to be in a Western Desert language form.

From all this data no clear conclusion can be drawn concerning the possible connection between the *wanji-wanji* and the *wantjiwantji*. The presence of three *wantjiwantji* songs whose isorhythmic structure differs from that of the others, however, suggests that the associated myth may not be confined in its entirety to Pintupi territory.

The second *tulku* with a claim to distinction outside as well as inside Pintupi territory is the *tarrkalpa*. The *tarrkalpa* series recorded at Kungkayunti was claimed to come from a long myth, only part of which was in the Pintupi language and known and performed by that particular group of singers. The series was not known at Balgo, although one man said he had heard of the name. De Graaf (1968:115) talks of a '*tulkarpa*' ceremony at the Warburton Ranges, but it has not been established that '*tarrkalpa*' and '*tulkarpa*' are the same. The Kungkayunti performance was accompanied by beating single sticks on the ground, which is found in only one other type of Pintupi singing—initiation series. This, combined with the apparently sectional nature of the associated myth, would seem to suggest that the *tarrkalpa* is not a *tulku* of the same type as those other series of this same generic name.

2. Held in the Australian National Library, Manuscript No. 365-36/2-104.

Yilpintji

The practice of love-magic ceremonies (*yilpintji*) has been widely reported from the Central Desert area (e.g. Meggitt 1962:209; A. Moyle 1974:120-21; Berndt and Berndt 1965:241-46), although use is not universally confined to either men or women. For the Pintupi, however, the *yilpintji* is an exclusively male ceremony.[3]

In two recorded cases, the *yilpintji* had two names; the one was known by all men, but the other was restricted to those men taking part in the performance. Thus the *tjilkamata* (Porcupine Man) *yilpintji* has the lesser-known name of *wangata*. Similarly, the *kinara* (Moon Man) *yilpintji* is referred to as *maanytja* by the performers.[4]

The *yilpintji* in the recorded sample recount Dreamtime myths in which the erotic adventures of the characters play a major part; the ceremonies appear to have two functions. Firstly, by enacting in ritual the activities of the mythical characters, the performers believe that they will acquire some of their irresistible sexual attraction. Secondly, by the manufacture of string crosses and by the singing of the appropriate songs, the women will immediately feel sexual desire which can be gratified only on the arrival of the performers. To this end, the bullroarer is the activating instrument. When, in the course of performance, the bullroarer is swung, its sound is believed to carry long distances and seek out the female victim who will think it is a bird or an animal, and not realise its power over her.[5] During the performance of the *wangata* at Kungkayunti, one of the singers assured me that the bullroarer had the range to affect women as far away as Papunya, some 80 km distant. The Balgo performance of the *maanytja*, on the other hand, did not feature a bullroarer, and the only spoken comments heard which related to the desired outcome of the ceremony were directed to local women, to the accompaniment of much laughter and mock denials of *wiya* (no) and *wanti* (leave it alone) from the Yuendumu men.

Typical *yilpintji* appear to consist of bodypainting by all the men present, the manufacture of one or more wooden crosses to which hairstring is attached, and solo dancing near or using such objects, all of which are accompanied by singing. The singing is timed so that particular activities are accompanied by the appropriate songs. However, songs may be sung also by themselves without any associated ritual activity.

The literature on *yilpintji* from other parts of the Central Desert is rather heavy on generalisations and functional analysis, but light on detailed first-hand accounts of performance procedure. The following description of the Balgo performance of the *maanytja*, which appears as originally written in the author's field notes, may be of value in this respect. (Explanatory notes are given within brackets and original measurements have been converted for uniformity).

4 March 1975
walked in single file to large tree some 200m out of camp (site 6, Plate 12)—ground cleared using boomerangs, feet, also pulling out grass; a circle some 4m in diameter cleared. Personnel:

Subsection

A	Tjapangati	(these are the two *tjatiwanpa*
B	Tjapangati	teachers from Yuendumu)
C	Tjungurayi	(this man is also C in the *tjatiwanpa* descriptions)
D	Tjungurayi	(later to be the messenger, taking the news of the new *tjatiwanpa* ownership to Papunya and Yayayi; a close friend of A)
E	Tjupurrula	(he is B in the *tjatiwanpa* ceremony)
F	Tjapanangka	
G	Tjapangati	
H	Tjapaltjarri,	an old man
J	Tjapangati,	an old man
K	Tjapaltjarri,	an elderly man
L	Tjapangati	

---

3. In Balgo, some women appear to use the term as synonymous with *yawulyu*. After mild complaints that I was recording too much of the men's *yilpintji* and thus neglecting the women, a group of them came up and insisted that they too had their own *yilpintji*; on recording this, however, it was discovered that the performance was in fact part of the *tjarata* ceremony (a female love-magic ceremony of non-Pintupi origin and language, although Pintupi women at Balgo participate in it).

4. Unlike *wangata*, which name appears to be unknown to women, the word *maanytja* is in common use by both men and women. The ceremony was performed in isolation by the Pintupi men at Balgo, together with two visitors from Yuendumu. When they strode back into camp after the performance, proudly displaying their bodypaint, they told the other men that it was simply a *yilpintji*, while whispering to me that it was not just a *yilpintji*, it was *maanytja*, their own private *yilpintji*.

5. In the Dreamtime narratives, a single woman is usually depicted. However, in current performances, it appears that each man taking part has his mind on a particular woman, and thus the desired outcome is on a greater scale than the original.

F brings a spear and woomera, C brings a *kutitji* [wide shield]—small hole dug in centre of circle by A—B collects a couple of branches, B and E straighten these in the fire, then pound the outer bark off them. A took handful of grass cinders to grass outside circle, put them in tin, urinated on them, returned [to make black colouring material]—central piece of wood rubbed with dry red ochre; held off ground by A and C; black stripe painted 20cm from bottom, 60cm from top, stripes circle wood—two black lines, on opposite sides of the pole, join these first stripes—white ochre painted on by C, chewing it as no water available—A paints series of 13 crescents about 5cm apart, though closer together at the top—*kaltji* [white ochre] applied—then painted identical row on opposite side: C helps, painting a few himself, though not starting from his own end—two balls of double-ply wool unravelled, made into single ball by E and L—dry red ochre dabbed on with finger between these [crescent] marks for greater colour contrast—white dots applied at base [three rows] and top [two rows].[6]

Crosspiece at bottom attached; wood has had bark scraped off by A, but ends ragged. This tied between lower two rows of dots using string—covered with cloth—crosspiece about 60cm long 2.5cm diameter; tied on by A—top crosspiece chopped to same length, attached 10cm above top row of dots, using cloth only—this tied on by C—cross leant back in its hole—C takes wool ball attached to bottom wood joint, starts to tie on—wool wound on; small hole scooped (in ground) at base to allow passage of hand holding ball—when all wool thus used, band is 10cm high—vertical stick is bent by tension and both crosspieces lean to left. No attempt to correct this—cross placed in hole, earth packed around, stick at rear to support it, *kutitji* laid there on back—all retire for lunch—A C E F G L.

1.35 pm—all return, along with B D H J K—C brings tin of flour [for making paste]—never used, though—almost immediately after first song, H J K leave to collect pension money [from the Mission]—red ochre scraped by knife into woomera, applied by A to himself and by D to himself—A removes shorts, sits playing with penis, joking about its appearance with D—F goes and finds two cement bricks, returns, rubs them together dry to remove loose parts, then grinds wood charcoal between them; a tin of the stuff has

been brought from camp—D and E collect [vegetable] down; A crushes this with his hands into large tins—B starts to paint himself, using *kantawarra* [yellow ochre].

D paints all but stomach and left breast pattern [on himself]; no red base is used—A urinates again into tin, adds crushed wood charcoal—D paints A, starts with waist band, then shoulders, then link, then back: waist, shoulders, link. F strips, takes *kutitji* and small sharpened stick, jabs at urethra, drips blood into shield grip recess. D strips and does same. Both do this on other side of tree. Both return naked, sit for some minutes, then re-don trousers—singing during this—E mixes more *kaltji*—D dabs blood on to A using small stick with cloth wound around the end; adds white down to blood, simply outlines previous charcoal pattern, 2.5cm—all other men take shirts off, apply red ochre, and start painting themselves—C and self paint B; J then paints E at his request—C asks me if I want a 'number' [i.e. pattern] painted on; I decline—all move from east side of tree and stand around cross—A gets two hand-clumps of bushes, sits crosslegged facing cross, some 3m away—accompanied by non-stop singing, he brushes path in front of himself, wriggles forward on his bottom, twists shoulders and on boomerang tremolo, quivers. This continues until he reaches base of cross. He lays bush clumps at base, gets up; all return to east side and continue with painting—this dancing started immediately after D had finished applying all down to A—at last minute D remembered that paint and down were required on A's face; applied it. On completion of all painting, cross lifted out, laid at tree base and covered with leafy branches—*kutitji* stuck up in tree—all left for camp, some remaining bare-chested—terminology: *wayili* = crosslegged stance, shuffling forward; *parrparrpa* = quivering of whole body—sexual attraction of ceremony worded 'pull im [i.e. 'er] out'.

By way of addition it should be pointed out that the *maanytja* is not currently owned by the Pintupi at Balgo, although from earlier experience in the south, they have become familiar with the ceremony. It is

---

6. In order to avoid distress to the performers by publishing a picture of the completed cross, which women may not see, a sketch is not presented here. The cross is, however, virtually identical in appearance to that appearing in Berndt and Berndt (1964: plate following p. 208).

owned by the Tjapangati subsection at Papunya and Yayayi, and thus the arrival in Balgo of the two teachers from Yuendumu (who had previously lived at both Papunya and Yayayi) gave sanction to the performance. There is no patrimoietal division of the participants into owners and managers; the more overtly aggressive of the two owners, A, directed the overall proceedings, took the leading dance part, and led most of the singing. There was no doubt that he was in charge of the ceremony.[7]

It should also be noted that singing was more or less continuous throughout the proceedings, mostly in an informal manner while the singers were preoccupied with making the cross, or preparing or applying their own bodypaint. Only during the solo dance did all the men devote their entire attention to singing, as an accompaniment to A's actions; in this instance, the same song was repeated ten times, until the dance was completed.

Although only three of the song texts were included in the original field notes, comparison of the activities with the particular songs (as recorded) shows that as in other ceremonies, the time at which the stages of preparation were completed determined the times for song change as, for example, in the first seven songs:

Activity	Song number	Expanded translation of song during the same period
Painting of vertical pole	1	The Moon Man made himself a decorated cross with crescents on it.
Painting of crescents	2	In his camp, he painted crescents on to the decorated cross.
Attaching of wool (a common substitute for hairstring)	3	Digging a hole for his hand, the Moon Man tied hairstring on to his cross.
Completion of tying; other men come and look at the result	4	I, Moon Man, sit in my camp, looking at the cross.
Cross erected	5	The erected cross distracted the women's minds.
Blood-letting into shield; painting of dancer	6	The Moon Man drips blood into his shield; the women sit pining for him.
Solo dancing	7	In his camp, he danced in front of his upright cross.

The corollary, that a mythological event referred to in the song text will necessarily be enacted in the performance, does not hold. For example, songs 20 and 21 in this series refer to the Moon Man swinging his bullroarer, but in the actual performance no bullroarer was used (for reasons unknown); there were a number of bullroarers in camp at the time, but none was brought out for this performance. Similarly, song 22 (which completed the performance) refers to the Moon Man's dancing, but no dancing took place at this point in the Balgo performance.

From his position as leader of the ceremony, A organised the activities in different ways: for the clearing of the ground he simply pointed out how large the area should be, but did not delegate the task to anybody in particular—several men immediately carried it out; for the painting of the cross, he himself took charge, and D's assistance in the latter stages was neither sought nor commented upon. By contrast, D, E and F were specifically asked to go and prepare the charcoal and vegetable down. The close friendship between A and D was such that the two were constantly together for the weeks prior to the *tjatiwanpa* ceremony; this may account for D's painting of A; although the two of them were sitting less than 1.8m from my own position, A made no overt request to D to paint him. E stood in a classificatory avuncular relationship to me, and this would normally make any request for my services quite normal; several of the men were helping complete each other's paint designs, and E's request to me was thus entirely in keeping with the general work pattern. C's asking me if I too wanted to be painted was partly out of friendship (he was one of the two main field consultants), but possibly partly a natural extension of my status as a minor participant (having assisted in the bodypainting).

7. As distinct from other song classifications, *yilpintji* ownership is not identical for all examples; some have the Owner-Manager system, while others, like the *maanytja*, are owned by one subsection.

The older men present, G, H, K and L, participated minimally during the morning's work, but they all joined in the singing; during the bodypainting, each painted himself in designs generally smaller than those of the younger men. Their senior status apparently excused them from the manual labour in making the cross, but although their degree of overall participation was noticeably less than that of the other men, they were not simply spectators.

Although one or two men donned shirts after the ceremony, and A removed the black down from his body, most walked back bare-chested into camp. One or two men spoke to them as they went to their respective homes, but without exception the women totally ignored their return. Some of the smaller children approached and examined their father's bodypainting, but at least in the three families observed, they were told nothing about their significance, and questions to this effect were either ignored, or countered with *wiyangka* (it's nothing). The designs were allowed to rub off naturally.

The site chosen for the performance was some 200m from the edge of the camp, but only about 100m from a women's love magic (*yawulyu*) site (site 4, Plate 12). Several times during the day, the women could be heard singing, and men would nod and say, '*Yawulyu*'; on a later date, some of these same women said they could hear the men's performance. This proxemic placement seems to be deliberate.[8]

The key point is that although members of the opposite sex may identify the performance as that of love magic, they should not be so close as to identify the song words and thus comprehend specifically the proceedings.[9]

Yawulyu

The *yawulyu* is the principal Pintupi women's love magic ceremony: in its overall organisation (bodypainting, manufacture of ceremonial objects, solo and group dancing) it parallels the men's *yilpintji*, although at least during the periods of fieldwork, it occurred more often (6 performances in three months at Kungkayunti; 16 performances in three months at Balgo).[10]

Like the *yilpintji*, the *yawulyu* aims to make the participants more sexually attractive; in addition, it is said to excite men's sexual urges (some Balgo women claimed their singing could produce an instant erection). At other performances, the women claimed that, Siren-like, their singing could cause a man to come to them.[11]

The activities of *yawulyu* ceremonies are such that most of the time is spent painting-up the participants (in a typical 4-hour performance at Balgo, anything up to 3½ hours would be taken up with painting); during this time, individual women might get up and dance, but the organised dancing did not start until the painting was completed. The bodypainting was rarely performed by individuals on themselves; at Kungkayunti, classificatory sisters painted each other, while at Balgo cousin painted cousin. In both areas, there was a speech taboo between painter and subject, although each could sing, or speak to a third party.[12]

Not everybody attending took part in the bodypainting or singing; at Balgo a few elderly women were among the first to arrive at the performance site, but they simply sat silently watching the proceedings. After an hour or so, they slept.[13]

Unlike the *yilpintji*, the recorded *yawulyu* (six different examples in all) cannot be performed in their entirety at one sitting because of the sheer number of songs involved in recounting the respective myths. The *yawulyu kungkayunti* at Balgo had already started when the writer arrived there; it continued for a further seven performances before the myth was completed. Likewise at Kungkayunti,[14] the *yawulyu* called *mungamunga* had been going for

---

8. C. H. Berndt confirms such arrangement (1965:243).

9. Apparently this does not always work. At Kungkayunti, one old woman sang two *yilpintji* items (previously performed by the men there) presumably to judge my reactions, and burst into laughter on catching my eye.

10. My presence may have stimulated the frequency of performance; at Balgo, especially, the ceremony leaders would delegate one or two women to come and inform me of the next performance, and sometimes even to escort me there.

11. On one occasion at Balgo, a man, apparently unaware of the performance, blundered out of the scrub on to the ceremonial area. The women immediately jumped to their feet, calling out for him to come right over to them; this was the living proof of the *yawulyu*'s power! With a look of utter terror, though, he fled.

12. Painters occasionally gave instructions to their subjects, however, telling them to turn around, lean back, etc. More often, though, they simply silently guided the subjects into the desired positions.

13. My own presence at such performances was a curious ignoring of my sex; the only explanation for this paradox was voiced almost identically at both Kungkayunti and Balgo—'You're all right, you're a white feller'. Munn (1973:xviii) notes a similar situation, with the sexes reversed, among the neighbouring Walbiri.

14. By sheer coincidence, the place called Kungkayunti, where fieldwork was first carried out, features in this particular *yawulyu* from Balgo; the Balgo women expressed considerable interest when the writer was able to describe from memory features of the landscape referred to in the songs.

several performances prior to my arrival and continued for a further four. The remaining four examples were shorter, but all took more than one performance to complete.

Although localising the numerous place names referred to in these two myths has not been undertaken, it appears that the Balgo and Kungkayunti *yawulyu* represent two portions of a single myth whose total narrative encompasses an even larger territory. The Balgo story moves from Karukati towards Kungkayunti, while the Kungkayunti story starts at Papunya (some 80km away) and heads west. If subsequent research proves this to be correct, then this *yawulyu* joins the *tingarri* and other so-called 'travelling' song series in their sectional treatment of total myths.

The ownership basis varies from example to example—some belong to individual women, while others are owned by a whole subsection, and depending on this, performance is led by either one or several women. Singing during the manufacture and application of bodypaint is informal, the loudest coming from those not actively engaged in the work at hand; in many cases, the other women cannot be heard even though they are visibly moving their lips. Accompaniment to the singing may consist of hand-clapping, with crotch and chest-slapping; however, it is usually sporadic, not necessarily performed by all the singers, and appears to be optional. During the more formal dancing which concludes each individual performance, the singers stay seated as they provide the musical support for the dancers.

Two further women's ceremonies apparently connected with love magic were recorded from Kungkayunti. The first was taped in five sessions spread over three weeks. The secrecy surrounding its nature was considerably greater than that of the same group of women's *yawulyu*, and the performances took place well out of earshot of camp. All children were forcibly removed (an unusual occurrence). Once, two other women from camp, both younger sisters of one of the participants, arrived at the site; all activities and singing stopped, and after a few minutes of pointed silence, the newcomers left.[15]

It appeared to differ from the *yawulyu* in only the songs, dances, bodypainting designs, and sacred paraphernalia, but the overall organisation of each performance however—a period of straight singing followed by bodypainting and group dancing using particular ceremonial objects—was identical to the other more widely-known ceremonies. Ownership is said to be limited to three classificatory sisters who claim that they, together with one other elderly woman, are the only people who know it. Their plans for the future of the ceremony appear hazy, although they were not pasing on their knowledge to even their closest relatives. In future, this series will be referred to as Restricted (b).

In the course of a brief return visit to Kungkayunti in March 1976, the same women were performing another series in their customary area a few hundred metres out of camp; the series was said to be a 'new one'. The name was known to one or two men, who claimed it originated in Pitjantjatjara country, but to be in the Pintupi language. In the later sections of this book, the series is referred to as Restricted (a). For the purposes of discussion and analysis, the Restricted (a) and (b) series will be included within the *yawulyu* category. While at Balgo on a final return visit in March 1977, this same series was being performed by the local women, and some 10 hours of the activities was recorded. The dreaming, it was said, started from Amata, in Pitjantjatjara country, and moved northwards, touching at Papunya, Yuendumu, and finally Balgo. It was also said to have been acquired recently, from Pintupi women at Yuendumu. Although the information was obtained too late for detailed transcription analysis and comparison with the Kungkayunti version, one important observation needs attention here. While the name for this Balgo ceremony was the same as the Kungkayunti Restricted (a) series, the melodic outline was that of the Restricted (b) series; the Balgo women were acquainted with the name of the (b) series—even asking me if I myself knew of it—but maintained that their ceremony and its series were called by the other name. I do not have explanations for the words in these names, nor was there sufficient time to enquire further into this paradox.

The same singers at Kungkayunti knew another women's ceremony, in which they had participated at Yayayi prior to moving to Kungkayunti, and were about to sing it for recording purposes, when one objected strongly, pointing out that they did not own it and therefore had no right to perform it independently. Reluctantly, the others agreed. From

---

15. The singers were specifically concerned that even the ceremony's name not be revealed, and berated the writer on one occasion when he inadvertently used it in front of other women.
16. Here too the ceremony's name appears to be secret, and is thus omitted here.

their general descriptions, it appears to have been similar to the *yawulyu*.[16]

As with men's love magic, so too with the *yawulyu* is there a verbalised desire that members of the opposite sex hear and see enough of the proceedings to identify the performance, but not be so close that they can hear the song words.[17]

Two notable exceptions were observed, however. At Kungkayunti, one man privately recited a number of songs from the *yawulyu* the women were currently performing, claiming that an un-named old woman 'olden time' had revealed them to him. After some hesitation, the writer asked one of the women performers if she was aware of this; to his relief, and confusion, he was told that all the women knew of this. Although they did not appear entirely happy with the whole business, they had not discontinued their performances. The second event occurred at Balgo, when during the first recordings of a *yawulyu* performance, one old man came across and sat beside the writer, remaining there all afternoon. The performers appeared to ignore him, and for his own part, he did not speak to them, being content to sit and smoke quietly as he watched. No reason for this exception was given.[18]

The function of the *yawulyu*, and other women's restricted ceremonies, appears to be undergoing change; although some women insist that the performances are connected with the generation of sexual attractiveness, others are of the opinion that they serve more to maintain good health. Whether or not this dual nature has always been present could not be established during fieldwork, and possibly the use of the word 'change' above presupposes that it has not. However, early accounts of such ceremonies tend not to contain references to the latter aspect, thus suggesting at least the association with health may be a recent addition.[19]

Kutitji

Within the framework of initiation, an all-night ceremony is held prior to the period of long seclusion; this is the *kutitji*. The ceremony signals the start of the initiation period proper and following the performance, the novice and his companions set out on their bush-journeying. The ceremony name derives from the type of shields, *kutitji*, on which have been painted representations from one or more myths; these shields are laid on the ground and beaten with single sticks or single boomerangs as an accompani-

ment to the men's singing during part of the ceremony.

Ngalungku

The series of initiation ceremonies (*ngalungku*) for males include some of the most secret ritual activities and singing, to the extent that no element of the proceedings, whether it is bodypainting, dance actions or song texts may be revealed to females or uninitiated males. For this reason conversations dealing with initiation generally are conducted in whispers and almost never inside the camp area. In the Alice Springs area, one of the effects of European-type education has been to disrupt traditional initiation practices by reducing the amount of time each year children are free from school.

According to local accounts, the duration of a novice's exclusion from camp might be from six months to a year, during which time he travelled widely (in the company of an older classificatory brother and a guardian), received instruction in bushcraft, and was gradually introduced to various initiation ceremonies; however, it appears that he was not necessarily told the meanings of the songs and rituals at this stage.[20]

Initiation culminates with the circumcision act, which takes place at night in isolation; some time later, the novice returns to camp.

From a musical point of view, initiation songs are readily identifiable by their frequent use of heavily accentuated enunciation (called *pangaltjuninpa*), rising glissands (called *ngutulmaninpa*) and by the accompaniment technique of beating single sticks on the ground.[21]

---

17. C. H. Berndt (1965:243) suggests that such proximity is instrumental to the success of the ceremony (presumably regardless of the magical attributes claimed by the participants).
18. He was not, however, the same man C. H. Berndt observed staying within earshot of a *yawulyu* performance at Balgo (1965:245) and who was said to 'understand' *yawulyu*.
19. Indeed, the attendance by decrepit individuals, who may make up as much as half the total number of participants, solely for the former aspect would need to be an act of tremendous faith.
20. There were no young males at Kungkayunti during the period of fieldwork, and it was said that the practice of initiation was not adhered to at Balgo. At Yayayi, however, some 46km from Kungkayunti, initiation of a kind was still practised in 1974-75, although the neophytes were kept only in local seclusion for a matter of weeks, and apparently did not undertake the more traditional journeying associated with the period.
21. One exception to this rule, as regards accompaniment technique, is the *tarrkalpa* series (*see tulku*); however, as this particular series is said to have come from Pitjantjatjara country it may represent a non-Pintupi practice.

Although initiation ceremonies are known collectively as *ngalungku*, individual ceremonies may be named according to the identity of the principal character, e.g., kangaroo, possum, perentie, etc. The myth of the kangaroo in particular is possibly the longest-travelling in the Pintupi repertoire, covering long distances in the Tomkinson and Rawlinson Ranges area, but starting further south, in Pitjantjatjara country. It is difficult to say precisely how many *ngalungku* myths are in general use, as the indications are that of the total number known by initiated men, only some are revealed to the neophytes during any given initiation period. I have no information of the current situation, wherein initiation takes place in the relatively short period of a few weeks.

Yarritjiti

Details of this ceremony are sketchy; the songs were performed at some distance from the camp at Kungkayunti, and I was warned not to divulge any information about them to the women and there was a general air of reluctance to discuss the series and its ceremonies. This attitude was due to a fear that one man who had banned the singing of it on an earlier occasion but who had been absent from camp on this present occasion, might get to hear of it and, because of his known ability as a sorcerer, cause trouble.

What is known of the ceremony is that it occurs at the end of the initiation period, and after it has run its all-night course, the initiates return to camp for the first time. The associated dreaming concerns the *mutilya kutjarra*, the two initiates, and also the *ngaturrpa*, a species of bird. What is less certain is the language—some say Pitjantjatjara, others Yagundjadjara, but all men say that it is now part of the Pintupi repertoire. The ceremony is known as *aratjiti* among the Pitjantjatjara.

Although they are part and parcel of the initiation process in its entirety, neither the *kutitji* nor the *yarritjiti* ceremonies are subsumed within the generic term 'ngalungku'.

Tingarri

Berndt (1974:7) and Ellis (1966:2) have observed that certain myths (of which the *tingarri* is one), with their attendant ceremonies and songs, are not owned or performed *in toto* by a group from any one geographical location; rather they suggest that each individual group has ownership of a section of the total myth. It is further suggested that as these myths tend to deal with characters who spent much of their time travelling, the geographical locations associated with the first and last songs in the respective series belonging to any given group constitute points on their traditional territorial boundaries. This, however, remains an unconfirmed possibility only.

Although it is not known how many complete *tingarri* series the Pintupi possess altogether, two different series were recorded at Kungkayunti, and a further two from Balgo; no attempt was made to localise the myths, and I have only the singers' word, on listening to examples from each series, that the four are separate. By contrast, referring to song texts he obtained from Balgo in 1958 and 1960 Berndt (1970:224) at first implies that there is only one *tingarri* myth, but several 'versions', a view on which he does not elaborate; later however (p.232), he speaks of 'the [*tingarri*] myths'. It may be that what Berndt describes as 'versions' or 'myth-sections' (p.232) correspond to what I was informed were discrete myths.

The *tingarri* ceremonies are secret and are for initiated men only, although not all of those participating possess the same degree of knowledge of the ritual and the myths; indeed many of the associated activities in both ritual and myth concern the socialising of novices. (For a list of some of these, *see* Berndt (1970:236-37.) As for the *yilpintji*, however, so too for the *tingarri*, songs from the associated series may also be sung informally without the customary ritual. Such performances take place inside the designated men's areas, which are on the outskirts of the camp living quarters. In these cases, individual songs sung at the same time that a bullroarer would be swung had the full rituals been observed, are sung unaccompanied. However, this, together with the tendency to reduce the number of consecutive repetitions of any given song before proceeding to the next (as described elsewhere), is the only change apparent in the music itself. As in the cases of the *yilpintji* and *yawulyu*, there is a concern on the part of the participants that members of the opposite sex be far enough away so as not to hear clearly the song words; by contrast, when the performance includes the rituals, everything occurs in isolation, far from the camp and the possible presence of females. Unlike the *yilpintji* and *yawulyu*, however, the in-camp performances of *tingarri* are not designed to give members of the opposite sex a tantalising aural or visual glimpse of the activities; most occur at night and consist entirely of singing. If any fire is lit it is not for light but for warmth. Although it is difficult to obtain detailed information beyond it being considered acceptable for the songs to be heard faintly by women and children, it appears that the music by itself in this context is not considered as secret as the full ritual. Moreover, such singing sessions seem to function to refresh the singers' memories of the songs and their sequence. On several occasions in both Kungkayunti and Balgo, a further downgrading of formality was seen, in which small groups of men, meeting in the men's area to fashion boomerangs or spears or just to talk and snooze, would sometimes sing quietly through a number of *tingarri* songs.[22]

Nomenclature for the three recorded series is identical—each is described simply as *tingarri*, with differentiation made by saying each is a '*tingarri kutjupa*'—a 'different *tingarri*' a view expanded by reference to the respective geographical routes of the *tingarri*. The term *tingarri* refers to a particular type of mythical man, sometimes alone, sometimes living with other *tingarri* as a group.[23] Those who figure individually in the episodes from the myths tend to have personal as well as subsection names, while those in a group are categorised by subsection name(s) only.

Kutatji *(Waṉapa)*

The subject of sorcery in general, and 'pointing the bone' in particular has received widespread and often sensational publicity in both popular and academic publications. Descriptions of such phenomena have often used the word 'sing', as in many areas song is an integral part of the sorcery act; however, the way in which the word is used in English is ambiguous. The sentence, 'The man is singing his song' is unequivocal, since 'song' is the cognate accusative for the verb form 'is singing'. Now take the sentence, 'The man is singing his enemy'; here the accusative does not repeat the idea already contained in the verb, and to make sense of the sentence, we must apply another meaning to 'is singing'. The most common interpretation of the verb in such a case would be 'is ensorcelling', that is, is performing a curse on the enemy by singing a magical song at him.[24] Finally, there are several descriptions of 'singing' an object, e.g. 'The man is singing the spear prior to hunting for his enemy', in which case yet another meaning of the verb is intended, namely that

the man is imparting magical properties to his spear so that it will fly true, or the like.[25]

It is perhaps recognition of the ambiguity in stressing the connotations of 'sing' rather than the denotations that most writers have chosen to enclose the word within inverted commas. On the other hand, it may be that they are translating the actual native terminology; for example, the Hansens list *yinkangu* as meaning both 'to sing or to laugh' and 'to curse by singing' (1974:292). Although the connotations of the term were not explored, it appears that provided the second meaning is not a gloss, a situation not unlike that existing in English may hold also in Pintupi.

Whatever terminology earlier writers have used to describe the activating of supernatural powers directly or indirectly (into an object which is then used against the victim) against another person, the accounts agree that singing is the mechanism whereby such powers are both unleashed and channelled specifically. In sorcery, however, the initial ceremony (in which the victim is ritually tracked and killed) appears to be the occasion on which the greatest supernatural power is activated, and the subsequent flicking of a small pointed stick at the victim is more the deed which sets into motion the final part of the sorcery, rather than the main act itself.

There is no suggestion in the literature that the activities occurring prior to flicking or pointing of a stick or bone or other object at the victim have any effect on the victim's body or psyche. Rather, the ceremonies concentrate on generating sufficient supernatural power in the ritual killing so that the subsequent act, which alone is directed proximically towards the victim, will have the desired result.

---

22. The practice was not confined to *tingarri* songs, however; with the exception of the highly secret initiation series, songs from virtually every genre were sung in this manner. They tended to be sung unaccompanied, and more slowly and quietly than in a formal situation.

23. In common with the nomenclature for other Pintupi song series, the same term may also refer to the complete ceremony, individual activities within that ceremony, the song series as a whole, and each individual song.

24. *See*, e.g. 'the medicine men . . . "sing" the killer' (Meggitt 1965:325), and 'the sorcerer releases it by singing it out' (Berndt and Berndt 1964:270).

25. *See*, e.g. 'they . . . imagined the weapon to have been "sung" . . .' (Spencer and Gillen 1899:537), '. . . they [small stones] are "sung" . . .' (Elkin 1964:290), and 'women's singing of the husbands' boomerangs' (C. H. Berndt 1965:245), 'they wear . . . shoes . . . which have been ritually sung . . .' (Berndt and Berndt (1964:272).

Without the ceremony, say the Pintupi at Kungkayunti, the stick-flicking cannot succeed.[26]

The Pintupi believe that sorcery is carried out by one or more *kutatji* (sorcerers), who are humans, but who on occasion may assume a spirit-form and perform superhuman feats, including periodic invisibility and travelling long distances at great speed. They are also known for their odd sleeping habits—they prefer dry creek beds or tree tops and lie on their backs with legs in the air (to keep them cool). At Kungkayunti, a few men claimed to have 'seen' such *kutatji*:

These men can travel enormous distances very quickly, e.g. to Alice Springs and back in one day (some 400 km). Ordinary men may see a horse going along complete with riding gear but no rider—this will be the *kutatji*'s mount, and he really is there, but invisible. He can also ride a camel or an emu. (Field notes 22 January, 1975)

The *kutatji* are known by a number of different names—*wanapa, tjanpa, wati kutjarra* (two men, so called for their habit of travelling in pairs), *tjina wantu* (magic feet), and *tjamana karrpilpa* (tied-on shoes). These last two names refer to the shoes made from emu feathers, which the *kutatji* are said to wear in order to leave no tracks. They are also worn by the human *kutatji* when he flicks his stick at the victim. Prior to donning them, the fourth toe is raised, and a stick slid across the foot, holding the toe up; this is to further disguise any tracks.

Two of the men at Kungkayunti were said to be *kutatji*, and they themselves verified this, showing as physical proof their dislocated little toes, which are believed to act as eyes, enabling the men to move freely in the dark. On the outside edge of each *kutatji* shoe is a small opening to allow the dislocated toe to protrude, and thus 'see'.[27]

These same men took part in the recording of the *kutatji* song series, referred to here by the alternative name, *wanapa,* although at least four other men in camp also knew it, and joined in the singing. Fear of sorcery in general, together with the dread of ever being accused of having performed it on someone (which would normally involve being killed in reprisal), make the subject a reluctant one for conversation among the Pintupi. The *wanapa* songs were performed several kilometres out of camp, and those included were chosen after some discussion between the two *kutatji* men, lest knowledge of the songs be given to unqualified men. (There appears to be some initiation process required before men may attend actual ceremonies of this nature, but details were not given.) The general proceedings of the ceremony are as follows:

All the qualified men meet secretly and sing the series of *wanapa* songs. One man is then chosen, along with perhaps two companions, to perform the ritual killing. They place a twig under the fourth toe to lift it off the ground, don emu-feather shoes to avoid leaving tracks, and set out in the direction of the victim. Then one will flick a small stick with a hairstring tail towards the victim. There are two methods of flicking: (a) held in the crooked index finger of one hand, flicked away with the third finger of the other hand; (b) second and fourth fingers raised, twig inserted along between these and fifth and third fingers, then jabbed with the other hand. In the latter case, the stick may travel underground to the victim; this method is preferred if secrecy of presence is impossible. The victim immediately feels a jab of pain (descriptions always refer to the area of the shoulder blade) but there is no mark; by next morning he will be dead. (Field notes 22 January, 1975).

Expanded translations of texts from the *wanapa* series are as follows:

Song number
(Field tape 55)

1 I (the *kutatji* man) see my victim; I arise from a sitting position and move into dense mulga to remain unseen.
2 I move directly towards him, closing in, my weapons at the ready (he carries boomerang, club and shield).
3 Dogs (who alone can detect the presence of the *kutatji* man) dig holes to lie in, unaware of my coming.
4 A flock of *nyinyi* birds discloses nearby water; I sit to drink.
5 Having chased and caught my victim, I choke him, then stab him on each shoulder with my bullroarer (carried inside the feet).
6 I go off, moving on *putunputun* grass.

---

26. During fieldwork, it was said that in Balgo, such sorcery was not practised, although R. M. Berndt (1965:170) describes a fight there in 1960 induced by accusations of this very thing.
27. Spencer and Gillen (1899:479) has a photograph of *kutatji* shoes.

7   I, Blackness, I, Penis, move on.

8   To avoid the smoke of a bushfire, I walk on my knees, carrying my bullroarer; then, I rest.

9   I arrive at a large camp area, by the water; I see that the people have all gone out looking for food.

10 I point, with a backward sweep of my left hand, towards a group of women asleep inside the camp; I cannot enter yet.

11 I dance, my feet lifted high.

12 I travel on, then sit to rest.

    (Field tape 77)

13 I don my boots made from emu feathers, tying them on tightly.

14 My feet feel heavy from the long journey; nevertheless, I get to my feet and dance on top of a flat rock.

15 I stride straight towards the place where my victim lies.

16 I arise from my cave and go to the top of a hill where I gaze around.

17 In the heat of the day, I carry my possessions to the shade.

18 I, Blackness, take my bullroarer and sit in the shade.

19 I, Blackness, I the Subincised Penis, sit in the dense shade, resting.

20 I, Penis, insert my painted stick into the victim's shoulders, killing him.

21 I make my escape, disappearing in a whirlwind.

22 I pause to drink rainwater.

23 I travel on, hidden in a whirlwind; coming to a dry creek bed, I stop to sleep.

24 I, Tjangala, sleep with my feet in the air; I scratch my large testicles.

25 I, Tjampitjinpa, stand upright.

Pukalkarra

Although the practice of revenge expeditions, following the death of a member of a group in circumstances considered unjustified, is reported widely in the Central Desert area (e.g. Meggitt 1962:325-26; Strehlow 1970:108, 114, 117, 120-21; 1971: 265-66, 622-25) and beyond (Berndt and Berndt 1943: 127-29, Elkin 1964: 327-28), most accounts lack detail. Two noteworthy exceptions are the Berndts (1943) who describe the procedures at Ooldea (some 750km to the south), and Strehlow 1971, who notes that the Aranda use texts in the Luridja language.

The most common Pintupi name for both the ceremony and the expedition as a whole is *pukalkarra*, although other terms are also in use.[28]

There appears to be a connection between this ceremony and that preceding the *wanapa* (sorcery) act; in both, following a ceremony of singing and dancing, those chosen to carry out the respective activities are fully fledged *kutatji* men wearing feather shoes to avoid leaving tracks. Detailed information was not available from the Pintupi, partly it seemed because of an understandable reluctance to discuss an activity now known to be illegal, and partly because the activity itself seems to occur less frequently than, say, a generation ago. Thus while Strehlow (1970:119) and the Berndts (1943:127) could find very recent cases of such killings, Meggitt (1962:326) and Tonkinson (1974:80) found the custom to have been discontinued at around the '50s. I myself found nobody at Kungkayunti or Balgo who said he had participated in such activities, but knowledge of the song series appears fairly widespread.[29]

Tuyutu

The classification of song series called *tuyutu* encompasses a number of healing practices which relate to both external and internal maladies; these in turn may be considered the result of direct injury or the malevolent workings of a supernatural creature.[30]

In the former cases, the songs sung deal with particular episodes in myths in which the Dreamtime character is afflicted with the same ailment; this character cures himself/herself by singing certain charms, and because of the success of these, the Pintupi too believe they will effect a cure by performing the same songs. In each *tuyutu* of the latter nature, however, it is believed that a specified and named creature from the mythological past is inhabiting the patient's body. Such an unfortunate

28. The Hansens (1974:166) give *pukalkurra*, and a number of men used the word *warrmala*; this latter term in various cognate forms is in widespread use, e.g. at Jigalong it is called *wanmala* (Tonkinson 1974:80) and at Ooldea it is *warnmala* (Berndt and Berndt 1943:127).

29. In 1969, a number of Pintupi men from Yayayi and Papunya performed the *pukalkarra* ceremony, apparently for sheer enjoyment, during an arranged visit to a distant ceremonial site (AIAS Film L66: PINTUPI REVISIT YARUYARU).

30. Although more than one singer may perform these *tuyutu*, it appears to be more the practice for one individual to sing alone; in this respect it may be considered the only solo song type in the traditional repertoire.

situation has an exact precedent in a particular Dreamtime episode, in which a mythological character is able to remove or kill or otherwise incapacitate the offending creature and thus effect a cure; in all such cures, singing accompanies whatever acts the character performs. The final act by the Doctorman is often to 'remove' from inside the patient's body, using sleight of hand, a small stone, piece of wood or bone, and, displaying this object as a symbol of the creature causing the sickness, to proclaim the treatment successful.[31]

The recorded version of the cure for a *yawarra*, a spear wound in the thigh (a traditional form of punishment as well as a common injury resulting from a fight), consists of five songs of which the fifth was, for some reason, not sung on this particular occasion:

Song number

1 The spear withdrew from the wound.
2 The spear withdrew from the wound; I arose.
3 I am able to walk to the place (? of convalescence).
4 I am able to walk to the place.
5 I am sore from the completed operation you performed on me.[32]

In explaining the use of the first person pronominal suffix *na* in the last three songs above, and songs 2, 3 and 7 below, the singers confirmed that in these cases the Dreamtime character's own words (i.e. the actual charms) constituted the texts. They also claimed that there were many more songs to the series, but that they had forgotten them; the above were enough, apparently, to be efficacious.[33]

There are two series of songs sung to induce rapid blood clotting after circumcision and subincision; the term *kirrpinpa* (sometimes appearing as *kirrpinkurra*) was used several times in describing the cure, but it is not clear if this refers specifically to the clotting, or to the song series. For the first of these two, seven song texts were dictated, but only five sung in the recorded performance:

Song number

1 The foreskin has been cut.
2 After the operation, I go to the fire. (*Note*: Often, the patient crouches over a small fire so that its heat will quicken the clotting, and relieve the post-operative pain (*see also* Dean and Carrel 1955:134 for a description of this from Yuendumu).)
3 I am sore after the operation.

4 A cold wind descends from the Milky Way, and enters the body to effect healing.
5 The subincision act is carried out swiftly.
6 You completed your operation on me.
7 I am sore from the completed operation you performed on me.

The second series designed to encourage clotting refers also to the chewing of yellow ochre, which was considered beneficial to a rapid recovery.

1 After the operation, the initiate chews yellow ochre.
2 After chewing it, he spits it out.
3 He squats over a smoky fire to ease the pain.

It is not known from which particular myth or myths these three episodes are taken.

The only healing ceremony observed during fieldwork took place at Kungkayunti when a young boy had fallen from a tree and injured his leg; he was carried to the men's customary meeting place on the edge of camp, and with his head cradled in his father's lap, lay back while two men, lying on their stomachs, sang a number of songs from the *yukurukuru* series, their mouths only a short distance away from the leg; at the end of each song, the two men spat on the affected area. After some ten minutes of this, they forcibly straightened out the injured leg, giving the boy considerable pain, and causing his mother (who was walking about the camp, club in hand, but afraid to approach the men's area) to call out repeatedly, '*Wanti!*' (Leave him alone!). The treatment was performed only once, and was judged to have been successful (even though the boy could not walk for another six days). The myth associated with the song series is said to originate at Broome (on the northwest coast of Australia and well outside Pintupi territory), but the songs performed in both the healing rites and subsequent recording sessions were said to be in Walbiri, which suggests that, like the *tingarri*, the *yukurukuru* may constitute a long myth covering several linguistic areas and only a portion of which is known and used by the Pintupi. Although a

---

31. Although the people at Kungkayunti and Balgo did not assert their own healing prowess openly, the Pintupi were, according to Meggitt (1962:41) held in some awe on account of it by the neighbouring Walbiri.

32. Both this series and the following two are not represented in the Analysis because of inferior recordings in which the melodic lines are unclear.

33. Barrett (1964) also notes that a few songs only from the appropriate series were effective in curing toothache among the Walbiri.

few of its song texts refer to healing and massage, the main concern of the myth is with the travels of the woman Yukurukuru (the relevant Dreamtime character) and how she dealt with her own injuries; the selection of such episodes from the myth and the singing of them appears identical to the practice employed in the first three examples above.

The songs sung to cure snakebite, likewise, represent only a small part of the *kuniya* (snake) ceremony, which involves costumed dancing, ceremonial objects and ritual activities, in addition to singing; the whole ceremony is restricted to initiated men, and thus the cure too can be performed only by men and for men.[34]

However, the women too have their own curing songs for snakebite, taken from the *kinyu* series. Both the *kuniya* and *kinyu* series are, however, claimed not to be in the Pintupi language, and are thus omitted from the analysis later in this present work.[35]

The following curing ceremony recorded was called *paniya*, and claimed to be beneficial for any eye ailments; as with previous examples, the particular songs used in the treatment are taken from a much longer myth. After each song, the Doctorman spits into the eye, and later produces a small piece of wood to the patient saying that he has removed this from the eye and that the treatment has been successful. This was the only curing ceremony whose immediate origin is known: the Balgo man in question learnt it from his father, although he says his real brothers also know and perform it.

1. *milpa*   *witingka*   *nyinanya*
    eagle-type clear-eyed sit-they-two,

    milpa   *tjantjingkin* *nyinanya*
    eagle-type eye-part   sit-they-two

    Two eagles, clear-eyed, sit looking out over the country.

2. *parral* *parral* *nyangu* *yalu* *karri*   *tjina*
    thin   thin   saw   plains expanse tracks

    Looking over the immense plains they saw faint tracks.

3. *larrantaya*   *karriya* *tiwurrku* *tiwurrkuya*
    foreign object hands   departs   departs

    The foreign object in one of the eagle's eyes is removed.

4. *kanapilyirrpa*   *tiwurru* *timparr* *timparrpaka<u>nu</u>*
    mulga country departs emerges emerges

    As they fly over mulga country, the foreign object is removed.

The final curing ritual appears to be in the Walbiri language, and the Pintupi man who dictated the song texts has had a long association with the Walbiri; nonetheless, he now calls it his own, and uses it at Balgo. The songs are from the *tjaputa* series (about which I have no further information), and are claimed to be useful in curing a variety of ailments in the upper body, including the head.

1. *yaltapayi*   *karalkaralpungka* *kumangka*
    sickness   healed   cured by singing

    karalkaralpungka
    healed
    The sickness is cured by singing.

2. *karalpana*   *karalpa*   *tjanarrinta*   *tjanari*
    healed-I   healed   cooled   cooled
    The healing lowers my temperature.

3. *tjakarrkarralu* *tjakarr* *kani<u>n</u>u* *kantirrirrilu*
    healing ritual   ?   brought   healed
    The healing ritual was brought, and enacted.

The songs illustrate graphically the relevance of events in the past to acts in the present. The cures described here obviously do not cover the entire range of possible disabilities; it is not known, however, what remedies are resorted to in cases where no mythological parallel can be cited and used.

Towards the end of fieldwork, two further series

---

34. In contrast with the Aranda concept of curing snakebite, in which the animal eventually chokes its victim to death (Strehlow 1971:258), one of the *kuniya* songs recorded at Balgo indicates that here the snake is considered as eating away at the internal organs of the victim; the cure in effect makes the human food inedible to the animal, thus starving it to death:

yalana	*tjampurr*	*wangka,*	*kamana*	*tjampurr wangka*
hungry-I	famished	speak	hindered-I	famished speak

I (i.e. the snake) speak, saying I am famished (here inside the victim's body).

35. There is some disagreement as to the location and identity of Kinyu. Men say it is a mountain southwest of Winparrku and strictly off-limits for women. The women maintain, however, that it is a deep cave some 320km north of Wiluna (whence several Pintupi people at Balgo have come in the past decade), and associated with the myth of the bush-cat. There may in fact be two distinct Kinyu place names.

were recorded, the name for each being given simply as *tuyutu*; they differ from the other *tuyutu* in having multiple melodies, and include the *tingarri* contour. Details are few, and the series are referred to in the analysis as *tuyutu* (a) and (b) respectively.

Wantapi

Although the Hansens (1974:247) list the term as synonymous with '*tulku*', there is one important musical difference. Whereas in the *tulku* women may sing together with the men, in the *wantapi* they may only crotch-slap; the men use boomerangs to accompany their singing. In contrast with the *tulku*, there are specific times during the *wantapi* when women and children are required to cover themselves with blankets or shield their eyes in some other way, to avoid seeing certain ceremonial objects which the men bring out. Generally, however, differentiation from the *tulku* is made more on social than musical grounds. Of the three recorded *wantapi* (all from Kungkayunti) two were said to be in the Pitjantjatjara language, and all were performed specifically for recording purposes; they consist of only portions of the song series.[36]

Although informants agreed that *wantapi* was not a type of *tulku* (or indeed a type of anything else), they could not specify differences beyond that of the women's role. There appears to be no cognate form of the term in neighbouring languages, unlike other song classifications. Individual people commented that the *wantapi* was 'like *tingarri*' or 'little bit *tingarri*', although the precise nature of the association with the all-male *tingarri* ceremonies (*see* below) was not defined, and indeed is still unclear. One or two others claimed that it was the 'same' as the *kurangara*, a ceremony accompanying the trading of pearl shells (Tindale 1974:84-85) from the Fitzroy area to the Warburton Ranges via the Murchison area, but there appears to be no definite proof that this ceremony involved the Pintupi in any large-scale or organised manner. Certainly no recordings were obtained, despite enquiries, of material generally acknowledged as *kurangara*, and those Pintupi who used the word denied that it was of Pintupi origin.

The evidence suggests that although some Pintupi, especially those at Kungkayunti, have knowledge of *wantapi* series, these series are of non-Pintupi origin; for this reason, the *wantapi* are excluded from analysis in this present volume.

---

36. During these performances, the men initially were dissatisfied with the small numbers of women present; to call over reinforcements, they uttered loud falsetto alveolar trills (*tjumpirrpa*) after each song.

Musical instruments

In the sense that they do not possess a discrete category of artefacts manufactured exclusively for musical purposes, the Pintupi have no musical instruments. There is no suggestion in the literature that the pairs of boomerangs used as song accompaniment have been anything other than hunting boomerangs temporarily featuring in a non-hunting situation, and the pairs of sticks and single lengths of wood used with particular musical genres are strictly *ad hoc* objects, discarded after the performance. (The current situation regarding the boomerang, however, is not clear-cut. Individual men at Balgo were seen making boomerangs for the *tjatiwanpa* ceremony in the first instance, but whether or not they were used thereafter for some other purpose could not be ascertained. Similarly, it could not be said for certain that all *kali* at Kungkayunti and Balgo were used for both fighting and musical accompaniment; some may indeed have figured only in the latter activity.) However, in the sense that these same instruments, together with hand-clapping, chest-slapping and crotch-slapping, are grouped together in nomenclature distinct from other sound-producing objects or devices, are considered essential to song performance, and are used only in musical circumstances, they may be said to be musical instruments.[1]

Although the Pintupi have no lexical term for music *per se*, there is a fairly well defined concept of music sound centring, understandably enough, around 'singing', and for most of this 'singing' an accompaniment device is used. This may be hand-clapping, chest-slapping, crotch-slapping, beating pairs of boomerangs or short sticks together, or

---

1. It might be argued that the term 'sound instrument' is more appropriate for such non-melodic instruments, but this only begs the question. For if we assume that not all aurally perceptible vibrations are considered musical to the Pintupi—and such an assumption is fundamental to the concept of music sound as opposed to non-music sound—then there will be 'non-musical instruments' as well as 'musical instruments', the latter term applying only to musical situations. The term 'sound instrument', however, does not imply any such distinction.

thumping a single stick on the ground. Although there are individual descriptive terms for most of these actions, two ethnoclassifications are in use: those sounds produced directly by the hand or hands (i.e. hand-clapping, chest- and crotch-slapping) are called *papunpa*,[2] and those using hand-held objects (i.e. pairs of boomerangs and sticks, and beating the ground with a single stick) are encompassed in the taxon *maya punganyi* (literally, loud beating). Insofar as these accompaniment devices are considered an integral part of most song performance, are not found in any non-musical situation, and are subsumed into distinct ethnoclassifications which are based on the means of sound production, these devices may justifiably be considered musical instruments; this term is used throughout this work.[3]

By the same token, the Pintupi do not consider the bullroarer a musical instrument. Although it figures in secret male ceremonies, it is an integral item in the ceremony as a whole rather than in the singing.[4] And although swinging the bullroarer may occur during singing, there is no indication in the literature of any pitch, intensity, rhythmic, durational or melodic relationship between the resultant sounds and those same elements of the particular song or songs being performed concurrently. Temporal contiguity alone does not establish a musical relationship. Whereas the sound producing devices described in the previous paragraph have no function or importance beyond that of a musical context, the bullroarer has a profound significance; sometimes it represents a spirit-voice, sometimes it is the means of transmitting an irresistible sexual impulse to an unsuspecting female (who may be many kilometres away), but whatever the particular supernatural connotations, the resultant sounds are considered 'speaking' rather than 'singing'. Thus, for the Pintupi, and despite its ritual importance and supernatural properties, the bullroarer is essentially a non-musical sound producing device.[5]

Boomerang

The Pintupi have two types of boomerang: the *kali*, currently used primarily for fighting, and the hooked variety, sometimes referred to as *kali pinatjarra* (kali-ear-with), which is used exclusively for fighting. There are few of this latter type to be seen, outside tourist shops; on one occasion one was seen hit against a *kali* at Balgo as accompaniment to singing.

Thomson (1964:410) noted that the Pintupi he

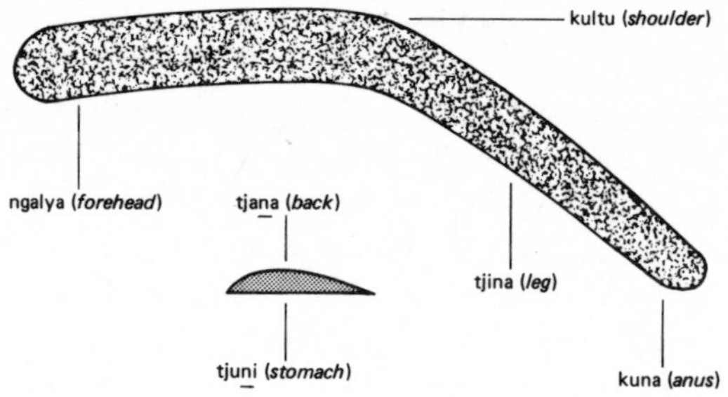

(All these terms are generic, and apply to both humans and animals).

Figure 7 Nomenclature for parts of the *kali* (boomerang).

encountered at Lapilapi in 1957 possessed boomerangs, but that they had been obtained from the Walbiri. Further, they were not seen in use as hunting, fighting or musical implements, but rather were valued more as ceremonial objects. He also noted that none of the people arriving at Lapilapi at that time from the adjacent areas of the Gibson Desert had boomerangs, neither did groups met south and west of Lake Mackay, or west of Lapilapi. Corroborating evidence for a recent acquisition by the Pintupi comes from Hanns Peter, AIAS Research Fellow specialising in boomerangs; he believes (personal communication) that the Pintupi obtained their boomerangs from the Walbiri in exchange for spears and spear-throwers, later passing on the artefact to the Pitjantjatjara. From this, one concludes that acquisition of the boomerang by the Pintupi may be relatively recent for more eastern groups, and

---

2. This is the present-participle form; the verbal forms *papu punganyi*, *papunmanu*, are also common.

3. The opinion given by one old Pintupi man, known over a wide area as a leader of men as well as of song, indicates the importance attached to instruments. When asked what would happen if the singers had no instruments, he replied that they would clap (for men) or slap their crotches (for women). If, for some reason, they could not do this, they simply could not sing at all.

4. At least at Balgo, knowledge of the bullroarer is not confined to men. I was shown several by a woman, who allowed me to photograph them and record details on their names and use. As she also requested that the pictures and tape be placed under a closed option at the AIAS, further comment is not possible here.

5. In *tingarri*, *yilpintji* and *ngalungku* ceremonies, there are prescribed occasions when men's bullroarers are to be swung. Although I did not attend any ceremony when this act occurred, it appears that the swinging of the bullroarer might occur during the singing of one or more particular songs, or in the periods between singing or repeating such songs, and is thus structurally related to the ceremony as a whole. For cases where it is swung during singing, it might well be argued that it is indeed functioning as a musical instrument—the Pintupi's claims notwithstanding—insofar as it is integral to the performance of those songs.

certainly very recent for more western and southern groups.[6]

Wanari (a type of mulga) and *walakara* (an unidentified species) are preferred woods. The various parts of the *kali* are shown in Fig. 7.

In performance, two boomerangs of the same size are clapped together, the flat surfaces of the *ngalya* and *kuna* coming into simultaneous contact. Two methods of performance are in common use:

(a) One boomerang is laid diagonally across the lap and the other hit down on to it. If the player is right-handed, the right-hand boomerang is uppermost; the corollary is also true.

(b) Both boomerangs are held vertically in front of the performer, and the one nearer the performer's face is slapped out against the other. According to some, boomerangs should always be held in this vertical position, but should a player tire, he will then lower them on to his lap. Others, however, maintained that the two positions were equally acceptable.

The first position seems to require slightly more space to execute, and it was noticed that when ceremonial managers told the singers to bunch up, most changed from (a) to (b). When standing to sing (as the *kutungulu* ceremonial managers do in the *tjatiwanpa* ceremony), all men use (b). Usually the boomerangs are hit from about 10cm apart, but this gap can increase to as much as 30cm if the player becomes excited, and the singing is loud. In both playing positions the *ngalya* is uppermost, or away from the player, and the *kuna* lowermost, or closer to the player (*see* Plate 1).

In addition to providing regular beats for song accompaniment, boomerangs also perform a tremolo effect, executed by rolling the wrists rapidly to bring *nyalya* and *kuna* into quick alternate contact. Such beating is called *titji* or *titjititji* (the latter more common in Balgo), and has two functions:

(a) During a recording of the *tjiwiri tulku* at Kungkayunti, many of the songs had a brief tremolo in mid-performance.[7] Two of the singers said separately afterwards that this indicated that the beater was dissatisfied with the unison of the singing or accompaniment. On hearing such beating, the other men with boomerangs would also start this rapid tremolo effect, before restarting their original beating rhythm, hopefully in tighter synchronisation. Meanwhile, the

Plate 1 Donkeyman Luuku (left) and Brandy Kunymangara demonstrate the two styles of beating boomerangs (Balgo 1975).

singing continued unabated. It was usually the song leader who initiated such a signal.

(b) In longer series of songs, rapid beating at the end of an item, i.e. during the last few seconds of singing indicated that this was the last item in one section of the ceremony; following the item there would be a short period of rest, usually about five minutes. Such beating, in which all the men participate, is called *yulutjarra* or *titutjarra* (lit. continuous). It is general practice for each individual song in a series to be repeated at least once before moving on to the next; the tremolo is used in all performances of such a last item.

There are a number of words in use referring specifically to boomerang beating as a song accompaniment; the more general are *timpilpa* (the beating itself) and *timpilpunganyi* (to beat boomerangs together). In some song series the beating starts at a rapid pace but in the middle of each item changes to half the earlier rate; in such cases terms used to describe the different rates are, for the faster: *wala* (lit. fast), *parrparrtu* (trembling) and *pulkapulka* (big, heavy); and for the slower, *purrpurrpa* (trotting), *manginpunginpa* (?), and *katapunginpa* (? lit. hitting the head).

---

6. In the course of the 1932 expedition to Mt Liebig, Tindale took films of Ngaliya and Pintupi people, and later (1963: plate 69) published a photograph of Ngaliya men singing and using the boomerang as accompaniment. No mention is made of Pintupi use of the artefact at that time, and possibly the incident represents early, if not initial, contact with the boomerang.
7. This particular *tulku* is not included for analysis later in this work, because of the relatively poor quality of singing and recording.

35

On one or two occasions, these terms were also used to describe the unchanging beating rate in a particular song series; on further enquiries, comparison was made to the beating rate of other series, thus suggesting the absence of any absolute speed criterion.

As mentioned earlier, importance is attached to unison, both instrumental and vocal; terminology relating to this unison is identical for both media: *tjukarurru* (parallel, straight), *kintilpa* (level) and *tjunguni* (to come together). Lack of unison is described simply as: *putaninypa* (to go wrong), *kuya* (wrong), *panytja* (rubbish) and *kurra* (bad).

In the **singing** for the *tjatiwanpa* ceremony, each item **contains a** change in boomerang beating from fast to **slow**, and there is aural preparation for this change, in the form of alternate accented and unaccented beats as shown in Example 5.

In other song series, however, formal divisions in each individual item may be cued in by other means.

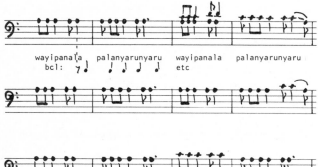

Example 5 Aural preparation for change in accompaniment rate in *tjatiwanpa* song.

Example 6 Single-beat accompaniment using boomerangs.

Boomerangs are the most frequently used means of song accompaniment among the Pintupi, and in performance at both Kungkayunti and Balgo it was frequently noted that all the men seemed anxious to provide some sort of accompaniment. Those who did not have boomerangs looked for small sticks and hit these together, but holding them in the same way as boomerangs; those who could not find sticks held imaginary ones, and performed beating actions in the air, including even the tremolo action perfectly mimed.

The boomerang is the only enduring artefact functioning occasionally as a musical instrument. There were no professional boomerang makers at Kungkayunti or Balgo, and most men made their own, although there was distribution between uncles and nephews, sons and fathers, and brothers. At the time of ceremonies it was not uncommon to see men taking two pairs of boomerangs to the performance area, ready to give the spare one to a relative who had none. (The writer himself was pleasantly surprised by such an act by a classificatory brother.) Because of their additional use as a fighting implement, however, most men have at least one boomerang stored in their house at all times. It is essentially the instrument of the initiated male, and it is not until subincision is completed that an initiate is given his first boomerang.

In the recorded sample, accompaniment using boomerangs consisted of the following variety:

(a) Tremolo, occurring for one or two seconds during songs from the *tjiwiri* series, and after selected songs in the *tjatiwanpa* series.

(b) Single beats, unchanging throughout the song; this is the most common boomerang accompaniment and is illustrated in Example 6.

(c) Augmentation of a steady beat in the middle of a song; this phenomenon is confined to *tjatiwanpa* songs, in the recorded sample.

All Pintupi song consists of the repetition several times of word groups which constitute the song text; the particular rhythmic accompaniment established during the first utterance of this word group is generally repeated in subsequent utterances, so that the relationship between particular syllables and strokes from the accompanying instrument is constant. (Obviously, though, this does not apply to cases where the accompaniment rhythm or rate changes in mid-performance.) In the case of the *tjatiwanpa* songs, it will be seen that there must be an even number of strokes per complete utterance of the text, otherwise after augmentation the beating will not recur on the same syllables in subsequent utterances. This practice holds for all but one song. During the singing of the 202nd song in the series, the beating started with thirteen beats per utterance of the text; on augmentation however, the beats could not recur in exactly the same places (*see* Example 7).

(d) A triplet formation (♪♩).

The *tulku yunpu* is the only recorded song series in which the triplet formation occurs performed by boomerangs (although it is commonly found in initiation series, where single sticks striking the ground beat it out); further, only one song from the *yunpu* series contains this particular rhythm. It would thus appear to be more typical of single stick-beating than of boomerang-beating.

(e) In a metric ratio of 2:3 against the melody, for example:

Single sticks beaten on the ground

This accompaniment device is restricted principally to those men's song series which, when performed with their associated ritual, must on no account be seen or heard by women or children. It is thus common to all initiation series. Meggitt (1962:287) suggests such beating simulates the thudding of kangaroo tails. The stick itself is called *pilypa*, a name applying to any short piece of wood, be it for firewood or musical purposes. In addition, however, men may refer to it as *lungurrtjuninpa*, or *lungurrmaninpa* (literal translations of which are not available). The beating itself may be called *yatuni*, *pilypa* or *wanmurr punganyi*; a term given for very loud beating is *lungku*; two-handed beating, which is usually applied to achieve this, is called just that—*marra kutjaralu*, and features also in some *tingarri* singing. As mentioned earlier this type of accompaniment is found also in the *tarrkalpa*.

The boomerang may be used in this way as an accompanying instrument, with either the flat side or the edge striking the ground. More often, however, a piece of wood 45-60cm long and 2-3cm in diameter is found near the singing site and used. If the wood is

Example 7 Exception to constant text-syllable-accompaniment beat relationship in *tjatiwanpa* songs.

Example 8 Changes in accompaniment using single sticks.

straight a small depression for the hands is dug, so that the entire length of the stick hits the ground; if the stick is naturally curved, however, no depression is necessary. The stick is most often held with both hands, and sometimes used with enough force to obscure the body of singers in a cloud of dust before

37

Example 9 Cross-rhythm ratio of 2:3 between accompaniment and voice in *pukalkarra* song.

Example 10 Cross-rhythm ratio of 3:5 between accompaniment and voice in *yarritjiti* song.

Example 11 Cross-rhythm ratio of 4:7 between accompaniment and voice in *yarritjiti* song.

Example 12 Cross-rhythm ratio of 14:25 between accompaniment and voice in *yarritjiti* song.

Example 13 Cross-rhythm ratio of 16:27 between accompaniment and voice in *yarritjiti* song.

38

each song is finished. When the depression formed by the length of the stick becomes more than one or two centimetres deep, the surrounding earth is pushed back to level the ground once more.

As with the pairs of boomerangs, so with the single stick there are a number of different rhythms and tempo ratios found in the accompaniment. Unlike the boomerangs, however, where maintenance of a single steady beat throughout each song is the general rule, stick beating is almost evenly divided between maintaining a single rhythm, and changing from one rhythm and/or rate to another (or alternation between two such different ones).

The most common change is from ♪♪ to ♩ as shown in Example 8. Where the beating is at a speed different from that of the melody, the most common ratio is 2:3 as shown in Example 9.

Other ratios however do occur, and are found not just in isolated instances, but wherever particular songs in a series recur; e.g. the ratios of 3:5 and 4:7 occur in two songs from the *yarritjiti* series (*see* Examples 10 and 11). Also in this series there are individual cases of what appear to be more complex ratios of 14:25 and 16:27 as shown in Examples 12 and 13.

The only other ratios in this series, 3:5 and 4:7, occur more frequently, however, and those of 14:25 and 16:27 are, respectively, only one unit different from them (15:25 = 3.5 and 16:28 = 4:7); it certainly seems possible under such circumstances that this is what the singers may have been trying to achieve.

A further difference between boomerang and single stick accompaniment lies in the position of the beats relative to the initial sounding of melodic notes; the former occur at the same time as the new note is sung, while the latter are often slightly before or after the note (*see* Examples 12 and 13), not only as in the two examples above where a relatively complex tempo ratio applies, but also where the beats may be aligned more precisely within the melody as, for instance, Example 14.

As mentioned earlier, the recorded sample is almost equally divided between maintenance of a single rhythm, and change from one rhythm or rate to another; in all but one case, these single rhythms comprise simply the regular repetition of a single beat, rather than repetition of a rhythmic figure which consists of more than one beat. The sole exception (*see* Example 15) occurs in the *ngintaka* (perentie lizard) series, an initiation ceremony.

With the exception of the *tarrkalpa*, whose precise nature is unclear (but whose origin is said to be non-Pintupi and thus is not really relevant to this present discussion), the only series accompanied by beating single sticks on the ground are associated with male initiation. All of these series are shared by other groups, chief among whom are the Pitjantjatjara, to the south and southwest. In the associated myths much of the Dreamtime activity occurs inside Pitjantjatjara territory before crossing, if at all, into Pintupi country (e.g. the Petermann and Rawlinson Ranges area). If one accepts that the ceremonies have their ultimate origin in Pitjantjatjara country—and while some Pintupi men assert this, the whole issue is still unresolved—then the inescapable conclusion would seem to be that prior to their adoption of these ceremonies, the Pintupi had no musical instruments other than the percussive use of their own bodies.

Paired sticks

There is doubt as to the authenticity of paired sticks as both a traditional Pintupi accompanying device, and an entirely separate musical instrument. Apart from *punu* (wood), the only name given was the Walbiri one, *dururu*, and the only recorded items accompanied solely by such sticks were, with one exception, of Walbiri, not Pintupi origin. There is no doubt, however, that the Pintupi are familiar with the sticks, and on several occasions when singers had no other means of accompanying their singing, they would pick up two sticks which happened to be at hand, and beat them together. It was thus more familiar as a boomerang-substitute than as a separate instrument. (By contrast, when the nature of the song series called for single sticks beaten on the ground, all the singers went and found one for themselves, and nobody used any other accompanying device.) In the sole song series in which it was the only accompaniment, the *wangata*, the beating consisted of regular single beats throughout the entire performance. Such beating, which is the most common boomerang style, together with the appearance of the sticks when individuals had not brought boomerangs of their own, suggest that the paired sticks may, at least in Pintupi music, be simply an *ad hoc* substitute for that other instrument.[8]

tingarri series

Example 14 Non-coincidence of initial sounding of note and accompaniment beat.

Example 15 Use of rhythmic figure in *ngintaka* song.

Hand-clapping

When performed by men, this appears to be another boomerang-substitute, and is not used if the singers have the wooden implements with them. With the women, it seems to be an alternative for crotch-slapping, and indeed, both devices are frequently observed together where women are providing vocal and/or rhythmic support for male singing, with individual women changing from one to the other during the overall performance. For both men and women, the procedure is the same: one hand lies across the lap, and the other hits down on to it (*see* Plate 2). Both hands are cupped, the thumb lying tight against the outer knuckle edge of the index finger. The striking hand drops at right-angles to the other to produce a muted hollow sound not unlike that of crotch-slapping.[9]

Crotch-slapping

This is possibly the most common female accompaniment to male group singing of *wantapi* series, to

8. *See* Thomson's description of singing at Kimai well, north-east of Lake Mackay: 'The Bindibu had no musical instruments and lacked even the "corroboree sticks"—the short sticks used by the "song man" in most parts of Australia to mark the rhythm.' (1962:156)
9. During one performance of a women's secret ceremony, an elderly woman was observed clapping briefly with her hands held parallel. When asked about it, she replied simply, '*Kutju*' (same).

mixed singing of *tulku*, and occasionally in *yawulyu* and other restricted women's series, and consists of holding the two hands cupped one over the other, and bringing them quite firmly down on to the crotch area (*see* Plate 3). When the woman is sitting with feet stretched out together in front, or tucked to one side, the natural cavity formed in this area acts as a resonance chamber, and the slapping produces a sound very similar to that of hand-clapping. At Kungkayunti during the singing of a *tulku*, several girls aged about 8-12 years were trying to slap in this manner, but to their great embarrassment, had trouble locating the correct spot to hit. After numerous periods of giggling failure, they all eventually succeeded in copying the women, and became so enthusiastic that the men had to caution them not to hit so loudly. For days afterwards, these girls could be seen in camp engaged in impromptu competition with each other as to who could produce the loudest slap.[10]

Chest-slapping

There is a problem here as to the authenticity of this device as a musical instrument *per se*, because in most observed cases (*see* Plates 4 and 5), the slapping is inaudible above the singing; it appears that the tactile sensation is more important than the audible, and unlike instances of hand-clapping and crotch-slapping, there are no calls of '*pulkara!*' or '*mayara!*' (louder!) from other singers. As far as can be determined, there is no vocal distortion produced or intended, and the device is used on an individual rather than a group basis. It may be described literally as *ngarrka punginpa* as well as by the more generic *papunpa*.

In all types of song accompaniment in the recorded sample, errors occasionally occur. In the case of *tjatiwanpa* songs, these errors may take the form of mistaking the point of change in the beating rate, or, because the songs have a precise end-point, of continuing when the others have stopped. Elsewhere, however, the musical form is less rigid, and melodic extension more frequent; in such cases, errors in accompaniment consist of an individual beating out of time with the majority of singers. The only method

10. Alice Moyle (1973:4) has introduced the term 'lapslap' for this activity; however, as the lap technically extends from waist to knee, and all observed Pintupi examples hit the crotch area, this term is not used here.

of correction observed during fieldwork was one of gradual alignment; the person in error continued thus for several seconds, moving progressively towards the general beating rate until synchronisation was achieved, whereupon the accompaniment was in good unison until the end of the song.

Such poor unison beating is a matter of some concern to the Pintupi, and on one occasion at both Balgo and Kungkayunti the lead singer called out 'Tjukarurru' (together) to the others. During the recording of one *wantapi*, as described earlier, a group of girls received criticism from the leader when he tired of their crotch-slapping incompetence. By contrast, there does not appear to be a single instance among the recordings of a breakdown in the melodic rhythm; the errors singers make are confined to text and pitch.

Fig. 8 is a summary in tabular form of the different accompaniment rhythms contained in the recorded sample (the *wantapi* have been omitted, on account of their foreign origin).

It should be pointed out that throughout this volume where accompaniment rhythms appear in transcriptions, the durational value of each note as indicated is not intended to represent the period for which the beat continues to sound. There is no evidence that even if it were possible to determine such a period, the Pintupi regard their percussive accompaniments as consisting of more than the initial moment of audible impact. In the transcriptions, rather than choosing an arbitrary durational value and following it with rests, which would tend to clutter the overall appearance, the accompaniments are written using durational values which cover the entire period from one beat to the next.

Accompaniment of one sort or another occurs in all genres of Pintupi music, with the exception of the *mungamunga*, *yawarra*, and *paniya* series. It is integral to performance in all except women's ceremonies, where use appears optional; it may or may not recur in repeats of the same song, and where it does figure, it is performed by individual women rather than by the group of participants as a whole, as in other genres. Whatever implements are used to function as musical instruments on such occasions are strictly *ad hoc* items—a stick against an empty tin or billycan is the most common.

In the recorded sample, only the *tjatiwanpa* uses a single rhythm in all the songs; this series, however, is considered of non-Pintupi origin and may be discounted from the present discussion. In the *yikuluku*,

Plate 4 Wimintji Tjapangati illustrates chest-slapping at Balgo 1975.

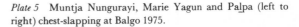

Plate 5 Muntja Nungurayi, Marie Yagun and Palpa (left to right) chest-slapping at Balgo 1975.

Series name and/or category   **Accomp.**

			♩	♩.	♪♪	♩/♩. before note	♩/♩. after note	none	trem	♩.→♩	♩→♪	♪♪→♩	♪♪→♩	♪→♩	2:3	3:4	3:5	4:7	14:25	16:25	16:27	♩♩
tulku	wantjiwantji	sts	●	●				●														
tulku	yunpu	bcl, hcl	●		●										●	●						
tulku	yikuluk	bcl, hcl, h/l	●					●														
tulku	tarrkalpa	st/g, h/l	●	●											●							●
tulku	tjatiwanpa	bcl												●								
tulku	yununtju	hcl	●					●														
yilpintji	maanytja	hcl	●					●														
yilpintji	kungka kutjarra	sts	●					●	●													
yilpintji	marali	sts		●	●			●							●							
yilpintji	wangata	sts	●		●			●														
yawulyu	kungkayunti							●														
yawulyu	mungamunga	hcl, st/tin, h/l	●					●	●						●							
	Restricted (a)	st/tin	●	●				●														
	Restricted (b)	hcl	●	●				●														
kutitji		bcl, bcl/shield	●												●							
ngalungku	malu	st/g	●	●	●									●	●							●
ngalungku	kipara	st/g	●											●	●							
ngalungku	wayuta	st/g	●		●									●	●							
ngalungku	ngintaka	st/g	●				●								●							
yarritjiti		st/g	●			●	●	●		●		●			●				●	●		●
tingarri		st/g	●	●	●	●	●	●			●				●		●					
kutatji	wanapa	hcl	●	●				●														
pukalkarra		bcl, bcl/shield	●				●		●						●						●	
tuyutu		bcl, hcl	●	●				●							●							
tuyutu	yawarra							●														
tuyutu	paniya							●														

Figure 8 Accompaniment rhythms for recorded sample.

st/tin   single stick against a metal tin

bcl/shield   single boomerangs on a shield which is lying on the ground, curved side up.

Key to the other vertical columns

♩   single beats where the duration of notes in the melody are in multiples of two—e.g. semiquavers, quavers, crotchets, minims.

♩.   single beats where the duration of notes in the melody are in multiples of three—e.g. dotted quavers, dotted crotchets, dotted minims.

♪♪   a triplet arrangement, often with the first beat louder than the second, occurring in melodies where the durational values are in multiples of two, or three.

♩/♩.   a repetition of the situation for the first and second columns, but with the beat sounding slightly before the sung note; the precise interval between the two varies from song to song, but is retained throughout the item.

♩/♩.   a similar situation to the former, but with the beat sounding slightly after the sung note.

none   in some cases very soft bcl or sts tremolo occurred during performances, but was inaudible on the field tapes; on the assumption that the purpose of accompaniment is to be heard, such items are considered as having no accompaniment, for the purposes of analysis.

trem.   a tremolo on bcl, sts or st/tin occurs in camp performances of an informal nature for selected songs which in full performance would be sung at the same time as a bullroarer was being swung, or some other sacred ceremonial object displayed.

♩.→♩. the next five columns concern changes in the rate or rate of the accompaniment. The first represents a diminution by a factor of 2 in a melody whose note durations are in multiples of three.

♩→♪   a diminution by a factor of 2 in a melody whose note durations are in multiples of two.

♩.→♩ a diminution by a factor of one third, both rhythms comprising single beats.

♪♩→♩ in effect, similar diminution by a factor of one third, but with the first rhythm comprising a triplet arrangement.

♪→♩ augmentation by a factor of two.

2:3   an accompaniment beat in simple duple time against a melody in triplet rhythms.

3:4   an accompaniment beat in triplet time against a melody in quadruple time.

3:5   three beats in the accompaniment against five units of similar durational value in the melody.

4:7   four beats in the accompaniment against seven units of similar durational value in the melody.

14:25   as mentioned earlier (*see* Example 12), this may represent a variation of, or an attempt at 3:5.

16:27   similarly, this may represent a variation of, or an attempt at 4:7 (*see* Example 13).

♩♩   single beats alternately loud and soft.

maanytja and *kungka kutjarra* series, single beats constitute the only means of accompaniment, but in each of these series there are also songs sung unaccompanied. For the remainder of the sample, two or more different rhythms appear the norm, with the *yarritjiti* and *tingarri* containing the greatest variety, having ten and eight respectively.

Certain types of accompaniment rhythm are peculiar to men's restricted series; these include changes of rhythm in mid-item, beating slightly before or after sung notes (i.e. never coinciding exactly), and the more complex accompaniment to melody ratios. By contrast, those series of a social nature, i.e., the *tulku*, tend to contain more simple accompaniment rhythms.

Musical ethnography

Song performance

Although the researcher may separate musical and textual elements of a song for the purposes of analysis, and examine individually the component parts of each, the Pintupi concept of singing welds the two together so powerfully that very little nomenclature exists, in either absolute or analogous terms, for individual aspects of song performance which may seem outstanding to an outsider, and about which he may wish to enquire in some detail. Ellis (1964a:24) has commented on the inability of Aborigines in some cases to merely recite song texts; so great is the association of word and note that they must be sung to be remembered. This observation was corroborated by the present writer on a few occasions, although four or five individuals, both men and women, were able to speak the words of various series without hesitation. In addition, older women at some of the *yawulyu* ceremonies would whisper the words of the next item to the leading singer if she herself could not recall it. Numerically, however, such people were exceptions.

Along with the concept of the essential unity of song text and music is the equally powerful inseparableness of song and song series, and song series and purpose. In longer ceremonies involving a succession of ritual acts, an individual song associated with one such act may be repeated over and over until that act is completed, before the singers proceed to the next song. Repetitions ten to fifteen times of a single song occurred eleven times in the recorded sample, and one section of the *tjatiwanpa* ceremony contained consecutive repetition fifty times of the same song. On a broader scale too; whole ceremonies are intrinsically linked to particular times of the day or night, particular periods of the seasonal year, particular stages of the life cycle, and with particular kinship subsections who may be the owners. These links are such that to perform whole ceremonies in any way out of context would not only be completely meaningless but in the case of more sacred ceremonies, invite punishment (*see*, e.g. Strehlow 1970). Songs by themselves seem not to fall into this same category, to the extent that *wanapa, pukalkarra, paniya, yilpintji* and *ngalungku* series were performed for recording purposes only with no apparent qualms.

Song is a known quantity insofar as for all song series familiar to a given group of Pintupi, the appropriate contexts are understood. However, geographical dispersal in at least the post-contact period has resulted in certain song series from one area being totally unknown in another area, or known only partially or through the accounts of other people; thus the total body of Pintupi song is not a known quantity to any individual, unless, of course, he or she has travelled extensively enough to be familiar with series whose use is limited geographically, and travelled frequently enough to have kept abreast of recent additions to the repertoire. Because of the restricted nature of some men's and women's private ceremonies, however, such an all-encompassing knowledge could not logically be obtained by one person. The writer did not meet anyone who claimed to know all the Pintupi song series in existence; on the contrary, during playback of Kungkayunti items at Balgo, and Balgo items at Kungkayunti, it became apparent that less than half the various series were known in both areas. This results in Pintupi from the one area hearing a recording and acknowledging that the language is Pintupi, but remaining ignorant of the context or the occasion of the recorded performance. To be sure, there are some aural clues for identifying particular genres—hand-clapping or crotch-slapping are exclusive to the *wantapi* and *tulku*, and women singing together with men is confined to the *tulku*—but these two aspects of the aural performance, while considered desirable, are not obligatory, and so absence of such features in any recording does not necessarily eliminate the *tulku* and the *wantapi* in any identification procedure. There are, on the other hand, a number of ceremonies—in particular, those associated with male initiation—which are known to all Pintupi men, and even though in some cases sections of them are openly acknowledged to be non-Pintupi in origin and their songs non-Pintupi in language, they have, since earliest records were made, been firmly transplanted into Pintupi culture. Only the song series associated with these ceremonies have purely musical features which the Pintupi point out as being identifiers; to them, the strong vocal accentuation (*pangaltjuninpa*)

and rising glissands (*ngutulmaninpa*) are infallible indicators of this song genre.

Merriam (1967:161) advances the opinion that 'theoretically, the number of songs in any community must be considered infinite', a statement whose logic would appear questionable. Merriam's premises are:

(a) . . . it seems impossible that the absolute number of songs of any group can be known. No matter how long or how thorough the recording program, there is always one more informant, and, presumably, one more song.
(b) . . . we assume that creativity is an on-going process, no matter how it may be shaped by the cultural framework in which it exists, and thus what is a 'total' sample today is presumably not tomorrow or the next day.
(c) . . . there has apparently never been a study which attempted a 'total' sample, and thus we have no real idea of how many songs we can expect to find in a given community.

Looking at each premise individually:

(a) Merriam appears to be confusing an infinite number with an unknown number; the three premises concern the latter, and only the conclusion deals with the former. For the Pintupi, at least, the total number indeed appears to be unknown to any individual, but it does not necessarily follow that the number is then infinite.
(b) By specifically limiting the scope of the research to the music of a given people at a particular period in time, there is no theoretical barrier to a subsequent attempt at a total sample.
(c) This objection is not relevant to the theoretical argument that a total number of songs is infinite, as by definition one cannot expect to find an infinite number.

Typical performance of Pintupi music may involve singing in correct order anything from 30 to 300 different songs, the often-arduous manufacture and decoration of ceremonial objects, and in the case of initiation ceremonies, ordeals generally accepted as painful. Despite this, however, it is not simplistic to say that they enjoy singing, and that the occasions for singing are often awaited with some excitement, and afterwards discussed and recounted with evident pleasure. During performances in both natural circumstances and those arranged specially for recording purposes, the singers would make jokes and laugh between songs, sometimes starting one or two seconds before the others stopped singing in order to make their comments heard. While actually singing too, there were often vigorous arm movements as singers described in sign language to each other the events about which they were currently singing; if such events were considered humorous there would be flashes of teeth as the singers tried to keep from laughing. On the other hand, there were occasions such as during healing ceremonies, when the greatest seriousness was evinced among the singers, and all those not singing sat quietly awaiting the outcome. The intervals between songs were in complete silence. Such silences in the Balgo performance of the *tjatiwanpa* ceremony made deep impressions on the Kungkayunti men who heard some of the recordings, commenting that the ceremony was 'proper *tulku*, that one'—that it was apparent from the recordings that full ceremonial formality was being observed. Apart from such times, however, the performers give every impression of enjoying the act of singing. Many of them closed their eyes in concentration, or especially in initiation items, where strong vocal accentuation and rising glissands feature, moved head and torso in time to the singing.

Attitudes towards the presence and participation of Europeans in Pintupi singing activities, with or without their attendant ceremonies, appeared to depend on how well known the foreigners were, how acceptable they were generally in camp life, and on which kinship subgroup they belonged to. (This last factor would, for example, exclude them from being present at the preparations for ceremonies if their 'skins' were not of the *kutungulu* or workers' division.) On one occasion a recently arrived European in Balgo was seen walking towards the ceremonial area in the middle of a performance. After much talk among both men and women as to his identity and intentions one man went over and told him that it was 'too dangerous' for him to stay; he left. For his own part at ceremonies occurring entirely at the Pintupi's initiative, the writer would stand conspicuously some distance off (with or without tape recorder) until he was called over verbally or by hand signs. Usually, however, he (and the rest of the camp) knew in advance of the performance occasion, time and place, and went along in the company of other men to sit with the singers. Non-Balgo individuals temporarily visiting the mission were asked to stay away from ceremonies considered to belong to Balgo alone, but were able to attend and participate in those whose ownership extended beyond the mission. Performance of important ceremonies was halted altogether during visits by groups of people, to be resumed after their departure.

Without exception, every attempt the writer made to join in the performances, either by singing, or by beating sticks or boomerangs, or by both, was met with obvious pleasure and encouragement by the Pintupi. Sitting with a small group of men who were themselves being taught a new *yilpintji*, the two teachers would catch the writer's eye and use exaggerated head and mouth movements to indicate the proper places in the songs for taking a breath, and spoke the song words to him after each time through. On another day when he was sitting with a large group of men who were singing and beating boomerangs, the writer was handed a spare pair of boomerangs by one classificatory elder brother, and men in front were constantly twisting around to see if he could manage them. (One or two local men who had come without boomerangs were also handed pairs by close relatives; these were returned to their donors after the ceremony.) Efforts to join in the singing were invariably met with vigorous nods of the head, smiles, and encouraging comments of '*Yuwa*' (yes), '*Palya*' (good), and the like.

On the surface, the mechanics of a recording situation seemed not to affect the singers. During recordings of live *yawulyu* performances at Balgo, however, one particularly influential singer would ask that the recorder be switched off between songs, but after the difficulties of capturing the spontaneous starts of new songs were demonstrated to her, she quite readily agreed to leave it running during their conversations. Elsewhere the visual distraction of microphones and cables and other equipment seemed to go progressively unnoticed as the performance continued, to the extent that late arrivals would sometimes bump into them or knock them over with a sudden arm movement. Comparison of recordings of live and elicited performances, however, reveals a consistently recurring difference in the number of times each individual song is sung before passing on to the next one, and also in the number of different songs constituting an acceptable performance. While the number of repetitions for each item averaged one to two for elicited performances, it averaged two to four in live performances, and while the greatest number of consecutive repetitions for any one item in the entire elicited sample was seven, instances of ten or more repetitions occurred quite frequently in the live sample, and one particular song was sung no less than fifty times successively before moving on to the next. The reason for this difference lies in the ceremonial activities associated with particular songs; these activities consist of continuous dancing, a lengthy preparatory activity (such as the body-painting of a principal actor), or a specific extended ritual act (such as the ritual burning of women in the final stage of the *tjatiwanpa* ceremony). In other words, while singing is an integral part of the total ceremony, the overall progression of songs may, at certain times, be governed by non-musical factors.

Most live performances among the Pintupi consist of what is considered a complete series of individual songs which,[1] in the recorded sample, may number more than 300. The only exceptions were women's *yawulyu* at both Kungkayunti and Balgo, two women's ceremonies at Kungkayunti and one at Balgo, and the *tjatiwanpa*, all of which were spread over several days.[2]

It has not been possible to determine on what basis the precise intermediate stopping points were selected, whether it be durational, ritual, musical, or otherwise. On one occasion, a sudden heavy shower of rain forced a premature end to the proceedings, which concluded with a spontaneous mass rush for shelter, but not before those in charge saw that the ceremonial objects on display had been gathered in. The Balgo women's ceremonies invariably started at around 11 am, continuing until 5 pm, when the siren announced the end of the mission employees' work day; likewise at Kungkayunti the women always returned to camp in the late afternoon to prepare the family evening meal, having spent some four or five hours in the bush at their private ceremonies.

Elicited performances, on the other hand, were made at the singers' convenience with performance duration depending on their mood in most cases. Where they had not sung an entire series at any single recording session, they would often say they would 'finish im up . . . all the way . . . right up' next time. Occasionally this 'next time' did not eventuate. In live performances however in some *tulku*, *tingarri* and *yilpintji* series, the singing may exist either alone or be part of a ceremony in which ritual behaviour occurs; if the former, then here too the entire series may not be performed at one sitting, so that singing, stripped of its normal ceremonial trappings, is not necessarily a non-traditional situation.

The physical demands made on singers, especially leaders, in performing over several hours, seem not to greatly trouble the Pintupi, although sometimes men complained during performances, '*Lirrina kampanyi*' (My throat is burning), and refrained from participating for a few minutes. Most singers, though, seemed able to last the entire performance. A few appeared to lose interest in elicited performances after a while, and left, and also in live performances individuals left to attend to urgent family matters, but such people were in a definite minority. The intervals between ending one song and starting the next lasted from a few seconds to several minutes, especially if the singers were unable to remember the next item. Often in such cases, they would repeat songs performed earlier in the series, until one of them recalled it. It was noticeable that more time elapsed between different songs than between repetitions of the same song. In addition, the period at the start of a song during which the leader sings alone becomes progressively shorter for each repetition, to the point where he or she sings only one note or syllable before the others join in. Among both men and women singers, the mouth tends to water during performance, and there is frequent spitting out of excess saliva. With the exception of the *kutungulu* in the *tjatiwanpa* ceremony, who stand around the group of seated *mayutju*, all Pintupi singers sit, the men crosslegged or kneeling, the women usually with their legs tucked to one side. Occasionally, individual singers have trouble hearing their own voices over the others' and in order to confirm that they are singing correctly, they may place a cupped hand over one ear (*see* Plate 6) to amplify their own efforts. As one Balgo man said, this helps to 'hear im right through'. The practice is called *pina muturra yinkanyi* or *pinatjarraku* (ear-with).

At both camps, relatively little interest was shown in hearing immediate playback of recorded performances, the singers drifting away after only a few minutes. In marked contrast, great interest was evident when listening to performances in the Pintupi language but by people other than themselves,

1. Earlier writers have used a variety of names for such series, e.g. 'song' (Strehlow 1971), (Ellis 1967), 'syllabic song' (Ellis 1968), 'song cycle' (Jones 1965), 'cycle' (Meggitt 1962:222), 'suite' (Tindale 1974:34), and 'songline' (Tonkinson 1974:71).
2. Tonkinson, by contrast, speaking of the people at Jigalong, to the west of Pintupi country, claims that the spreading of complete performances over a number of days or nights is the rule rather than the exception (1974:284).

Plate 6 Brandy Kunymangara singing with a hand cupped over his ear (Balgo 1975).

especially when they recognised the voice of any individual on the tape. It was noticeable that where the song series on tape was totally unknown to them, the listeners were more interested in hearing the conversations in the intervals between songs than in the songs themselves, which they often dismissed, saying, 'We don't know that one', or the like. In fact, one comment made by a Balgo man on a recording became something of a joke at Kungkayunti, and for days afterwards was repeated by the men among themselves with glee whenever the subject of Balgo arose. On another occasion, the Kungkayunti men listened to part of a Balgo performance, then asked to have themselves recorded, because they considered they could sing this particular series better; this however was the only time that a recorded performance acted as such a stimulus to other singers.

Handsigns

There are a number of handsigns which pertain to musical activities, and which are sometimes seen during singing, as well as in the course of conversations on other occasions. Those observed during fieldwork were all made by men, although women are acquainted with them as well; the various signs are demonstrated by Donkeyman Luuku of Balgo Mission, Plates 7-11.

Singing (*yinkanyi*) (Plate 7)

One hand is held in front of the body, fingers together and the thumb upright from the palm; the fingers are moved back and forwards very quickly.

Male dancing (*kantuṇi*) (Plate 8)

The forefinger and thumb of each hand are extended, the other fingers held together; the arms are moved up and down from the elbow, each arm alternately. The action represents the high-stepping movements of this dance style.

Female dancing (*nyanpinyi*) (Plate 9)

The hands are held out loosely, then fluttered back and forth from the wrist. The action represents the forward-jumping movements of women's feet as they dance.

Beating single sticks on the ground (*yatuṇi*) (Plate 10)

With the fingers held straight but separated, the hands are raised and lowered together, from the wrist.

Beating boomerangs together (*timpilpa*) (Plate 11)

The fingernails of one hand are beaten against the fingerpads of the other hand.

Withdrawal of individual songs

The Pintupi attitude towards the dead involves the immediate shifting of camp following a death from whatever cause, the destruction of the deceased's

48

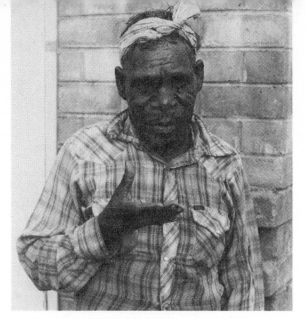

Plate 7 Handsign indicating singing.

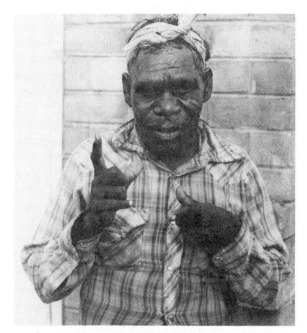

Plate 8 Handsign indicating male dancing.

Plate 9 Handsign indicating female dancing.

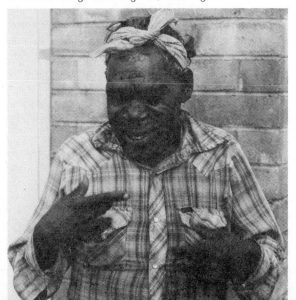

Plate 10 Handsign indicating beating single sticks on ground.

Plate 11 Handsign indicating beating boomerangs together.

personal property in some cases, and a ban on the use of his name. Should another individual either in the same camp or nearby have the same name, he will change it and not use the former name for several years. One man near Alice Springs with the name Billycan died, and four years later, the substitute term *wayatjarra* (having wire) was still in wide use as referring to this metal cooking pot, although a few individuals had reverted to the former name. It sometimes happens that a person's name occurs in a song text, in which case the whole song is omitted from the series. A singer, however, may forget the ban on the use of this word and this song and start singing it at its normal position in the series. The performance is immediately stopped by the other men in a variety of ways—holding up the hand (like a traffic policeman), inhaling through tightly compressed lips (similar to an exaggerated kissing noise), or calling out *'yulingka'*, *'mirringka'* (lit., corpse-at) or *'wurra'* (wait). The offender quickly replies, *'Yuwa yuwa yuwa'* (yes yes yes) or similar, and they all move on to the next song in the series. By reason of this speech ban, it is almost impossible to discuss the nature of the offending references in the texts, e.g. whether it contains the deceased's name only, or perhaps an identifiable link of some other sort. Likewise in the literature, no specifics are given (*see*, e.g. Meggitt 1962:222; Strehlow 1971:601; de Graaf 1963:22).

In 1966, R. A. Gould recorded a number of initiation series from the Warburton Range area; during my own fieldwork, selections from such series were played to Pintupi men, who immediately identified them as part of their own initiation complex, even though the language was not entirely Pintupi. At Balgo, one man noted that there was a man called Nyukali said to be living in Warburton Range Mission, and that this same name occurred in the kangaroo dreaming, which is sung at circumcision. The man then isolated eight songs from the series, saying that when Nyukali died these might be omitted from subsequent performance. Expanded translations of these are as follows:

1. The old kangaroo met and fought with a pack of dogs on the grasslands. The head dog's name was Nyukali; the dogs killed the 'roo, but his spirit escaped and reformed another 'roo body. The dogs followed his scent.

2. 'They bit off my testicles, but I slipped away,' sang the kangaroo.

3. The kangaroo saw Nyukali and the other dogs with gore on their faces as they feasted on his old body. He went a long way off and stood erect, watching them.

4. He stood watching as the pack devoured his body.

5. He made a string cross, and attached it to his head.

6. After wandering about collecting further string crosses, he was again attacked by dogs.

7. The Old Man kangaroo was devoured by the dogs and left lying on the ground.

8. The kangaroo became mere meat, and was eaten and left lying on the ground.

Of these items, it was said songs 1 and 3 would definitely be omitted, and such was the close (though implicit) association of Nyukali and the remaining songs that they too might well be dropped from the series. Time will tell. No estimation of the duration of such omissions was given.

Proxemic arrangements

As already stated, *tulku*, *tingarri* and *yilpintji* may be sung with or without their associated dancing, ritual behaviour, manufacture and use of ritual objects, and still be considered acceptable. All other genres are normally performed complete with their respective rituals. Performance of these three genres where only singing occurs tends to take place within, or close to, the camp area, and thus usually within earshot of those inside the camp. Where the full ceremonials occur in *tingarri* and *yilpintji* series, however, it is imperative that women are not present, or be within hearing or viewing distance of the activities, but when singing alone takes place, the performance restrictions are eased somewhat. These camp performances function to introduce suitably qualified visitors to the series in an informal manner, and thereby teach them the items, and also refresh the other men's memories with the songs. One or two men added that they sang like this when they felt 'happy' (but presumably not 'happy' enough to perform the whole ceremony).

Tulku and *wantapi*, on the other hand, appear primarily for entertainment, and while the enjoyment may well be enhanced by dancing by decorated or non-decorated performers, singing by itself seems to give considerable pleasure. Where only singing takes place in these two genres, men and women sit closer to each other than they do when organised dancing takes place. A seating arrangement for *tulku* seen several times on such occasions is for a tight circle of men facing inwards to be flanked by all the women sitting in a group as shown in Fig. 9.

The preferred proxemic arrangement for singers is that they sit in as compact a group as possible. On one or two occasions during the formal rehearsals of the *tjatiwanpa* ceremony at Balgo, the *kuntungulu* ordered the seated *mayutju* to move closer together, although most latecomers took up sitting positions on this and other occasions for singing immediately beside those already there without any direction from the leader. By contrast, at the formal performances, the *kutungulu* were the only ones to stand to sing for the whole of the ceremony, and were sometimes several metres from each other as there were simply not enough of them to stand shoulder to shoulder and still entirely surround the *mayutju*, as required by tradition. An indication of one reason for such proxemics was given at a performance of a *yawalyu* at Balgo in which insufficient shade was available for all the women to sit together. They sat under a line of bushes stretching for some six metres, remaining there for the entire ceremony. The singing on this occasion was characterised by frequent loss of melodic unison, caused apparently by the comparatively greater distance between the singers than was normal. The leader, in exasperation after several minutes of this, called out in English, 'You fellers want to sing im properly level', but despite her complaint, the others continued to be out of time for some time, until lengthening shadows allowed them to sit as a single unit. The problem seemed to be simply that at that distance they could not hear each other sing, and thus could not achieve unison.

At Kungkayunti, where eleven *tulku* and three *wantapi* were performed, all without dancing, it was a cause for frequent complaint that there were too few singers present to provide music loud enough for the dancing.

There is little doubt that all adult male Pintupi wish to be considered as competent singers, since knowledge of, and executant ability in, a variety of song series is a significant part of the initiation process. Therefore if any man is ignorant of, or incompetent in, participating in such performances,

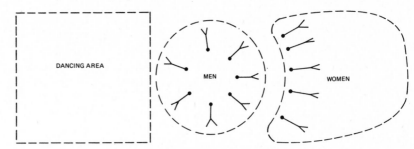

Figure 9   Typical spatial arrangement for *tulku* performance.

he is something less than a man, and thus unfit to join the camp's religious life, which is primarily a male prerogative. Men who are incompetent and unable to participate orally in song series nevertheless prefer to sit with the performers rather than not attend at all, and seem content to beat sticks or boomerangs together with the rest. The corollary also holds true: at most occasions for singing there are no spectators (children attending *tulku* or *wantapi* were the main exceptions seen during fieldwork). At both Kungkayunti and Balgo, very young children were sometimes permitted to attend women's *yawalyu*, those condoning the action saying that they were *tjukutjuku* (young) and therefore unable to comprehend the significance of the ceremonies. Those who are disqualified from attending on account of their age, sex, social status or subsection remain in camp or otherwise stay away from the performance area.

The precise locations of initiation ceremonies only are kept secret from outsiders.

The sites for ceremonies and singing relative to the camp living area appear to be determined by two factors. Firstly, the ceremony category determines the degree of secrecy required for the performance and thus the physical distance from the areas normally used by those who are not qualified to attend or hear; in general, the more secret the ceremony the further from the camp it is held. Secondly, the direction, relative to the living area, in which the ceremonies are held seems to be determined by the geographical location of the mythological events described in the respective song series. For example, all the Pintupi ceremonies held, and song series sung at Balgo were to the south or southwest of the camp, and references to the mythological events were frequently accompanied by pointing to these same directions, along with finger-snapping to indicate great distance. Also at Kungkayunti, the route taken to the place where the women's ceremonies and the

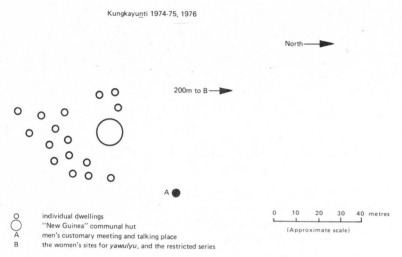

Kungkayunti 1974-75, 1976

North→

200m to B→

○	individual dwellings
⊖	"New Guinea" communal hut
A	men's customary meeting and talking place
B	the women's sites for *yawulyu*, and the restricted series

0   10   20   30   40 metres
(Approximate scale)

Note In 1976, there were only eight dwellings, all on the south side of the New Guinea hut.

Figure 10 Living and performance areas at Kungkayunti during fieldwork.

men's secret songs were recorded coincided with the direction given by the participants when asked which way the respective mythological characters had travelled.[3]

The layout of the living areas of such camps with composite populations appears to be a microcosm of the original traditional territories, reflecting the directional relationships between each group.

Fig. 10 and Plate 12 indicate performance areas in relation to the living areas at Kungkayunti and Balgo.

Participation and leadership

With the possible exception of some *tulku* (whose function seems to be primarily entertainment), the ceremonies exist to be perpetuated; active participation rather than passive observation is the keynote. Whereas the secret male ceremonies are normally open to all initiated local men in camp, the women's private ceremonies may be more restricted. At Kungkayunti the Restricted (b) and *yawulyu* were attended only by women of Napaltjarri and Napanangka subsections, whose numbers started at six and later dwindled to three. At Balgo, the camp was divided into a 'north' and 'west' side each having its own separate women's *yawulyu* ceremonies (a division which at times produced slight rivalry for the writer's presence). Occasionally, however, a woman from one side would attend the performance

put on by the other side, and showed enough familiarity to join the singing and dancing without visible hesitation. Older women both at Kungkayunti and Balgo who attended these ceremonies sometimes did not participate at all; after an hour or two watching the others, they would lie down and sleep. If at all possible, both men and women wish to associate themselves with those ritual activities (of which singing is invariably a part) to which their social, marital and sex status entitle them, regardless of their current executant ability. To this extent they will attend preparatory and ceremonial activities, but not necessarily participate actively.

At Kungkayunti and Balgo singing is essentially an adult activity.[4] There are, however, some exceptions. Children and unmarried adults do not participate in the camp's musical activities. Pintupi children appear to have no music of their own, and were not seen imitating adult performances; adults confirmed that they have no songs of their own. Unmarried girls sometimes take part in providing accompaniment to the men's *wantapi* songs, by slapping their crotches at the same rate as the men's boomerangs, but they do not join in the women's singing in a *tulku*. Likewise, they are specifically excluded from attending a *yawulyu* ceremony, let alone participating, for fear they may reveal secret material. Prior to initiation, boys take no part in the camp's music, and it is only during initiation that they are obliged to take careful note of ceremonies and singing. It is not until they are fully initiated that they are given boomerangs and taught songs.

Insofar as song is an integral part of the information revealed to neophytes during the initiation

---

3. It was also noteworthy at Balgo, where the Pintupi represent a minority among the total population, that (apart from cases where Pintupi women had married non-Pintupi men and subsequently lived on their husband's side of the camp) they lived in a compact group to the south of the others, that is, a location closest to their traditional homeland. One man verbalised quite specifically about this, pointing out that the whole housing arrangement at Balgo consisted of clusters of people having common geographic or linguistic origins. To some extent, the Mission's housing programme regulated the choice of a place of residence; rather than be accommodated elsewhere in the camp, two Pintupi men built their own shelters on this south side. At Kungkayunti, those claiming Pintupi ancestry lived along the west side of camp. Long (1970:322-23) describes a situation at Haasts Bluff in which Pintupi people lived on the west side of the settlement. The situation is not unique to the Desert; Hiatt (1965:33) reports a similar situation at Maningrida, to mention but one other instance.
4. This situation may not hold true for all Pintupi, as is discussed later in the section The Sample.

Balgo Mission 1975

1 old ceremonial ground
2 new ceremonial ground
3 women's *yawulyu* site, north side
4 women's *yawulyu* sites, west side
5 men's *yilpintji* and *tingarri* sites
6 men's *maanytja* site
7 Pintupi camp area
8 Pintupi men's secret storage area

0   15   30   45   60 metres
approximate scale

Plate 12   Living and performance areas at Balgo during fieldwork.

process, musical executant ability is a general attribute among adult male Pintupi. As far as can be ascertained, women's initiation processes do not involve comparable singing, and although most women are familiar enough with local *tulku* to be able to sing them, their role is also to provide an audible accompaniment to the men's singing, in the form of hand-clapping or crotch-slapping. Although individual songs in some series are performed unaccompanied, the vast majority have audible accompaniment in one form or another provided by the singers themselves (who may be reinforced by women in certain types of series); to this extent it is assumed by the Pintupi that singing ability implies accompaniment ability, although, as was indicated earlier, mistakes do occur.

It would be inaccurate to talk of musical specialisation among the Pintupi, despite the recognition of certain individuals as being superior singers, not only because executant ability is assumed for all adult males (and probably for adult females as well, although less evidence is available on this), but also because among the behavioural restrictions

operating during non-Pintupi ceremonies sung at Balgo and Kungkayunti are some pertaining to music; the nature of these is such that they may preclude an individual acknowledged as a good singer from performance or even attendance.

These restrictions pertain more particularly to song and ceremony ownership, and may be divided into two types. There are certain categories of ceremonies, all involving singing, in which those attending are divided into patrimoieties: the *mayutju* (often called owners, or bosses) and the *kutungulu* (commonly called the workers, managers or policemen). The duties of the *kutungulu* include the demarcation and clearing of the ceremonial ground, manufacture and decoration of any necessary ceremonial objects, the care and preservation of more permanent sacred objects (e.g. bullroarers, carved boards), the manufacture of bodypaint and its application on fellow *kutungulu*, and providing adequate firewood for the duration of the ceremony, if this occurs at night. All these duties take place prior to the commencement of the ceremony proper. During the ceremony, the *kutungulu* act as masters-

53

of-ceremony, informing the *mayutju* when all is ready and then escorting them on, directing their seating positions, leading the singing, providing a food gift for the *mayutju*, painting up the principal actors and shouting instructions to them as they perform. At the conclusion of the ceremony they dismantle the temporary ceremonial objects, take away for safe-keeping the permanent ones, and ensure everybody leaves the area. The preparatory activities listed above may take a whole day to conclude, and generally at a place out of sight from the others and are attended only by the *kutungulu*, who often sing informally songs from the ceremony while they work. This singing is intended to instill into the ceremonial objects the supernatural power of the Dreamtime character each represents or is associated with. Older members of the patrimoiety may be too old to take any active part in this work, but they attend nonetheless, and join in the singing.

While all this is going on, the other patrimoiety, the *mayutju*, will be gathering (although this may be delayed until an hour or so before the ceremony is due to start) and as they wait they may also start singing quietly through some of the songs they will perform later formally. In the period after the *kutungulu* have entered the ceremonial ground and started singing among themselves, the two groups may sometimes be heard singing simultaneously, but still independently. On the other hand, the *mayutju* may prefer to sit quietly awaiting their entrance cue. In either case, once all the performers are assembled on the ground, leadership of the ceremony as a whole though not always of the singing (*see* below), is in the hands of the *kutungulu*.

Although overall organisation of a ceremony may be on the basis of moieties, ownership is usually on a smaller scale, involving people of particular locations, single kinship subsections (of which there are eight in Pintupi society), or individuals (in which case the conception totem establishes the ownership). On several occasions at Kungkayunti, performance of particular song series was either started and immediately stopped, or not started at all, because a person belonging to the appropriate subsection, or the individual owner himself as the case might have been, was not present. Such a restriction also operates with women's ceremonies; three Kungkayunti women were about to start a song series originating at Yayayi Outstation (where they all had previously lived) when a fourth woman pointed out that they might get into trouble if they sang it in another location, because it was *tjanampa tjanampa* (lit, their's)—it belonged exclusively to women at that place. The others agreed, and did not sing it.

Technically, an owner has the sole right to act as leader, and start each song by himself or herself, the others joining in after a second or two; in most observed cases this practice was adhered to even though, in cases where the owner's voice was weaker, he could not be heard after the others joined in. The song leadership changed hands only

(a) in a case where ownership was by a single subsection, when another individual senior to the first leader and having a louder voice and more forceful personality, but more important—also of that same subsection and therefore also an owner—arrived and assumed control for the rest of the recording session;

(b) when, on one occasion at Kungkayunti, the sole owner was an old man with a noticeably weak speaking and singing voice. He led the singing for only a few songs, whereupon another man, the acknowledged 'boss' of the whole camp, took over the lead. The original owner continued to sing with the other men, and showed no outward signs of disapproval;

(c) when it was said that 'everybody' was the owner; this situation applied only to the *wanapa* and certain healing series. By the same token, however, any individual who disapproved of performance had the right to veto it (as occurred once at Kungkayunti). Further, such a situation did not mean that while anybody had the theoretical right to lead, anybody at all necessarily *should* lead. At Kungkayunti during the singing of one series, one rather young aggressive individual who had merely joined in with the others on previous singing occasions, started singing by himself, as a leader does at the start of a song. To a man, the others just sat, until this one individual had sung the whole song by himself, their silence an eloquent rebuke for his precocity. Never again was he the first to start singing.

The proxemic and social organisation of several men's ceremonies and series acknowledged as Pintupi, however, divides the participants into *tjintulukultulpa* (sun) and *ngumpalurrungkatja* (shade) moieties; the former category comprises Tjupurrula, Tjungurayi, Tjangala and Tjapanangka subsections, and the latter includes the Tjapaltjarri,

54

Tjapangati, Tjakamarra and Tjampitjinpa subsections, and the two groups remain separate for the duration of the activities. (I do not have specific information on which group, if any, leads the performance, or as to who within the groups plays a leading role.) Such a pattern applies to the following series: *pukalkarra, tingarri, ngalungku, maanytja, yilpintji* and *wanapa*. The *tarrkalpa* series, claimed to be a 'mix-up' of Pintupi and Pitjantjatjara, is also organised along these lines. The *wangata* ceremony and song series is said to be led by the local *nintipuka*, a term meaning 'knowledgeable one', and corresponding roughly to the English 'sage' or 'elder'. Performance of all categories of series not involving spatial separation of individual participants from others—i.e. *tulku*, as well as the women's *yawulyu* and other restricted series—is led by one or more individuals considered as owning the respective ceremonies.

Song leadership is integrally connected with ceremonial leadership, which in turn is determined by the notions of ownership. Song leaders are thus not necessarily those with the best voices; considerations of subsection, seniority, ceremonial knowledge and conception totem are of greater importance, and exceptions to this rule are rare.

To say outright that there are no individuals in Pintupi society who would qualify as music specialists is not to imply any casual attitude towards song performance. On the contrary, while non-musical factors may determine who leads any given song series, certain people are identified as being superior singers generally, regardless of whether they are leaders or not. The criteria for distinction in such cases involve two factors: the ability to remember in correct order the songs comprising a song series (together with details of the associated myth and ceremony), and the ability to perform them in a loud, carrying voice called by the Pintupi 'big throat' (*lirri pulka*), 'good throat' (*lirri palya*), or 'good tongue' (*nyalinpa palya* or *yuntju palya*). Pintupi song texts contain acceptable and intelligible deviant pronunciation of lexically meaningful words, using colloquial terms as well as some apparently confined exclusively to song texts and not necessarily understood or understood identically by all the singers. These deviations stem initially from a stated preference for the 'big throat' singing style, which corresponds approximately to the chest register in European vocal production. One of the criteria for a 'good' singer is the ability to sustain this 'big throat' sound over as wide a vocal range as possible so that

A	B	C	D
Elements of the ideal performance		*Errors*	
in kind	of degree	of degree	in kind
Those categorised as 'good', and essential:	Those categorised as 'good', and preferable:	Those categorised as 'bad', but tolerable:	Those categorised as 'bad', and unacceptable:
text word-perfect	loud, using 'big throat'	softly sung	textual errors
songs in proper order	many singers	few singers	songs out of proper order
contour and rhythm correct	high pitch	medium or low pitch	contour or rhythm incorrect
accompaniment rhythm correct	all accompanying instruments in unison	accompanying instruments out of unison	textual reference to the dead

A Elements in this category are not normally discussed if the singing is proceeding well; rather, they are taken for granted. Specific terminology is used for all but the first item.

B Elements in this category may elicit comments of approval from the singers; specific terminology is used for all items listed here.

C Elements in this category may be criticised during or after the singing by individual singers, which usually results in their being remedied by a change to the appropriate element in column B.

D The presence of any element in this category is generally sufficient to stop the singing immediately; all the items are discussed and treated with serious concern.[5]

Figure 11 Positive and negative features of song performance.

5. Further information of performance errors is included in the Analytical Technique and Analysis sections.

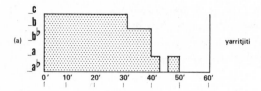

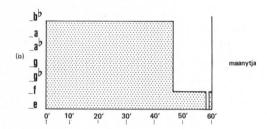

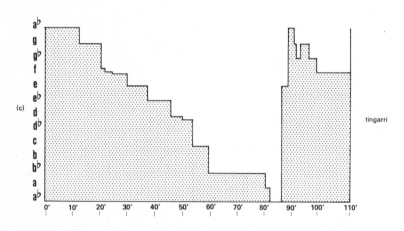

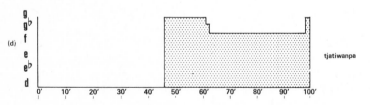

Figure 12 Typical overall pitch for *yarritjiti*, *maanytja*, *tingarri* and *tjatiwanpa* songs.

Note The vertical axes indicate the notes through which the pitch changes move, and the horizontal axes show elapsed time in minutes from the start of singing.

the entire song is delivered in a loud, carrying manner. In order to achieve this, the lower jaw is thrust forward during performance, and the mouth opened only partially, actions which affect not only the tone quality but also the phonetic composition of the resultant sounds, e.g. tjuṉu [ṯuṉu] becomes [ṯuṉei] ngawa [ŋʌawa] becomes [ŋʌwai] kalkani [kʌlkʌni] becomes [kʌlkʌnei].[6]

Performance errors

References in the ethnomusicological literature to performance errors are very rare indeed, the general attitude appearing to concentrate on what is 'right' rather than on what is 'wrong', however those values might be formulated or expressed. Indeed, so strong is this attitude that in most cases, simply from lack of reference to the contrary, the reader might well assume that performance errors do not occur. However, if one reverses the argument and says that by lack of explicit confirmation *no* errors occur, and by adding the assumption that however well-trained the musicians may be, this does not suggest that they are somehow incapable of making mistakes, then the reader might reasonably conclude that technical performance perfection is not always achieved.

The absence of mention of performance errors is regrettable, not only because making errors is common in one major part of musical enculturation—that of learning new songs—and thus is worthy of comment, but also because in the teaching situation, and specifically in the manner in which errors are corrected, identification and categorisation of errors may be found, together with positive statements of musical values. Rather than thinking of the situation entirely in terms of such mutually exclusive categories as 'rightness' and 'wrongness', the Pintupi appear to recognize degrees and kinds of deviations from an explicit ideal. These form a kind of evaluation continuum, which may be expressed as shown in Fig. 11.

Pitch fluctuation

In all the recorded series there was a certain amount of overall pitch fluctuation. This tended to take the form of a gradual lowering of the pitch, which continued for the entire duration of the shorter recordings of an hour or less. In longer performances,

---

6. Strehlow (1933:197ff; 1971:67ff) has reported similar changes in Aranda songs, and classified these in some detail.

however, this lowering continued only to a point where their song leader considered that the singing was no longer comfortable or sufficiently loud; at this point he/she raised the pitch, in many cases returning to the one at which the series had originally started. The process of gradual lowering and sudden raising continued for the remainder of the performance. During these longer performances there were occasional pauses lasting about five minutes in the singing while the people rested or took refreshments, everyone tending to remain in his/her place. Generally, when singing resumed after these breaks, it was on a relatively high pitch, followed by the gradual lowering process described above. In some cases it was also noticeable that the pitch which commenced the performance was not necessarily the highest reached during the course of that performance. After an initial period at a relatively low overall pitch, the leader might raise it, sometimes by as much as an octave. Singers' spoken comments such as *lirri kuya* (bad throat), at the start of a series, suggested that it took some time before they considered they were in good vocal form.

Typical pitch changes for the tonic in *yarritjiti*, *maanytja*, *tingarri* and *tjatiwanpa* songs are illustrated in Fig. 12.

Comparison of overall pitches for series spread over more than one day, or which were repeated after a period of several days, indicates a certain amount of variation, suggesting that there is no concept of any particular pitch being considered more, or less, 'correct' than any other. Also, in the sole recorded example of a prolonged period separating performances of the same series, the overall pitches for each varied considerably. Current vocal ability appears to be the chief criterion in determining such pitch.

Song origins and ownership

Song series are ascribed origins both ancient and modern. Most of the recorded sample is said to have come from the *tjukurrpa* (lit. dreaming), the past world with an indefinable time span. During this *tjukurrpa*, the Aboriginal world was populated by a variety of mythological beings who travelled widely, performed acts both human and superhuman, formed and reformed features of the natural landscape, transformed people into physical features of the country, carried out certain activities (many of which have now become ritualised ceremonies), set precedents for kinship behaviour patterns, and composed songs describing some of their deeds. Composition of series of this type as a whole, however, is not ascribed to any individual in either the Dreamtime or the historical past and the events are related in the third person. Individual songs may contain words with the first person singular suffix *na*, and the Pintupi agree that in such cases it is in fact the Dreamtime character singing or speaking.

Assuming that the construction of the individual texts reflects strict narrational accuracy (and the Pintupi certainly believe this) the various song series can be seen as anonymously composed contemporary accounts of the mythological past in which individual songs sung by the characters are included verbatim within the poetic and musical constraints. The musical construction of such songs differs in no way from other items in the series, and information on composition of complete series appears to go no further than a general ascription to the *tjukurrpa*. For example, there is no explanation of how the boundary between Dreamtime and historical time was crossed in order to teach the series to mortals. To the Pintupi, there is no questioning of the authenticity of the Dreamtime origin; whatever processes enable people to come into possession of them now are not subject to enquiry, however rational, and are insignificant in comparison with the necessity for accurate performance, without which, efficacy is impeded.

Unlike the music of neighbouring areas, Pintupi song series do not always consist of a single melodic contour repeated for each individual song. Where a series has more than one melody, each contour is considered as representing a separate character or group of characters in the original myth. Because of limitations of time and linguistic ability, the subject was not examined to the extent that I would have liked, and the following should be seen in this light. The Pintupi describe the situation by holding out the hand, fingers spread wide apart and each representing a separate melody. Two explanations of the phenomenon of multiple melodies, referred to as *tarrpirarra*, were given by men at both Kungkayunti and Balgo:

(a) that the melodies originate from the Dreamtime, i.e. that each melody has always existed in its particular form;

(b) that at some time long ago (*kurralpa*), as opposed to the Dreamtime, a tribal elder (*nintipuka*) taught the new melodies (and presumably new songs), which were added to the series as it then existed.

For example, one man at Balgo was able to identify only two of the four *yarritjiti* melodies during a test conducted there in 1977. When told later of the identity of the other two, he remarked that the performance style to which he personally was accustomed used only two, and he attributed the other two ultimately to the activities of a *nintipuka* in some other area. He was also unfamiliar with the texts of the songs using the different melodies. (The performance this man heard had been recorded at Kungkayunti.)

The second explanation raises a whole host of implications concerning the stability of melodic forms and the immutability of myths and their associated songs—implications which could not be evaluated or examined adequately in the current fieldwork circumstances. Suffice it to say here that those giving the explanations did not appear to see any inconsistency between them and their understanding of song origins; elucidation of the phenomenon must await further research.

Inscrutable though their origins may be, these *tjukurrpa* ceremonies carry with them a rigidly followed ownership system, whether it be by kinship subsection or by geographical location. In some cases there is also a division of participants by patrimoieties or, in the case of *yawulyu*, matrimoieties into 'owners' and 'workers', but although such a division neatly accounts for all Pintupi society, there always are one or two subsections considered to be the *mama* (father) of the ceremony. Such a position is determined by the subsection of the Dreamtime individual concerned in the myth, and just as the whole song series recounts his exploits, so in real life the *mama* (or one of their number) is the chief actor in the ceremony.

The Dreamtime origin thus establishes an inviolate precedent for the ceremony in its entirety, including song texts, melodies, dances, and the whole gamut of ritual objects and acts.

To describe song series ascribed recent origins as 'compositions' is something of a misnomer, as that term implies a creative act occurring at a definite point in time, or over a definite period of time. The only category of Pintupi song, examples of which the people at Balgo and Kungkayunti claimed was not of Dreamtime or non-Pintupi origin, was the *tulku*, and only one example of a recent *tulku* was recorded at each location.[7] However, far from being considered the result of an inventive process, the Pintupi say that the whole *tulku* song series already existed just waiting to be discovered. They commonly used the words *witinu* (caught in the hand) or *ngalunu* (grabbed) to refer to the actual acquisition of the *tulku*, implying that it is both visible and tangible, at least to the catcher. This catcher is always a man's spirit, not the man himself. Accounts agree generally that at night when a man (and no stories speak of this happening to a woman) is sleeping, his spirit leaves the body, exiting through the navel from its normal position in the stomach region, and departs, sometimes up to the stars, sometimes to other areas on earth far from places normally inhabited as camps. Searching for songs is not the only nocturnal activity of the spirit; the desire to travel is the main object, whether alone, or in the protective company of a *mapantjarra* (Doctorman), who is able to see any dangerous spirits and deal with them. Having found and captured the *tulku* the spirit returns to the body of the still-sleeping man, entering through the navel. When he awakens, the man will remember the activities of his spirit the previous night perfectly,[8] and is able to perform and teach the details to others.

By contrast, one informant claimed the songs were taught by an eaglehawk, but in all the other descriptions, people say they simply do not know in what form the *tulku* existed, or how it was located and identified. Most Pintupi talk freely about such things, recounting what they themselves have heard and believe, but in only one case was first-hand experience claimed. *Tulku*-acquisition is but one activity among many engaged in by human spirits, essentially no different from the others, and the marked contrast between the number of people able to verbalise about the acquisition process on the one hand, and the number of specific cases cited on the other, presents no problem to Pintupi thinking.

Prior to recording, the present owner of the *tulku yunpu* (the sole example from Balgo ascribed a recent origin) stressed the episode in the story dealing with the death of an old woman who, he said, was his own mother and was adamant that the events recounted in the songs were absolutely true, and had taken place in the desert in his own lifetime. He also claimed that he himself had 'found' this *tulku*.[9]

---

7. The women's Restricted (a) series was claimed to be a 'new one' in 1976, but further details could not be obtained.
8. Indeed, he may claim to be physically exhausted from the trip! *See* Tonkinson 1974:79.
9. He left Balgo shortly afterwards, and did not return during the fieldwork period; regrettably, no elaboration of his statements was thus possible.

The other *tulku* in the recorded sample said to have originated from a known individual is the *yikuluku* (eaglehawk), which is well-known at Papunya, Yayayi and Haasts Bluff, as well as at Kungkayunti. At the time a group of Pintupi were living at Alumbra Bore (probably in the '60s), between Papunya and Yayayi, one man of the Tjapangati subsection, together with a companion, went on a spirit journey to a distant place where they saw an eaglehawk circling high above them; this bird taught them the entire *tulku*. Here, there is reference in one song text to the acquisition process:

nyakula	*watjanu*	*waringka*	*tulkintjunu*
having seen	spoke	sky	turned

puntunya	*tjananya*
men	they two

The two men saw an eaglehawk circling in the sky; it spoke to them.

In essence, the Pintupi believe that all of the song series in their repertoire originate either in the Dreamtime or from the activities of human spirits. Any non-Pintupi material in this repertoire is believed to share these same ultimate sources, although in most cases only the immediate origin is known, and usually expressed in a geographical location.[10]

Acquired song ownership is achieved by a variety of means:

Personal inheritance

This method seems to apply only to ownership held by an individual, with the transference achieved by verbal donation to the eldest son. If there are no sons, another close male relative may receive it. One Kungkayunti man claims a particular *tulku* he owns was given to him by his elder brother. There is also one case, widely known and told among Pintupi men, in which the eldest son of the man who 'found' the *tulku yikuluku* described earlier went to his father's grave, and was taught the songs by the spirit still living there.[11]

This son had been absent from camp when his father died, and arrived back too late to receive the bequest personally. His subsequent actions were aimed at improving a then-imperfect knowledge of the *tulku*. In the case of certain ceremonies, ownership was said to be on the basis of one or more subsections; however, within those subsections there were always individuals who had inherited a greater claim to ownership than the others.

General inheritance

There are a number of ceremonies common to the Central Desert as a whole, comprising initiation and pre- and post-initiation rites. There is some disagreement among the Pintupi, who are familiar with these ceremonies, as to the language of their song texts. Some say they are Pitjantjatjara, and others that they are Mayidjarra, but the majority opinion is that the language is, to use their own term, 'mix-up', an amalgam of Pintupi and several related languages which border on traditional Pintupi territory.[12]

Examination of the geographical areas encompassed by the Dreamtime characters in these initiation myths tends to confirm this latter opinion, as they include the Warburton and Tomkinson Ranges, and The Granites (all of which lie outside Pintupi territory), as well as Christopher Lake, the Walter James Range, and other sites north of the Rawlinson Ranges (all of which are considered inside Pintupi country).

When photographs of an initiation ceremony specially-staged by Pintupi men from Balgo were shown to Kungkayunti men, they were unable to identify the particular series, but when they listened to the music, recognition was immediate, thus suggesting that within Pintupi territory itself some variation in the rites had been established, but that the music has remained more stable. The Pintupi claim no exclusive ownership for these ceremonies, nor do they attribute it to any single area or group of

10. Such locations may be of two types. On the one hand they may be the places where the Pintupi heard and learnt the series; on the other, they may be the geographical places at which the *tulku* narratives start.

11. At Balgo, this particular *tulku* was well-known and referred to as '*mirringuru*' (from a dead person).

12. Of the *malu* (kangaroo) initiation ceremony, Meggitt recorded the declaration from the Walbiri: 'We Walbiri follow the same kangaroo dreaming track as do the Bidjabidja (Pitjantjatjara) and Pintupi; we sing the same songs, recite the same myths and make the same sacred string-crosses'(1965:41). Strehlow (1969:11), writing of an undefined 'Centralia' confirms this, '. . . ownership of the myths and songs describing these travels was shared out among the various tribal groups through whose territories these mythical wanderings were believed to have taken place.' So does Tonkinson (1974:77), 'The major rituals and songline, which have diffused widely throughout the Western Desert, have long ceased to be the property of any one group and are instead held in common and performed by responsible elders and initiated men, regardless of ancestral or other kinds of totemic affiliation.'

people. Common use has affected common ownership.

The all-night ceremony, *kutitji*, is a similar example, and Kungkayunti men claim it has songs comprising a 'mix-up' of Pintupi, Luridja, Aranda and Walbiri, but that they have no knowledge of why this should be. Details are lacking, but it appears that the events occurring in the myth cover more than one traditional territory, which might conceivably explain the variety of languages, although no Pintupi ever made such a suggestion.

Likewise, the ceremony called *yarritjiti* is said to have originated from Pitjantjatjara speakers, to the west, and that the language of its songs is a mixture of that and Pintupi. It is claimed to be in use by all Pintupi groups.

The major difficulty in working with song texts from series such as these is that, with the exception of Walbiri and Aranda, the similarities between Pintupi and the other languages claimed to be present in the 'mix-up' make positive identification of non-Pintupi elements almost impossible beyond isolating individual words. The issue is further complicated by the nature of song words from the Central and Western Deserts as a whole; much of the text material uses words not found in everyday speech, and thus the presence of a word whose meaning is unknown to the Pintupi does not necessarily mean that it is a non-Pintupi word.

General inheritance as a result of widened ownership

Among the recorded samples at Kungkayunti are two Walbiri series. The one, a *pulapa*, is said to have been formerly the personal property of a man of the Tjangala subsection living in Arnhem Land. Since his death, however, all performance restrictions have been lifted and the series, the equivalent of the *tulku*, may be sung by anybody. The sole caveat still in force is a reduction in the number of songs comprising the series, since several in the original form apparently related to this man, and therefore had to be omitted in subsequent performances. The other Walbiri series is an emu *yilpintji* which, according to two informants, used to be known and used only by people in the Cockatoo Creek area, near Yuendumu, but now it too may be freely sung by any men. The restricted features associated with *yilpintji* in general are, however, retained. No information was given as to the means of ownership extension in these two cases.

Exchange

While the whole issue of corroborees as trade goods is dealt with in Micha (1970:301-302) as one element in a broader process of exchange of goods leading to close culture contact and subsequent culture change, and while individual cases of so-called 'travelling' ceremonies are described in the literature e.g. de Graaf (1968:115); McCarthy (1939:83-85); Bates (1938:123-26); Strehlow (1970:94)[13] the mechanics of the transaction are not specified.

While I was at Balgo in 1975, an instance of such an exchange (or rather the first steps in an exchange process, the whole of which will probably take several years to complete) occurred, and is described in some detail here.

Preparation

The exchange concerned the giving of full performance rights of the *tjatiwanpa* or *winparrku tulku*[14] ceremony by the Walbiri of Yuendumu to the Balgo community, who in turn had already begun the first stages of giving one of their own ceremonies (whose name I was specifically asked not to reveal, on account of its secrecy) to Yuendumu. The decision to give the *tjatiwanpa* ceremony to the Balgo people was apparently made in late 1974, and this part of the exchange act concluded some six months later.

The *tjatiwanpa* is claimed by the Pintupi people at Kungkayunti to be of Luridja origin, though in the Pintupi language.[15] Prior to 1975, Pintupi at Papunya, Yayayi and Kungkayunti did not have the authority (i.e. of ownership) to perform the *tjatiwanpa* ceremony themselves, although they had participated often enough in the company of Walbiri at Yuendumu to know many, if not all, of the songs and rituals. At Yuendumu it was claimed that the ceremony was of Walbiri origin, and in the Walbiri

---

13. The title of Ellis' paper *Folk song migration in Aboriginal South Australia* (1967) is misleading in this respect, as the contents deal with the distribution of singing styles rather than the geographical movement of specific songs.

14. The ceremony is also called *winparrku*, after Winparrku Mountain (Blanche Tower, some 40km west of Haasts Bluff) where the associated myth starts.

15. Tindale (1974:155) claims this name is a derogatory term used by Walbiri to refer to the Gugadja, whereas Long (1970:331, note 6) claims Aranda origin and an application to all Pitjantjatjara speakers to the southeast and west of Aranda territory.

language. The Pintupi at Balgo claimed that although an occasional Walbiri word occurred in the songs, the texts were mainly Pintupi. In his book tracing the mythical path covered by characters in the *tjatiwanpa* saga, Mountford claims that part of the myth belongs to the Ngaliya people, and part to the Walbiri (1968:xviii), the division corresponding to the territorial boundary between the two groups; he does not, however, refer to the language or languages of the song texts.[16]

As mentioned earlier, difficulties arise in identifying the language used in song texts where the possibility of multiple languages exist, and especially where these languages are cognate to begin with. What is more important is that in 1974, the *tjatiwanpa* ceremony was considered by the Yuendumu Walbiri to belong to them, a claim generally acknowledged at Balgo.

The Walbiri and Pintupi kinship subsections are identical, and their names cognate. For this particular ceremony, the patrimoiety Tjakamarra, Tjupurrula, Tjangala and Tjampitjinpa constituted the *mayutju* (ceremonial owners), while the other patrimoiety of Tjungurayi, Tjapangati, Tjapanangka and Tjapaltjarri were the *kutungulu* (ceremonial workers). Within the *mayutju*, Tjakamarra and Tjupurrula are the two *mama* (fathers) of the ceremony, as the whole myth centres round characters from these two subsections, one individual from each of which is chosen to be the principal actor, although on what basis the Yuendumu individuals were chosen is not known.

Women play an integral part in the *tjatiwanpa* ceremony, especially those belonging to the female equivalents of the *mayutju* patrimoiety (Nakamarra, Napurrula, Nangala and Nampitjinpa). It is not known, however, if these women consider themselves *mayutju* in their own right.

A, a man from Balgo, was a Tjakamarra, and while on holiday at Yuendumu on a number of occasions in the 1970s, became friendly with local men of the same subsection, including the man who was one of the two principal actors in the *tjatiwanpa* ceremony. B, a Tjupurrula man from Balgo, had an elder brother at Yuendumu who was the other principal actor. When the decision was made to give the ceremony to the Balgo people, A and B were chosen to be the new main actors; they were informed of the choice, and spent further time at Yuendumu learning more of the myth and of the roles they would be playing in its enactment. The Yuendumu *kutungulu*

was led by one man, who directed the preparation activities and led the singing; he was referred to as the *mangaya* (big one) or 'boss' during the Balgo ceremonies. He was a Tjungurayi and had a younger brother, C, at Balgo. C was informed that he would become the new *mangaya*. On return from Yuendumu in January 1974, C brought with him a small bull-roarer for use in the rites leading up to the *tjatiwanpa* ceremony; it was a gift from his elder brother.

Towards the middle of March 1975, two Tjapangati men from Yuendumu arrived, specifically to give final teaching to the Balgo people before the arrival of the main party who would lead a joint performance of the whole ceremony. Prior to this, however, the Balgo camp had gathered *en masse* on at least two occasions to sing the first hour or so of songs from this ceremony, but each time the performance was halted at the point when the principal dancers would normally have featured. Although the appropriate songs and dances were known well enough, lack of total performance rights at that stage stopped them from continuing. After continued shouted warnings of 'We can't sing im, that one', 'Too much *tulku* that one', and similar comments in Gugadja language (the principal language spoken at Balgo, and cognate with Pintupi), the gathering dispersed. The two Yuendumu teachers were Pintupi, and had lived earlier at Papunya and Yayayi; during their two week stay at Balgo they lived with classificatory brothers. In the days immediately following their arrival, they spent much time with a group of about fifteen men of the *kutungulu* moiety (especially Tjapangati and Tjungurayi) making new boomerangs to beat at the ceremony, and also to rehearse informally the *tjatiwanpa* songs. From time to time these two teachers would inform the others of performance details, or of the actions occurring in the myth associated with particular songs. C attended all these sessions, and was already demonstrating his knowledge gained earlier by occasionally adding to the teachers' comments with further details of his own. To all that was told them, the other men would reply *Yuwa yuwa* (yes yes), *mularrpa* (true), or the like.

---

16. Strehlow (1970:137, note 12) in a strong criticism of Mountford's book, claims the myth to be owned by the Gugadja, and in that language; Tindale too (1974:139) claims Gugadja ownership, at the same time disclaiming Mountford's assertion that the mountain is in Ngaliya territory. Meggitt (1962:47) compounds the issue by claiming Ngaliya to be a 'subgroup of the Walbiri tribe', whereas Long (1970:331, note 5) says this is a Pitjantjatjara term meaning 'people to the north'.

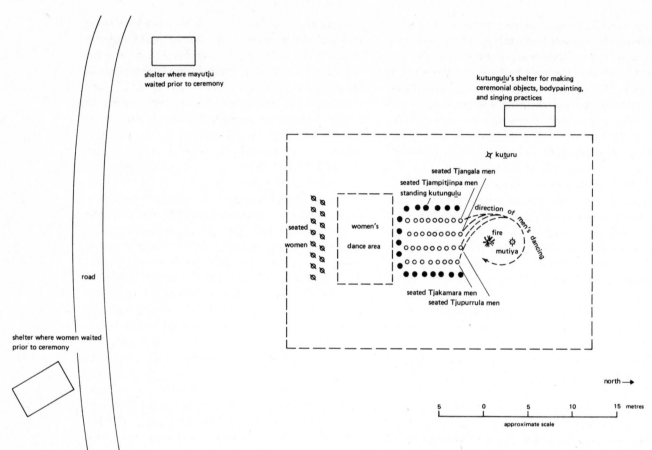

shelter where mayutju
waited prior to ceremony

kutungulu's shelter for making
ceremonial objects, bodypainting,
and singing practices

kuṯuru

seated Tjangala men
seated Tjampitjinpa men
standing kutungulu

direction of men's dancing

seated
women

women's
dance area

fire
mutiya

seated Tjakamara men
seated Tjupurrula men

road

shelter where women waited
prior to ceremony

north →

5   0   5   10   15 metres

approximate scale

Figure 13 Ground plan for second night of rehearsal of *tjatiwanpa* ceremony; the larger rectangle outlined in broken lines indicates the area of ground cleared for this purpose.

Formal rehearsal

One week before the anticipated arrival date (4 April) of the main party from Yuendumu (heavy rains had flooded the roads, and there was doubt that they would come at all), the two teachers announced what turned out to be a full dress rehearsal performance, to be spread over three days. On 26 March, 1975 the performance started, consisting solely of male singing and female dancing, and the only ceremonial object on display was the small bullroarer recently acquired from Yuendumu. On the following day, the performance was more elaborate, and Tjungurayi and Tjapangaṯi men spent from 9 am to 5 pm making large ceremonial objects and decorating these and themselves.

From 2-4 pm these men sat in a small shelter on the edge of the normal ceremonial ground, singing *tja-tiwanpa* songs as they worked. Although they were the same men who had been gathering there for singing

practice for some days before, the Yuendumu teachers did not lead the singing on this occasion, leaving many of the songs to one particular Tjapanangka, whose singing voice was generally acknowledged as the best in the camp.[17]

At one stage the singers were unable to remember the words of the next song; one teacher spoke the words—*palyanyin kantuwarra*—but made no move to demonstrate the melody or rhythm. The local singers made several attempts to sing it, and eventually succeeded. The rehearsal on the second night was delayed until after 5 pm to allow Mission employees to attend. During this rehearsal, the teachers again allowed the same Tjapanangka man to lead most of the singing, and the only intervention they made in the entire proceedings was to stand in front of all the

17. C also bowed to the other's better voice, and did not lead any of the singing himself, even though his brother at Yuendumu had given him the right to do so.

men at one stage and instruct them in the proper procedure for one set of solo dances. The layout of the ceremonial and adjacent areas is shown in Fig. 13.

When all the local men had arrived, the senior of the two Yuendumu teachers went to the shelter where the *mayutju* were waiting, and escorted them to their place, the whole party arriving in single file. Although they were stripped to the waist and carried pairs of boomerangs, they had no bodypaint; by contrast the *kutungulu* wore bodypaint, and had donned loin cloths. Some few minutes previously, the women had been called over from their shelter across the road, where they had been sitting for more than an hour; on arrival, they sat quietly at the southernmost end of the ground. The senior teacher initially directed the *mayutju* to kneel in four lines, corresponding to the four subsections of the patri-moiety, and the *kutungulu* stood surrounding them on three sides. Several minutes of singing followed, performed by the *kuntungulu* only although the *mayutju* beat their boomerangs too.

The next stage of proceedings was the formal introduction of the *mayutju* to the ceremonial objects. Flanking the line of Tjupurrula men, several of the *kutungulu* (including C and the two teachers) led them out and clockwise around the *mutiya* (a short decorated stump representing Winparrku Mountain) and back to their places. The men moved in a slow synchronised gait, their feet performing sliding circles to each side (in a movement called *kupunguranyi*), their backs stooped and their hands clasped behind their heads in imitation of the snake whose exploits feature prominently in the *tjatiwanpa* saga. During this the *kutungulu* kept up shouted warnings, of 'Look out for the snake', 'Mind he doesn't bite you', and the like. In similar fashion, the lines of Tjampitjinpa, Tjangala and Tjakamara men were then led out successively to circle clockwise the *kuturu* (a large nullanulla representing the emu which figures in the myth), first hopping along on one foot, then copying the sweeping foot movements of the Tjupurrula. The *mayutju* then returned to where they had been kneeling earlier, and sat down.

Following more singing, in which the *mayutju* joined for the first time, A was painted up for a solo dance featuring his ritual death by burning and subsequent loss of sacred objects (including a tall hat). During this dance he was flanked by two women each from the Nakamarra and Napurrula subsections, as well as the two teachers, C, and several other *kutungulu* members. These women were obviously

nervous and unsure of what to do; twice they stood still until the teachers, using hand signs, told them to dance along behind the main actor. One teacher demonstrated how a single *kutungulu* man was to crouch over the solo dancer, A, during his act, and later snatch away his hat. Another brief period of singing followed, during which B was painted up by the *kutungulu*. He then performed an identical solo dance, accompanied by two women each from the Nangala and Nampitjinpa subsections, as well as some of the *kutungulu*.

The teachers appeared to be dissatisfied with the actions of the one *kutungulu* man who was copying the example shown during A's solo dance, and went and stood alongside him, demonstrating how to crouch lower and parallel the solo dancer's movements.

After further singing, two Tjampitjinpa men were painted up and performed an identical dance around the *kuturu*, supported by four Nampitjinpa and Nangala women. The teachers were apparently satisfied with the performance, and although they walked along beside the two men, they offered no directions to them or to the women.

From this point until the end of the ceremony, at about 6.45 pm, only male singing and group female dancing behind the men's area took place. The following day being payday, there were no activities, but on the next night, the final stage of the rehearsal was held; this consisted solely of singing by the men. The women did not attend. The singing was led mainly by the same Tjapanangka who had led earlier.

The three day rehearsal involved elements of both instruction and ownership. The instruction was basically remedial, occurring only when a performance error needed correction, and was achieved by word of mouth, hand-signs, and personal example. The introduction of the *mayutju* to the ritual objects, which constituted the first formal step on their part towards assumption of ownership of the ceremony, was accompanied by the shouts and singing of the *kutungulu*, who in a more informal manner, had already taken on the role of managers by their presence and participation in the earlier singing practices, manufacture and decoration of the ritual objects, and by their own bodypaint designs. Although no separate action occurred during the performance which established their corporate role, each individual man acquired full *kutungulu* status earlier that afternoon when, on arrival at the shelter on the west side of the ground, he was taken by the hand by a classificatory brother and shown the completed ritual objects lying hidden in the grass, and made to touch them and thus receive a little of their inherent power. Mission employees belonging to the *kutungulu* subsections were, of course, unable to leave work before 5 pm, and on arrival at the ground stood fully clothed at the rear of the *mayutju*; they took no part in painting up or escorting the solo dancers, rekindling the fire, or any other activity beyond singing.

To summarise the acquisition process so far:

(a) A and B had performed their solo dances, and thus established their roles as the two *mama* of the *tjatiwanpa* ceremony;

(b) C's role as *mangaya* of the ceremony was not yet fully established; not only did the two teachers continue to oversee the rehearsals, but C himself did not lead the singing. (By contrast, there was verbal recognition of his imminent status as *mangaya* by the other Balgo men);

(c) the *mayutju* had been formally installed, and had been introduced to the ritual objects;

(d) by the preparing of the ritual objects, the leading of the singing, and general managing of the proceedings, the *kutungulu* had been effectively established in their role;

(e) only the women were still rather unsure of their part in accompanying the solo dancers, although this was mainly ignorance of procedure. They were perfectly at ease performing their group dancing behind the men's area.

Acquisition procedure

At noon on 4 April, the Yuendumu group arrived, and that evening the first night's ceremonies were held. A new ground immediately to the north of the old one had been cleared by the *kutungulu* (and with the help of Mission machinery), and green leaves spread for the men and women visitors to sit on. The only ritual object on display was one small bullroarer suspended from a thin pole in front of the men's area. At around 4.00 pm the *kutungulu*, who had been gathering all afternoon in their shelter beside the old ground to make bodypaint and to complete new boomerangs, arrived at the new ground, standing around the leaf-covered areas; shortly after, the *mayutju* and women came and sat down, the women on the east side of their leafy area, and the *mayutju* at the feet of the standing *kutungulu*. Singing started, led by the same Tjapanangka who had been prominent earlier, until at 4.40 the Yuendumu people were

sighted approaching in single file from an area on the far side of the camp where they had been painting up and arranging temporary shelters. Singing continued until the newcomers were at the edge of the ground, whereupon all the Yuendumu group danced on, four of the men in front holding behind their heads thin poles with small bullroarers attached; immediately behind them danced four women. Together these eight people represented the *kutungulu* patri- and matrimoieties. While dancing up to the area in front of the assembled Balgo men, the Yuendumu people led by C's brother who dominated the proceedings for the rest of the ceremonies, started singing. The Balgo men remained silent, watching as the four leading visitors planted their bullroarers next to their own; then the Yuendumu *mayutju* men went and sat on the leaves, with the Balgo *mayutju* joining them; the Yuendumu *kutungulu* stood on the west side of the *mayutju*, their Balgo counterparts on the east side.

For the whole of this afternoon performance, the Balgo women simply sat and watched the Yuendumu women dance; likewise the Balgo men joined in the singing, but did not dance. The solo exception was C, who joined a group of Yuendumu Tjungurayi for one brief dance in front of the other men. The performance concluded at 5.25 pm, and Yuendumu and Balgo men and women moved about freely, greeting each other, with old acquaintances and relatives occasionally weeping at the memory of dead friends.

The following night's performance featured two solo male dances by the two *mama* from Yuendumu (and accompanied by Yuendumu women only) and dancing by Balgo women for the first time (although they both sat and performed slightly apart from the other group). Singing was again led by the Yuendumu *mangaya*, who also controlled the groups of male dancers performing in front of the men's area, announcing in a loud voice who would dance next. He also deliberately prolonged the singing at one stage, when his younger brother, C, danced, calling out 'Winner!' at the end. Sudden heavy rain forced a premature end to proceedings 90 minutes after they started.

It was during this particular night's performance that the same *mangaya* ratified Balgo's ownership of the *tjatiwanpa* ceremony, by calling out in English, 'This one belong all Balgo now,' during one interval in the singing, at which several of the other Yuendumu men replied, '*Yuwa yuwa*' (Yes yes). This proclamation constituted the only public statement of ownership acquisition, and to some extent was the culmination of months of planning and weeks of active preparation. In another sense, however, the climax of this period was not to come until Balgo first performed the whole ceremony by itself, some five weeks later.

On the morning of the third day of ceremonies, all the Yuendumu and Balgo kutungulu went to a secluded area to the north of the camp, where the ritual objects for that night's all-night performance were being made. When these were completed the Balgo mayutju, who had been waiting inside the camp were summoned, and the significance of each explained to them by the Yuendumu mangaya, who was still very much in charge. Solo dances were then performed by A and B in what amounted to a validation of their roles by the whole assembly. During these dances, as in actual performances on the ceremonial ground, the mayutju were made to sit with the kutungulu standing around them. Only the females were absent from the performance. Afterwards, the ceremonial objects were taken to the main ground and set up.

The all-night performance which followed was not marked by any great changes in content from the previous two, although A and B performed their solo acts for the first time in front of all the gathering, and were flanked by local as well as visiting women. In the group dancing, too, local men performed for the first time. Shortly after 2 am a group of women singed their pubic hair as part of the ritual. This had not occurred in the performances of the previous week, and both men and women at Balgo were reluctant to discuss it (as they said, because it was 'heathen' and they were afraid of possible punitive action by the Mission); it is known, however, that local as well as visiting women participated in this.

The fourth (the final) night of ceremonies centred around the ritual death by 'burning' of all the women and male mayutju. Tall poles of leafy branches bound together were set alight and shaken over the victims, who waved smaller branches over their heads for protection. Both Balgo and Yuendumu men participated in this act, then the whole gathering dispersed and the complete tjatiwanpa ceremony was over. The following morning, the Yuendumu group returned home, taking with them one Balgo Tjungurayi, and leaving one of their own Tjakamarra. The Tjungurayi was to travel to Papunya and Yayayi, acting as messenger and informing the Pintupi there that from then on they too could perform the ceremony by reason of their having so many close relatives in the Balgo community.

On 4 June 1975, while passing through Papunya, the writer was stopped by one highly excited man from Kungkayunti, who informed him that the tjatiwanpa ceremony was to be held that night in Papunya, and that he had 'gotta come'. Although illness prevented detailed questioning, it appeared that this may have been the first performance at Papunya unaided by Yuendumu representatives, and indicative of the success of the Tjungurayi's mission. According to other Balgo men, he was also intending to try and persuade people at Papunya and Yayayi to travel to Balgo and participate in the first all-Balgo performance of the complete tjatiwanpa some five weeks later; however they were unable to go because of impassable roads. The Tjakamarra man who had remained at Balgo was to act as adviser if needed at this first local performance.

Independent Balgo performance

Since the Yuendumu people left, a small group of Balgo kutungulu had been meeting virtually daily in the shelter adjacent to the old ceremonial ground, to talk about the recent events, to make spears, shields and boomerangs for sale, and to sing tjatiwanpa songs. The first independent local performance started on 12 May, and incorporated solo dancing by A and B, male group dancing by the kutungulu, and the manufacture of a limited number of ritual objects. This performance, and another on the following day, were more by way of rehearsals of particular sections of the ceremony, rather than attempts to repeat independent of the Yuendumu people, and in their entirety, the same rituals they had only just acquired. As noted above, the first complete all-Balgo performance occurred some time later.

The singing was led primarily by the same Tjapanangka who had been prominent earlier, but occasionally other men would start individual songs. One musical phenomenon which had not occurred previously was a rise in overall pitch of a 4th occurring in mid-performance, that is, not following a break in singing lasting several minutes. (In the combined performances five weeks earlier, several pitch changes of up to a 4th had occurred, but always following a brief break for food or rest; in the present performance, however, an anonymous singer started to lead, but was soon interrupted by the same Tjapanangka who started a 4th higher; for a while the two men continued at their respective pitches,

65

until the rest of the men followed the higher lead, and this anonymous singer was drowned in their voices.)

At another stage, a song was stopped with cries of 'Wurra!' (Wait!), because it contained a reference to the dead; this particular item had been omitted in the combined performances, and its inclusion here was apparently pure accident.

The only procedural differences noted by the writer were that A and B were painted up at the places where they were to dance, rather than in the centre of the men's group, and that the small group of kutungulu accompanying the painters sang independently of the main group (with the inevitable result that they were always drowned by the larger group). When asked about this latter point, C declined to explain beyond assuring that it was palyalingku (very good).

Details are not available for the first night's performance, but on the second night 25 of the 58 different songs performed had not been sung during the combined performances. These new songs accompanied dancing by B in which his painting and dress differed from that worn when the Yuendumu people were there; it was said that the differences reflected a part of the tjatiwanpa myth not mentioned in the Yuendumu version they had so recently acquired.

When asked the reason for this, C replied that it was 'too much tulku'. 'They [i.e. the Yuendumu people] can't manage im', and pulkalingku (very big one), which would seem to indicate that nowadays Yuendumu regularly performs only part of the total tjatiwanpa myth and that Balgo already has performance rights to another section of this myth (although by what means they gained possession is not known).[18]

To place Yuendumu's donation of the tjatiwanpa into cultural perspective, it should be pointed out that they expected to receive something in return, or rather, to continue receiving something. (One of the teachers told me that Balgo's payment for the ceremony would, in the first instance, consist of $20 from each man, plus blankets, boomerangs, shields, spears and hairstring. This, however, was not corroborated by Balgo men. By contrast, the mangaya told the Mission Superintendent that they were giving the ceremony 'free' to Balgo 'because they wanted it'.) At Christmas 1974, four Yuendumu men went to Balgo specifically to observe the annual performance of ceremonies associated with the creation of new Doctormen. By so doing, the reciprocal part of the overall exchange was set in motion. Prior to this, no outsiders had been permitted to attend, but during that year, the Balgo owners had agreed to let Yuendumu men observe part of the proceedings over a period of several years (some say five), with the view to eventually granting them performance rights and thus extending the ownership. Presumably at that same time in 1974, the whole exchange mechanism was set in motion.

Conclusion

From the details in the past several pages, a number of concluding observations may be drawn. Song, in its broad context of ceremony performance, is considered as property, and may not be used except in the presence of approving owners. Further, not only is performance of the singing controlled directly by the kutungulu, but also within this patrimoiety a certain individual has the responsibility for leading the singing. (In the Balgo case, it appears that the Tjapanangka's age seniority and apparently superior knowledge of the songs are the present factors in his position as song leader; whether or not in times to come C attempts some sort of self-assertion to assume the full status of mangaya of this particular ceremony cannot be predicted.) Transference of ownership, or more accurately, extension of ownership, is viewed as an act of cultural economics, involving the expectation of reciprocity, although nowhere in the literature of the region is there any indication of a set pattern in this respect—e.g. a song series for a song series, a ceremony for a ceremony—or of what socio-economic or psycho-cultural valuations apply in any group decision to offer, or to accept, ownership of this nature. What was most apparent after the Yuendumu party returned home was the verbal phasis by the Balgo people on the fact that the ceremony was now theirs as opposed to the fact that it was not a local creation; present ownership prevailed over past origin.

Ownership of a song series implies ownership of each individual song in that series, and there do not appear to be any references in the literature to songs from one series featuring in another series. However, in the course of fieldwork, one particular song was found to occur in no less than four different series—a tingarri, a yilpintji, a yawulyu, and one restricted women's series. The text is as follows: kukatjanya kukatja

18. A view supported by Mountford who claims sectional ownership by several groups on the basis of the geographical areas encompassed by the mythical characters (1968:xviii).

66

ngaliyanya ngaliya 'They (two) are Kukatja (people), Kukatja; they (two) [i.e. two others] are Ngaliya (people), Ngaliya'. In each series in which it occurred, this song was explained as referring to a meeting of mythological characters from the two tribes. The creation of this text, four times, each time independently, seems unlikely, but although men and women knew it occurred twice within their own subculture's repertoire, no explanation for the duplication was offered. I did not inform the men and women of the existence of this song in the other's repertoire, nor did I enquire whether or not they were aware of this. Likewise I myself have no explanation for the phenomenon.

Although Pintupi music in its entirety is not a known quantity to any individual man or woman, that particular corpus of material known and performed by a given group will be ascribed one of a number of origins:

(a) the *tjukurrpa* (Dreamtime);
(b) the spirit activities of a known local individual within living memory (an origin apparently restricted to *tulku* song series);
(c) the spirit activities of a *nintipuka* (elder) at some time in the distant past (*kurralpa*), as opposed to the Dreamtime, who added new individual songs to an already existing series. This explanation was given by men at both Balgo and Kungkayunti only for those song series having more than one melodic contour. As mentioned in the Song Performance section, the men did not see any inconsistency between this view and that of the immutability of Dreamtime precedents. There is evidence to suggest that where such series are known and sung over a wide geographical area, not all performances employ the same number of contours, or the same songs, thus supporting the notion which the men themselves put forward. The ramifications of these views could not be examined to any useful extent, since the information was given on the last day of fieldwork at Balgo in 1977; likewise at Kungkayunti, little more than corroboration was obtained, before the entire camp moved to Haasts Bluff for extended trachoma treatment, thus cutting short the fieldwork;
(d) a location or group of people outside Pintupi territory; in most cases, the language of the song texts is acknowledged as foreign.

In the cases of (a) and (b) there is general agreement as to the origin, but in (d) the stated origin may, on different occasions, be given as the people speaking one particular foreign language, or a location within that language area, depending on the extent of the individual's familiarity with the series or with the foreign territory. Series in category (a) may also involve notions of ownership based on territory.

Sectional myth-ownership

All recorded examples of song series of the *tingarri* type were said to be but one part of a much larger myth, with portions occurring both before and after the particular ones sung.[19]

At both Balgo and Kungkayunti performances of *tingarri* series, the singers recognised that each myth was larger than the part they performed, but that nonetheless there were boundaries in the form of particular first and last songs, which could not be crossed. These particular songs described mythological events occurring at specified places during the Dreamtime but still identifiable today. There is growing support in the literature for the view that boundaries delineated in song series such as the *tingarri* (i.e. in the myth as a whole, which is normally presented in song form) represents points on actual boundaries for traditional travel and living (e.g. Ellis 1962:2; Strehlow 1965:138), and that the particular travels undertaken by the characters in these myths were along trails which represent actual trade or migration routes (e.g. Strehlow 1970:94; Tindale 1974:84; Berndt 1976:140). Neither of these views was investigated separately by the present writer. This phenomenon is not limited to the *tingarri*; in the recorded sample, the *tjatiwanpa* and *tulku kalaya* were said to be *tulku yanngu yananyi* (travelling *tulku*), which meant that the events described in the associated myths covered a geographical area greater than the one with which the singers were familiar. What has yet to be fully investigated is whether, within the total country the various groups of Pintupi consider their own, there are divisions, delineated in such myths and representing what each group claims as its own particular territory.[20]

19. Berndt (1970:222) has also noted this phenomenon in regard to the *tingarri*.
20. There is some support in the literature for divisions within the term 'Pintupi'. The Hansens (1974:113) list *ngaatjatjarra* as a dialect name for what they term 'North Pintupi', and Tindale (1974:235) also mentions 'northwestern hordes of the true Pintubi' who 'call themselves Kolo'. This same author notes that '*Wanka'winan*' was 'the name given by Pitjandjara to western Pintubi' (*ibid.*), suggesting another division.

In a related context, Berndt (1976:136ff) has expressed the view that land ownership in the Western Desert area is initially in terms of specific sites rather than large areas of the country; these sites are named and localised in myth. Over time, general association of each site with its immediate surrounding country enlarges the concept of ownership to include that country, thus producing an areal concept from a series of purely localised ones. The routes taken by mythical ancestors between such sites are commonly referred to in the literature as 'tracks' or 'dreamings'; Berndt (1976:140) notes that these often follow existing water-lines, and that formerly, Aboriginal nomads also moved along such tracks, sometimes moving from one to another, gaining both physical and spiritual sustenance thereby. Earlier, Strehlow (1970:94) had expressed essentially the same opinion regarding what he termed 'linking myths' which, he said, 'were almost certainly based on actual long-distance travels and on historical events'. However, neither Berndt nor Strehlow offers comment on the song series associated with such myths, even though the songs are the *sine qua non* of the preservation and presentation of such stories. While each group through whose territory the myth passes has autonomous performance rights, the possibility of changes in the music from one group to another is not raised.

In this respect, a number of Ellis' publications are of interest. In a paper called 'Central and South Australian song styles' (1966), she traced two such 'linking myths' (which she terms 'historical songs'), comparing the musical styles from four groups owning different portions of the Native Cat series, and three groups owning different portions of the Song Relating to the Two Women from Parachilna. Her conclusion is worded in a curiously negative fashion:

It may seem at a casual hearing that there is little in common between the various local forms of the one song. However, the common element appears to occur in the intervals which are not used, rather than in those which are. (1966:8)

She subsequently explains stylistic differences as being indicative of music areas within those parts of Australia, a view expanded a year later (Ellis 1967). Speaking of 'overall melodic shape in Central Australia' in a later publication, however, Ellis notes that

It is the broad definition of the melodic movement to firmly established pitch frequencies that con-

stitutes the 'flavour' (or melodies) of the ancestor. This melodic pattern crosses tribal and language barriers tracing the ancestor's mythical travels. (1975:31)

Such a 'melodic pattern' moving within 'firmly established pitch frequencies' strongly suggests similarities based on intervals which *are* used, rather than those which are not, and if so her earlier conclusion has been reversed. The somewhat uneven state of ethnomusicological research in Australia at present does little to encourage further immediate work on stylistic change between different groups' musical treatment of individual portions of the same myths; this must be preceded by further base studies of individual groups. However, Ellis' work, which, in the light of ongoing research, must be regarded as preliminary, has shown that once such studies have been made, valuable cross-cultural comparisons of this nature may follow.

With the exception of the *tingarri* and *kungkayunti*, those song series whose myths are acknowledged to cross tribal boundaries contain individual songs whose structural organisation differs from that described in this present work. These exceptional cases include a different number of isorhythmic divisions per word group, so that, for example, lower-octave repetition of part of a contour starts on a different word from that of the earlier, upper-octave, version. In other words, the 'first word' concept is absent from such songs, and the repetition of melodic material is not paralleled by an exact repetition of textual material in the way Pintupi music does. Given the location of the myth over more than one tribal territory, one tantalising explanation for this stylistic disparity suggests itself. If individual groups of singers are familiar with the entire myth, or with sections of it which move outside their own traditional lands, the different musical treatment of the same melodic contour may reflect the styles of the various areas through which the myth passes. Songs relating to the portion of the myth occurring within traditional Pintupi territory are organised according to the system described later in the Chapter Analytical Method. Songs relating to portions of the myth occurring outside Pintupi country are organised according to the systems operating within those particular countries. Admittedly this is hypothesis, and must be tested against the results of base studies in areas adjacent to Pintupi country, and tested also in terms of the precise localising of the numerous sites named in the myth. Unfortunately, the state of ethnographic and musical research in Australia is such that neither of these tests is possible at present, and so the theory must remain just that for the time being.

Teaching and enculturation

In quite another sense of the word, all songs 'originate' from a learning process, either alone (i.e. by imitation) or through conscious and deliberate teaching. The degree of formality, the identity of those who are to be taught, and the location of the teaching are determined by the nature of the ceremony as a whole and the music is an integral part. In brief, musical material which may be heard by both sexes is taught within the camp area, while material of a restricted nature is taught away from the hearing (if not always the sight) of those forbidden to attend, thus paralleling the general performance procedures.

The only time that formal teaching sessions as such take place is when a new song series (with or without its attendant rituals) is taught by one person to a group. In all other cases, where the initiates represent a minority, learning new musical material consists of silent observation followed by gradual participation; to this end, the repetition of an individual song in the series before moving on to the next, which is customary in performance of all categories of Pintupi song, is seen as a decided aid to the learner. (In regular performances, too, where presumably all the singers were familiar with the material, it was noticeable that the first occurrence of any individual song was often hesitant; subsequent repetitions of that song, however, were more confident. Analysis has revealed that where a given song is performed more than twice successively, there is likely to be closer similarity of melody and accompaniment between the second and subsequent times, than between the first and subsequent times.) One concludes that a function of repetition of individual songs (where they do not accompany specific ritual activities requiring duration longer than that of a single performance) is to impress more precisely on the singers' minds the text and rhythm peculiar to those songs. One or two singers also indicated that it was sometimes difficult to remember the song which occurred subsequent to the one they were currently performing; rather than endure a long silence, they would repeat the song they had just finished until someone remembered the correct sequence.

The following description of a teaching session is presented as written in the field notes. Explanatory notes are made within parentheses.

4 April 1975 Teaching a *yilpintji* (men's love magic series) *wati kutjarra*, from Yayayi [not recorded] (attended by twelve Pintupi men, at area 8 on Plate 12)

fairly casual attitude; some crosslegged, others had one leg up, or both legs straight out in front—items taught by younger Tjapangaṯi from Yuendumu (the same one who, together with another classificatory brother, had arrived only two days earlier for the purpose of completing the teaching of the *tjatiwanpa* ceremony *see* p. 61)—each item sung only two or three times—pitch kept low—stages of singing:
motionless
stickbeating, but no singing
stickbeating, lip movement seen
audible singing, with stickbeating
—accompaniment: one boomerang on ground (using) either end; one man used flat surface (of boomerang)—little explanation of text between singing—some errors in keeping beating time—texts as heard, after some five minutes of singing (dictated by the elder Tjapangaṯi):

—*winpangarangu winpangarangu tukulpungarangu tukulpungarangu*
—*kantul pangarangu kantul pangarangu tukulpu ngarangu tukulpu ngarangu*
—leader (i.e. the teacher) left to pee, told others '*yinkama*' (keep singing); they sang last item *mantapurrutu ngarangu, winpangarangu ngarangu* 2 times
mantarawurrka kumpangu, tirrutirru kumpangu 3 times
tirrutirru kumpangu, tunga pala paluru 4 times
tirrutirru kumpangu, mitji pala paluru 1 time

—N.B. only one word different from previous time, so once through enough, apparently.

manantara tjunu, mitjintara tjunu	2 times
pakara tjurrurru, matala urru	3 times
pakara nyinantu, matala urru	1 time
linti lantji walungana pinpaka panga	2 times
yilpalpupalyu pungu, ngalu ngalya lupalu pungu	5 times
patjina tjuturru nyarra	2 times

—total teaching time about one hour, 9-10 am—at

one stage, leader called 'Kutjupa?' (another one?); others replied 'Yuwa' (yes), and all continued. Afternoon teaching session had slightly less people comprising five Tjapangati, two Tjungurayi, one Tjupurrula, one Tjapaltjarri—session lasted about 2½ hours, from 2-4.30 pm—started with items previously learnt, then proceeded until the end of series—Talkatjarra (a Tjungarayi man) took song lead on two occasions, using items learnt that morning—all singers used sticks beating the ground—if stick is straight, hand hole is dug; if stick is curved, no hole needed—one Yuendumu Tjapangati (elder) held hand over ear during much of the singing—recognition of text-music structure:

if text form is A [= two words]: ‖:B [= two words], then music form is ‖ : A : ‖ : B :‖

most of the singers started in on repeat of B, then continued on—this type of construction accompanied by same rhythm ♩♩—at around 5.30 all singers took boomerangs to dance/song area (area 1 on Plate 11) and performed for the rest of the men, who also took boomerangs—this was to teach them in turn—I myself arrived too late to hear/see/tape the performance.[21]

Features of this teaching session which were also observed at the teaching of *tjatiwanpa* items, and on several other performance occasions, were:

(a) gradual participation, starting with silent observation, then accompanying, quiet singing, and finally on the second or subsequent repeat of an item, audible singing together with accompaniment;

(b) the greater the textual similarity between successive songs, the faster the learning process. Analysis of *tjatiwanpa* items shows that successive songs with only one word different contain the same isorhythmic pattern, thus further reducing the amount of new material to be learnt;[22]

(c) very little explanation of the text or of the myth in the intervals between singing. Nobody asked the meaning of individual words in the text during the teaching sessions, although some men asked the teacher about such details on later occasions. At this stage, however, the teaching concentrated on performance ability rather than understanding of the text or the myth;

(d) errors in the accompaniment were rectified only

gradually, as in actual performance, whereas singers making errors in the melody or melodic rhythm stopped immediately.

The Pintupi method of learning new songs, that is, by gradual participation after a period of silent listening, requires no technical explanations from those already proficient, (or in more formal settings, from the teacher(s)) nor, in both the formal and informal teaching sessions attended, were any requested; demonstration is its own explanation.

Only one case was witnessed during fieldwork where individuals were formally admitted into a restricted ceremony. This occurred at Balgo during the performance of the Restricted (b) series there. Two women, recent arrivals from Yuendumu, attended a performance of this ceremony in a bush clearing on 13 March 1977; for two days prior to that date, songs from the associated series had been sung in a shelter on the fringe of the camp living area, and several participants had been painted, but there had been no dancing or use of ceremonial objects. On the third day, these two women sat with the others, neither singing nor being painted, as indeed had been the case on the earlier occasions. At the end of the proceedings, however, they stood, and the two owners of the ceremony together with a few other women danced in a circle around them, repeating the same song several times before the two women themselves joined in the actions. Afterwards, the two presented cash and dress material to the owners, and are said to be now able to learn the songs and be painted in future performances of the series and ceremony.

Musical nomenclature

In contrast to some exclusively musical terms associated with boomerang accompaniment (*see* pp. 35), the words used to describe aspects of song performance are not exclusive, being borrowings from analogous non-musical situations, e.g.

Tempo slow: *purrka* (tired), Kungkayunti only
                pulkara (heavy)
                The two are not identical; the second refers more specifically to beating single sticks on the

21. During the later performance, boomerangs beaten together provided the accompaniment.
22. A phenomenon observed among the Aranda by Strehlow (1971:96).

70

ground, where particularly spirited beating in a ♩♩ rhythm may be slower than a simple ♩ rhythm elsewhere in the series; this former style is considered 'heavy'.

fast: *wala* (occasionally, the Pintupi translate this word as 'light'—as opposed to 'heavy'; applying it to both accompaniment and dancers' leg actions).
yaru (light)

Dynamics soft: *purrka* (tired), Balgo only
kanma (slowly, carefully)

loud: *katu* (high, up)—there is a tendency to link high pitch with loud singing, both of which are desired in 'good' performance.
kankarra (above, up)
maya or *mayarra* (strongly, greatly)

Pitch high: *katu* (high, up)
kankarra (above, up)
katuringanyi (to ascend, or be in the upper octave when other voices are lower)

low: *wataringanyi* (to descend, or be in the lower octave when other voices are higher)

Melody *mayu* ('scent', a Luridja term in wide use)
yatjila, *yakuntjirra* (taste), applied to the hummed or soft vocalising prior to a singer's starting a song.
ngurru (taste) (Balgo only). This may not be a Pintupi word.

Form *tjarra kutjarra* (twin forks) the bipartite structure of one particular song in the *tjatiwanpa* series; the 'forks' were sung both separately and together, but the two parts together formed only 'one *tulku*' (i.e. one song).

Similarly, in nomenclature for song performance, the verbalisations use essentially non-musical terms:

To sing a song out of correct order: *kawalinyi* (to forget)
to be unable to remember the next song: *walpapinanyi* (to lose)

to omit the next song and continue: *pititjunanyi* (to make a hole)
to correct a textual error: *waratjalu* (Balgo only)
to apply the wrong melodic rhythm to a song: *lurrpa* (obliterated) or *yurinyi* (to erase)
singing in unison: *kintilpa* (level) or *tjukarurru* (straight)
singing out of unison: *putaninpa* (to miss)

It may be noted that explicit verbalisations expressing a negative or adversely critical opinion outnumber those indicating correct performance; this is possible because of the variety of errors possible in singing. The Pintupi know when a song performance is going badly or well, and they are quick to criticise the one, but treat the other only with satisfied silence, or give expression to their excitement with emotional descriptions of the events portrayed in the song texts, or, especially in initiation series, use strong vocal accents (*pangaltjuninpa*) which they say indicate 'happy' singers.[23]

There is also a verbalised preference for 'lightness' in singing. To this end, the accompanying instruments are the means; this preference was expressed as follows, on one occasion:[24]

RM How do you know how fast to beat?
NP *Kulininpa* (by listening).
RM What do you listen for; do you listen to the *wangka* (words)?
NP Yeh, level. Level this one [sticks] and this one [mouth]. Same, same [as] you catch im now, you catch im me [in the tape recorder]. That's im, that's what-you-call-im *timpilpa* (beating sticks together as accompaniment). Sometime go wrong, you gotta be, you gotta be come and level im up this way. This one not this one (gives weak stick beat). No, this one: (beats more loudly) . . . *Timpilpa* all the time. Only this one (indicates sticks) no good, mine.

---

23. *yinkantja pangaltjuninpa* refers specifically to one's spirit, which lives in the stomach region; singing in this manner shows that the spirit is 'happy', a word often used by the Pintupi to explain the phenomenon.
24. Extracts from interview, field tape 76 AIAS tape A3588, with Nosepeg Tjupurrula, Kungkayunti.

RM   What's this one, then (demonstrates ♩♩ beat)? What's that one?

NP   That's a song, there, song, same as this one. *Timpilpa* make im light, this one make im light, this one ... Pintupi me tell im, like 'light' ... Pintupi call im *yaru* ... *wangka yaru*, that's im, *wangka yaru* [light words].

In description of song performance, this 'lightness' is often coupled with speed and loudness, and it is difficult to identify it as any single element; rather, it appears as one ingredient of singing where the performers say they are 'happy'.[25]

---

25. In describing male dancing, the Pintupi often say a good performer has 'light feet'.

The sample

In cases where anything less than the total recorded collection is subjected to musical analysis, sampling of one sort or another is called for, on the assumption that the size and nature of this sample will allow reasonably accurate generalisations about the recorded collection as a whole.[1] Thus a kind of four-tiered rationale emerges, in which the published transcriptions (which, for reasons of economy of space as much as anything else, tend to be fewer than those in the analysed sample) present typical examples from the various song types in the analysed sample and is presumed to reflect accurately the overall stylistic features of the recorded sample. The recorded sample, likewise, is presumed to be representative of the entire repertoire of the people concerned. Fundamental to the sampling process as a whole is the presupposition of the stylistic homogeneity of the music in its totality, or in its various subgroupings (usually determined on the basis of use categories).

Looking at the Pintupi sample, a number of matters deserve mention in the context of such a rationale. By way of introduction, the circumstances of the recording situations should be explained at this point. At Kungkayunti, the only material not sung specifically for recording purposes consisted of the women's *mungamunga* and Restricted (a) and (b) series, and the men's *yukurukuru*. The other series were solicited; after a number of these had been taped, there was usually a period of prolonged discussion prior to the commencement of the singing, during which the singers debated which particular series had not already been recorded and could therefore be sung on that occasion. As the weeks passed, and repetitions of series already recorded recurred, it became apparent that their repertoire had been virtually exhausted. At Balgo, by comparison, only

1. Thus, e.g. Densmore (1918) includes 240 out of 689 recorded Teton Sioux songs, Christensen (1964) analyses 69 out of 282 songs obtained from the Ellice Islands (now Tuvalu), and Merriam (1967) discusses 138 of 226 songs from the Flathead Indians.

the *ngintaka*, *paniya* and *kuniya* series were solicited. For various reasons it was not possible to duplicate the recording situation used at Kungkayunti and actively seek an exhaustive collection of the local repertoire; to this extent, there is a greater theoretical possibility that a number of series at Balgo were overlooked. There are indications, however, that this possibility is only slight; these are discussed below.

Although there is no published ethnology centring on the Pintupi, several accounts dealing with adjacent groups make mention of them (e.g. Spencer and Gillen 1899; Strehlow 1971; Meggitt 1962); these accounts tend to emphasise similarities and shared characteristics rather than differences between the neighbouring groups (Pitjantjatjara, Aranda, Walbiri) and the Pintupi, and suggest that any such differences (in social organisation and material culture) are of degree rather than kind. All opinions agree that the Pintupi fit securely into the Western Desert culture complex. By reference to these sources, and to the Hansens' *Pintupi Dictionary* (1974), it was possible to draw up a list of song series categories which might reasonably be expected to hold for the Pintupi at Kungkayunti and Balgo in 1974-77. These expectations were in the main realised, the sole exceptions being two women's series whose existence was not suspected prior to fieldwork. In the cases of the men's *kutitji*, *yarritjiti* and *tuyutu* series, their existence was anticipated, but their precise nomenclature was not discovered until fieldwork had commenced. The relatively small numbers of Pintupi at both Kungkayunti and Balgo meant that it was possible to observe if any group left the camp area for hunting, travel, or singing. With the exception of the performance of the *mungamunga* at Kungkayunti (during which I was making enquiries as to the propriety of recording it), it can be said with reasonable certainty that the recorded sample includes, at the very least, all song categories and all examples within those song categories performed at both locations during the periods of fieldwork. This repertoire was enlarged by the addition of material solicited for recording purposes; in the case of Kungkayunti, such additions were considerable.

Turning to the question that certain types of song series may have been deliberately withheld, this is known to have been so. In the case of men's initiation series, a general feeling of strong resentment over certain earlier researchers in the area who had published information and material of a secret na-

ture was such that I was wary of recording them. The *kutitji* and *yarritjiti* series from Kungkayunti, and the *ngintaka* series from Balgo (all of which fall into this category) while performed for recording purposes, were nonetheless volunteered for such recording after several weeks of residence, and after good rapport had been established. Another reason why I did not seek recordings of initiation series as actively as for other song categories was that suc recordings had already been made. In 1958, while working for the Department of Supply, Mr R. A. Macaulay made a number of recordings of initiation series sung by a large group of men from the Rawlinson Ranges. A copy of them was taken to Kungkayunti and, under conditions of careful secrecy, played to the men there; the enthusiastic reception given these recordings, together with the resultant hours of discussion and frequent outbursts of singing on their own part, confirmed that they were part of the Pintupi initiation series. However, because of the prevailing attitude towards current recordings of such material, I did not request the Kungkayunti men to sing them.

During the nine months of fieldwork, a total of 1021 different Pintupi songs was recorded. As the normal practice is for each individual song in a given series to be sung more than once before proceeding to the next song, the total number of times singing occurs in a performance will exceed the number of different songs in that performance. In the following table, the two (a) columns represent the number of times singing occurred in each series, while the two (b) columns indicated the number of the different songs for each series. Reasons for the differences between the figures in the recorded and transcribed samples are discussed in the table opposite.

The question now arises as to how representative this recorded sample is in terms of all known Pintupi song categories. While it includes examples of all categories (and all examples within those categories) which could be performed at Kungkayunti and Balgo during the periods of fieldwork, one women's series, known to three Kungkayunti women, as mentioned earlier in this work, was started and then stopped abruptly because the series' owners were in another settlement and performance without them was not permissible; to this extent, the list is incomplete. In addition, among the recordings of Pintupi singing made by an earlier researcher are individual songs which do not fall into any of the above categories (at least on the basis of the

Recorded sample (a)	(b)	Song series		Transcribed sample (a)	(b)
		Kungkayunti			
96	26	tulku:	yikuluku	37	25
52	18		tjiwiri	21	7
49	18		tarrkalpa	28	15
77	21		yununtju	26	11
115	32		wantjiwantji	29	17
52	10	yilpintji:	marali	7	6
45	19		kungka kutjarra	23	18
121	71		wangata	28	15
449	106	yawulyu:	mungamunga	50	28
103	48		Restricted (a)	40	34
654	136		Restricted (b)	38	24
62	26	kutitji		23	22
69	35	yarritjiti		66	34
114	59	tingarri (i)		100	53
73	34	(ii)		29	28
54	26	wanapa		49	26
18	11	pukalkarra		10	9
2203	696			604	372
		Balgo			
66	20	tulku:	yunpu	21	20
134	22	yilpintji:	maanytja	28	15
710	51	yawulyu:	kungkayunti	58	31
208	56	ngalungku:	ngintaka	74	26
14	9		miscellaneous	—	—
169	79	tingarri (iii)		35	33
156	71	(iv)		52	50
11	4	tuyutu:	yawarra	4	4
5	5		kirrpinpa	3	3
7	4		paniya	4	4
12	4		kuniya	7	4
1492	325			286	190
		R. A. Gould Collection (1966)			
93	34	ngalungku:	malu	36	33
34	15		kipara	16	12
127	49			52	45

documentation provided for the recordings). Among the early recordings of Norman B. Tindale are:

(a) A 'song by boys and girls' from Yuendumu, dated 24 August 1951 (documentation sheet 394) and claimed to be of Pintupi origin. No children's songs were heard during my own fieldwork. (Hansen also has not heard song in such a category [personal communication].)

(b) 'Songs by children', recorded at Haasts Bluff on 28 August 1957 (documentation sheet 442.6).

Unfortunately, copies of these recordings were not available during the research period and their authenticity was not checked by playback to the Pintupi at Kungkayunti and Balgo. To this extent, the present sample may be judged incomplete.

The figures in the table above are concerned with the next stage in the processing of raw field material, namely the analysed, or more specifically in this case, the transcribed sample. At the outset it must be stressed that the two samples are not numerically identical. Over the course of almost a whole year, every individual song recorded was played back as part of the analytical process—this included both different songs and repetitions of the same songs. At first, series were transcribed almost in their entirety (except where obviously poor performances occurred)—e.g. the first *tingarri* series from Kungkayunti (100 out of 114), *yarritjiti* (66 out of 69), and *wanapa* (49 out of 54)—but as familiarity with the singing style in general and the respective melodic contours in particular was gained, it was found that the ear could be trusted to locate any differences between repetitions of the same songs, and (after the conceptual basis for the music structure became apparent), between different songs. To this extent, comparison of the figures in the two (a) columns may be misleading at first glance. In the course of transcribing, it was found that the conceptual framework for some series became apparent more easily than for others; in general, this is reflected in the cases of greater disparity between the figures in the two (b) columns. The corollary also holds true, with the rider that where only a few different songs from a series had been recorded, it was considered advisable to transcribe as many as possible, if not all of them, to test the theory of structural organisation. The 'miscellaneous' initiation items from Balgo completing the list from that location were not included in the analysis as the performances were made by one man in great secrecy, the songs being sung at an almost inaudible level.

Analytical method

It has been noted for some time that the consistently recurring features of Central Australian songs have to do principally with their melodies. Strehlow (1955:37) reduces the contour for a series of Aranda Honeyant songs to skeletal form, indicating those pitches on which the melody remains longest. Ellis (1969a) essentially repeats this procedure, though in graphic rather than staff notation. However, neither writer ventures beyond informed and often detailed observation to real analysis in which broad patterns become evident.

Ellis (1968:36, 48) speaks of 'the underlying systems' of Central Australian music, which 'are not known'. In this work as well as in 1969a, Ellis examines individual elements of songs in an effort to determine these systems, but her conclusions tend to be in the form of suggestions rather than demonstrables. She plots melodic movement according to particular poetic metres (1969a:11), noting, for example, that groups with two syllables used different pitches for each note, and 'in groups with four syllables, there was melodic movement followed by repeated notes, and followed again by more than one note on one syllable . . .' and so on. The author herself then observes that such a practice 'was not adhered to meticulously' (*ibid.*) in her sample. The exceptions she subsequently describes appear, however, to be more significant than her original argument, mainly because she leaves the ranks of minutiae for the broader perspective of melodic contour in general, and thus comes one step closer to the necessary comprehensiveness of any 'underlying system'. Basically, she claims that if the contour at one point consists of, say, level movement, but the metric grouping at that same point has only two syllables (and therefore according to her system requires a non-level movement), then the contour has precedence over the metric grouping. However, apart from noting that the melodic contour is thus 'more important', she does not examine further this higher order of constraints, and passes to another topic. This present analysis, by contrast, seeks to establish links between songs and between whole series on the broadest possible levels.

The key to the structural and conceptual organisation of Pintupi music appears to be its isorhythm. By implication more often than specific statement, definitions of isorhythm both inside and outside the ethnomusicological literature are restricted to *exact* repetition of a rhythmic figure, e.g.

> . . . repeating the same rhythm although the notes are different (*Concise Oxford Dictionary of Music* 1955:301)
>
> . . . the employment of a reiterated scheme of time-values for the presentation of a liturgical cantus firmus. (*Harvard Dictionary of Music* 1965:367)
>
> Some characteristic metrical pattern . . . is forced upon a melody . . . Consequently, subsequent measures . . . though melodically different, have the exact metrical organization of measure 1. (Sachs 1953:47)

The corollary to such definitions is that variation, of even a single durational value, cannot be accommodated. This contrasts with the definition of isorhythm as applied to Australian Aboriginal music by Ellis:

> . . . the regular repetition (with culturally acceptable deviations) of the one rhythmic pattern throughout a musical item, irrespective of the melodic content of that item. (1968:25)

The phrase 'with culturally acceptable deviations' is problematic, for two reasons:

(a) It involves two unsubstantiated (and perhaps unsubstantiatable) presuppositions. Firstly, that in the minds of the singers and/or the listeners, certain group elements of the rhythm are recognised as deviations from certain other group elements of the rhythm. Secondly, insofar as a deviation must deviate *from* something, the phrase presupposes that whatever is being deviated from consists of an exact isorhythmic unit.

(b) It comprises a *non sequitur* to the rest of the definition. Whereas other definitions of isorhythm cannot include variations in time-values between units, Ellis is saying that variations may in fact be included provided that the singers are satisfied with their performance in such a manner.

Example 16 Examples of isorhythm.

Despite these semantic weaknesses, Ellis has drawn attention to a situation common also in Pintupi music, something that might be described as the 'almost isorhythm' phenomenon.

At the outset, one must distinguish between levels of isorhythm. As already described, the text of a Pintupi song consists of a number of words, called here the word group, which is repeated several times in the course of singing the prescribed melodic line. The rhythm of this word group constitutes the broadest level on which isorhythm operates, and is maintained in isorhythmic units for the duration of the song. Within this large unit lie two, and in some cases four, further isorhythmic units;[1] consider the examples shown in Example 16.

At this point, the question might be asked as to how the start of the isorhythmic unit is determined; for instance, in number 6 of Example 16, the unit could possibly be rewritten as

If the answer given is that the start of the isorhythmic unit coincides with the start of the word group, then two further questions follow:

(a) If, as has already been mentioned, successive repetitions of the same song do not necessarily start on the same word in the word group, does this entail a corresponding shifting of the start of the isorhythmic unit? Or does the isorhythmic pattern remain constant, so that when changes in the initial word sung occur, the different words must still be sung in the same rhythms as the first word of the earlier singing of that song?

---

1. There are a few exceptions to this, in which the word group is divided into three rhythmic units; these are discussed later.

(b) Given the situation in (a), can we justify talking in terms of a 'first' word, and therefore of the 'start' of an isorhythmic unit?

The answers are, I believe, no to (a) and yes to (b). The justification for these answers involves a considerable amount of induction aided by the sheer size of the sample, against which any theories may be tested, and supported by a small but crucial piece of spoken evidence. The justification is not limited to isorhythm, but encompasses the conceptual framework of Pintupi music as a whole.

As already mentioned, not all the songs in any given series may have the same melodic outline, in which case, they fall into groups, the individual songs of which having, respectively, the same melodic outlines. The analysis below applies to groups of songs with the same melodic outline, whether such groups constitute the whole, or only part, of the song series.

The word group of each individual song differs from those of the other songs, in some cases by as little as one word, in others by as much as every word. As mentioned earlier, the word group is repeated several times in the course of singing the song (*see* Example 17).

In common with songs from other areas in the Central Desert, Pintupi items have words in the word group which may or may not be identical in form to those in normal conversational speech; in general, the construction of the word group differs from that of normal speech in its compression, that is, by the omission of certain classes of words normally found in speech.[2]

In any song series, the word groups present linguistically condensed accounts of episodes from a myth; in addition, in all types of series, portions of the myth are also presented in ritual form, usually simultaneous with the singing. And finally, the myth may also be recounted in spoken form, although description in this manner is generally restricted to comments made in the periods between singing the individual songs, and relating directly to the events described in them, rather than covering the entire story. Typical performance of a Pintupi song series thus involves the recounting of the myth on the levels of music and ritual, with optional amplification and explanation provided through speech.

There is no evidence at all to suggest the use of any mnemonic device in remembering the exact words of a given song text; to be sure, knowledge of the relevant portion of the myth is of some help, but straight memorisation appears to be the only way in which the precise content of the word group is preserved. A second element of Pintupi song which appears to be based purely on memorisation is the rhythm. Although a detailed presentation of this subject is more appropriate at a later stage of the analysis, it will suffice here to say that there is no evidence of any mnemonic device for remembering the rhythm applicable to the respective songs in a given series. Word group and rhythm appear to be conceived of almost as a single entity; errors in the one usually coincide with errors in the other, and most people have difficulty in *speaking* a word group without first singing it over quietly.

By contrast, the phenomenon of identical melodies for whole song series (or whole sections of song series in the case of several Pintupi performances, *see* Song Performance) has been corroborated explicitly by Aborigines from a wide area of Australia. Ellis *et al.* have been especially active in reporting this phenomenon—from the Aranda (1969a:7) and Pitjantjatjara peoples (1974:4, 6-7,

Example 17 Repetition of word group throughout song.

2. For detailed treatment of this subject, *see* especially Strehlow 1971:67ff; also R. M. and C. H. Berndt 1964:319-20; C. H. Berndt 1965:249-54.

13), as well as from the broader areas of 'Central Australian choral songs' (1964b:6), the 'non-secret songs' of 'Aboriginal music' (1969b:20), and by strong implication, 'all tribal areas' (1975:30). For the Pintupi, the situation is as follows. Taking, as a working example, three songs from one *tingarri* series, the melodic contours are represented in Example 18 in continuous lines (transposed for analytical purposes so that their finals are on the same pitch).[3]

At this stage, certain generalised similarities are apparent—the initial almost-level section followed by a fall and immediate rise of approximately an octave, followed in turn by a more gradual fall broken by one large and several smaller rises. By omitting consecutive repetitions of the same pitch, the similarities become more apparent (to this end, the contours are rewritten (Example 19) using noteheads).

The Pintupi themselves verbalise specifically about such a similarity, saying that the songs have the same *mayu* (scent),[4] or the same *yatjila* or *ngurru* (taste), the latter term occurring at Balgo only.

From the contours in Example 19 it will be seen that if, as the Pintupi claim, each song has the same melody (*mayu kutju*), then this 'sameness' does not consist of the exact number of pitch changes per song (since these vary from song to song, and even among repetitions of the same song), but rather a selective combination of them. Let us summarise the situation thus far:

(a) texts and rhythms are preserved by straight memorisation;
(b) there is a 'sameness' in melodic contours.

The question is now asked as to how the singers know how to fit each new text and rhythm into this 'same' contour. (It will be remembered that vocal unison is a feature of Pintupi music openly preferred and sought.) Types of answers to such a question would probably form points on a continuum, representing at the one end straight memorisation, and at the other extreme pure chance. However, recognition of the 'sameness' of the melodic contour implies a denial of memorisation, and while a degree of chance may be acceptable, a totality is not. Between these extremes lies a concept of form applied in the shape of a rule or rules, and it is to the identification of such that attention is now turned.

Examination of the transcribed sample revealed that on successive repetitions of the same song, the singing was likely to start on a different word or a

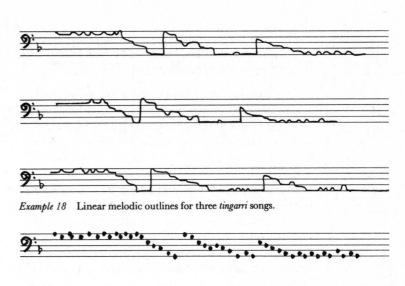

Example 18   Linear melodic outlines for three *tingarri* songs.

Example 19   Notated melodic outlines for three *tingarri* songs.

Example 20   Points of repetition of word group in notated melodic outlines of three *tingarri* songs.

different syllable of a word; in contrast with this, at the point where the melody rose a M9, a word, always the same despite any variation in the first word which started the song, commenced on this higher pitch. Plotting the positions in the melodic contour where this particular word in the word group recurred yielded the result shown in Example 20 (still using

3. The songs are found, respectively on field tapes 56, 58 and 59.
4. *Mayu* is said by the Pintupi at Kungkayunti to be a Pintupi and Luridja word, and by others (e.g. Ellis 1974:13; Ernabella Mission 1976:18) to be a Pitjantjatjara word.

Example 21   Three *tingarri* songs with starts of word groups in vertical alignment.

the same three songs as in the two previous figures).

Having noted the degree of coincidence of pitches for recurrences of this particular word, the phenomenon was then tested against the full transcriptions (the start of each word isolated above in vertical alignment, as indicated by bar lines) as shown in Example 21.

At this point, let us return to the matter of isorhythm, which has not been defined as regards Pintupi music. Turning to the first song in Example 21, let us attempt to identify any isorhythm; the word group as a whole has already been acknowledged as

the largest level on which isorhythm operates, and for this reason the study must start at point A on the transcription (since what occurs before A does not constitute a whole word group in all three examples). Firstly, let us write out the durational values for each individual note in the melody for this particular utterance of the word group—that is the *melodic rhythm*:

This can be divided into four similar rhythmic groups, thus:

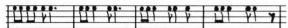

However, if we adhere to the definition of isorhythm which requires exact repetition of a rhythmic figure, then obviously what we have here is not isorhythm. By transcribing in instrumental as opposed to vocal notation, and thus indicating (even when a text is not underpinned) with slur marks where a syllable occupies more than one consecutive pitch, it is possible to determine the durational rate at which the syllables in the word group change—that is, the *syllabic rhythm*. This yields the following result for this same utterance of the word group:

Unmistakably, this *is* isorhythm.

It will be noticed that in the last isorhythmic division, the rest appearing in the original transcription is absent. This is because the syllabic rhythm takes no account of whether or not the duration between the start of one syllable and the start of the next is fully occupied with sound. Theoretically, there are no rests in Pintupi music between the start of a song and its ending; the syllabic rhythm continues inexorably, and if any singer stops to draw breath, the music will not wait, as it were, and he or she must recommence singing at some point further along in both the melodic contour and the word group, the precise point determined by the duration of the breath-break.

Turning to the second and third songs (Examples 22 and 23), we find an identical situation (again limiting ourselves to this one word group).

It will be noted that division of the word group in this way does not cut up individual words into more than one isorhythmic unit; in each division, whole words are the linguistic units. (There is one exception—which does not disprove the rule—and this is discussed later.)

Returning to the original transcription, let us place in vertical alignment the division into four of each of the word groups in the songs shown in Example 24.

In order to highlight further the melodic similarities between the respective divisions of each song, they are written out in terms of pitch changes only, (*see* Example 25). Striking though the similarities between these songs may be, they all have word

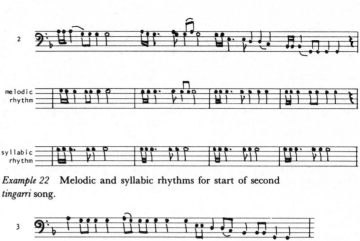

Example 22 Melodic and syllabic rhythms for start of second *tingarri* song.

Example 23 Melodic and syllabic rhythms for start of third *tingarri* song.

groups comprising four isorhythmic units; however, as indicated earlier, not all Pintupi songs fall into this overt pattern. Indeed (with one exception which is discussed on p. 97) *within* each song series there is variation in the number of isorhythmic units per complete utterance of the individual word groups. In this particular *tingarri* series, there are no less than eight different ways in which the rhythmic material within each complete word group is organised. Starting their respective syllabic rhythms from the first note of the rise of M9, these are shown in Example 26 (bar lines separating explicit units). (These have been assigned a working title, whose rationale will become apparent shortly; for the time being, however, they will be referred to by number only.) Using the same system of vertical alignment of identical or similar melodic movement in the respective songs, transcriptions exemplifying these eight types of rhythmic organisation are shown in Example 27.

The similarities observed earlier between the melodic contours of the three examples whose word groups each contained four isorhythmic units are evident here too, though in a more generalised sense due to the apparent disparity of word group divisions—some have four, others two, and one other three. It is possible however, to refine the divisions of

Example 24 Three *tingarri* songs with iorhythmic units in vertical alignment.

82

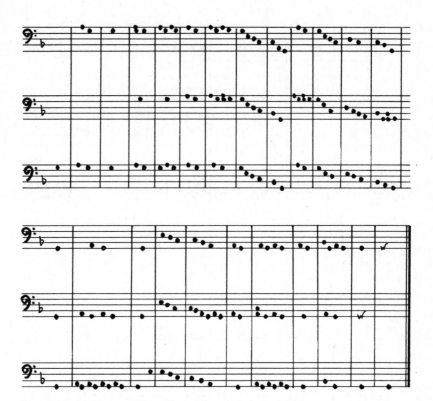

Example 25   Notated melodic outlines of three *tingarri* songs with isorhythmic units in vertical alignment.

Example 26   Variety of isorhythmic organisation in *tingarri* songs.

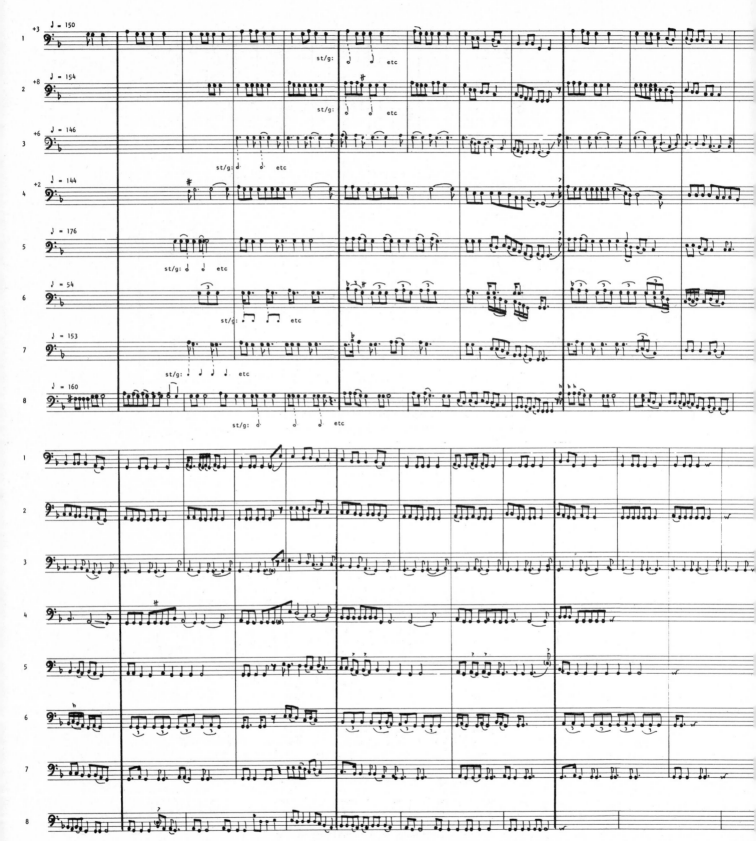

Example 27 Eight *tingarri* songs illustrating different types of isorhythmic organisation.

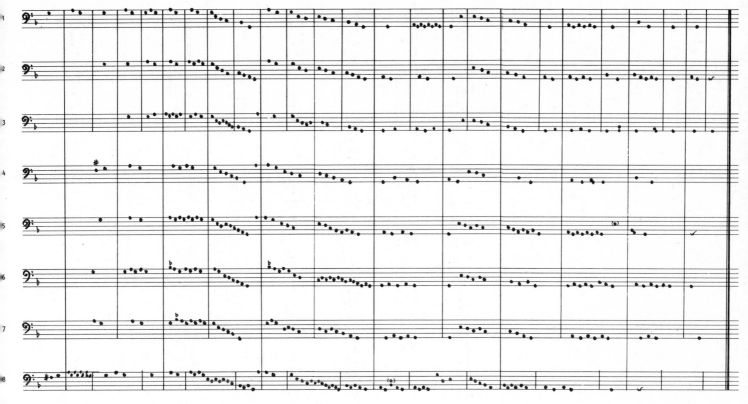

Example 28   Notated melodic outlines of eight *tingarri* songs with the respective isorhythmic units in vertical alignment.

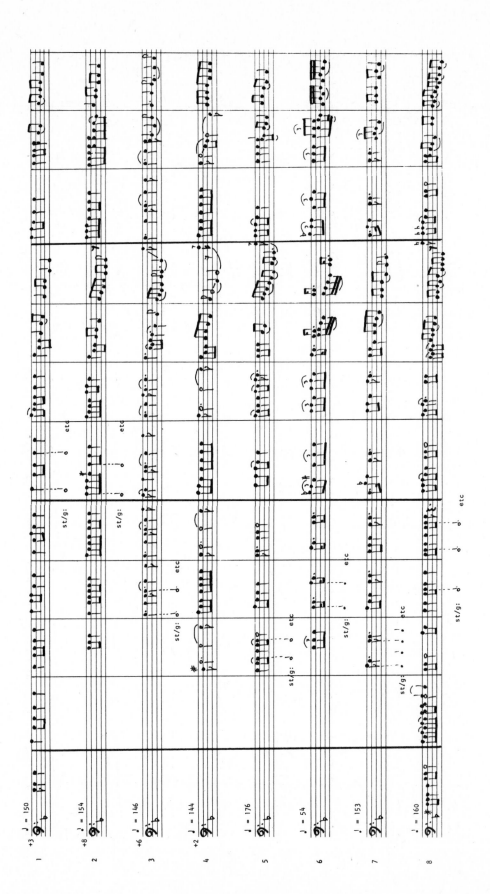

Example 29 Eight *tingarri* songs with equal numbers of isorhythmic units in vertical alignment.

87

Example 30 Changes to four isorhythmic divisions.

numbers 4-7 in Example 26, which at present have two each. These refinements are perhaps hinted at in the reduction of the sample as a whole to a presentation of pitch changes only (*see* Example 28).

By referring to the melodic movement in each successive division of examples 1-3 in the original transcriptions (Example 24) it is possible to subdivide each of the present divisions into two to give a result in which the melodic movement matches closely, if not always exactly, that of each of the four-part divisions of these first three examples (*see* Example 29).

It will be observed that subdivision in this manner does not break the rule observed earlier of treating whole words in the word group as the linguistic unit within each rhythmic unit. The changes to the respective isorhythms for examples 4-7 produced by this subdivision are shown in Example 30.

The working titles assigned to these types of rhythmic organisation are:

4   x2   (There are two explicit isorhythmic divisions per word group, each capable of further division into two. It will be noted that both the overall durations and the specific rhythms of subdivisions 1 and 3, 2 and 4, respectively, are identical.)

5   ≃x2   (There are two rhythmic divisions of the word group which show a sufficient degree of mutual similarity to appear related and, for the purposes of analysis, are considered to approximate isorhythm. Admittedly, this involves subjective judgement as to what specific degree of similarity is or is not

defined as approximating isorhythm. From the above, it will be seen that the first and third, and second and fourth subdivision, respectively, of Example 4 have identical overall durations. In cases considered otherwise ambiguous, comparison was made of these respective pairs of subdivisions—if they were identical in overall duration, the rhythm was considered to approximate isorhythm. No examples to the contrary appear in this particular song series.)

6   (x2) + (x2)   (Two rhythmically unrelated divisions are each internally repetitive.)

7   ≃(x2) + (x2)   (The situation for number 6 is approximated only; in ambiguous cases, a comparison of the duration of each internal division was the deciding factor, as in number 5).

The working titles for numbers 1-3 are:

1   x4   (Four explicit isorhythmic divisions per word group.)

2   ≃x4   (Three explicit isorhythmic divisions together with a fourth of identical overall duration and considered to approximate the rhythm of the other three.)

3   (x3) + 1   (Three explicit isorhythmic divisions together with a fourth of no apparent similarity.)

Subdivision of number 8 in the same manner, and still retaining whole words as the linguistic unit in the text, is also possible, and yields the following format:

This has been assigned the working title (x2) + 2. (It involves two identical rhythmic groups together with two further units which are considered unrelated to either each other or to the first two; each has an overall duration different from the first two.)

Presentation of all eight types of rhythmic organisation according to pitch changes within subdivisions confirms the overall unity of structural procedure (*see* Example 31).

(To be sure, there are variations from what appears to be the trend of melodic movement for each subdivision, but these are more of degree than kind, e.g. the most common variation consists of additional repetition of alternation between two pitches M2 apart—a and g, e and d, d and c, A and G.) In other words, despite differences in the rhythmic construction of each of the eight examples, melodic construction is identical, involving the division of each word group the same number of times in each song, and the allocation of a particular portion of the overall melodic contour to each division. In this particular song series there are four such divisions, but although the precise number may differ in other series, the above statement appears to outline the basis for the structural framework of Pintupi music as a whole. Whether or not such a situation should be labelled isorhythm, or any other term, seems relatively unimportant; what *is* important, however, is that:

(a) the rhythm of the word group as a whole appears to consist of four units;

(b) regardless of whether or not isorhythm occurs in two or more of these units, the four divisions function identically in each individual song—to separate the melodic contour into compartments and thus regulate melodic movement.

On the question of the stability of the text-melody relationship in terms of individual isorhythmic units and specific sections of the melodic contour, one particular type of variation occurs throughout the recorded sample. The phenomenon is restricted to those songs having x4, (x2) + (x2) or x2 isorhythmic constructions, and consists of a change in the 'first word' to that word beginning the third isorhythmic unit in songs of the x4 or (x2) + (x2) type, or that word beginning the second unit in songs of the x2 type (*see* Example 32).

The isorhythmic form for this song is (x2) + (x2). From the transcriptions it will be clear that the second time the song is sung, the order of the words in

each (x2) division has been reversed; the melodic contour for each isorhythmic unit has, however, been retained. Identical procedures are found in songs with x4 or x2 isorhythmic structures. There is no indication of any numerical preference for one form or another, or that the change is considered a performance error. The process is referred to hereafter as 'text reversal'.

While rhythm is the key to the structural organisation, what of the conceptual organisation of the music as verbalised by the Pintupi? In normal circumstances, that is, when the singers seemed quite content with their singing, nothing at all was heard, but during a particularly bad performance by one man at Balgo, the other singers present were thrown into confusion. At first they stopped singing whenever this man made an error, but later, in desperation, they told him outright '*wiya! wanti!*' (no! stop!).[5]

When the recording was played back privately to the other singers, their comments were either '*munkara yinkin*' (he is singing on the other side) or '*kalkuni yinkin*' (he is singing on the near side), according to the nature of each particular error. At that time, the precise meaning of these phrases was not understood, but relating them later to the nature of the errors and then to the melodic contour of the songs, it appeared that the singers were referring to a concept of structural organisation identical to that described earlier. It so happened that they were singing part of a *tingarri* series, having the same contour as that outlined above, and thus it is possible to describe the nature of the errors without introducing new melodic material into the analysis at this point. In the two examples (Example 33), the upper staff indicates the melodic movement as sung by the other singers, and the lower staff shows the melodic movement as sung by this one man; the former will be seen to be identical with that for the first two complete word groups for the Kungkayunti *tingarri* sample in Example 31. In the first of these, the singer in the lower staff began his descent at point A too soon—this was *munkara yinkin*—singing on the other side. In the second, the singer in the lower staff is too late with his descent at point B—this was *kalkuni yinkin*—singing on the near side.[6]

The question now arises—'on the far side', and 'on the near side' of what? Presumably, the answer was something known beforehand by the other singers

5. The singing, by three men only, appears on field tape 264.
6. An example of this latter error is found in number 6 of the Kungkayunti *tingarri* sample (Example 29).

90

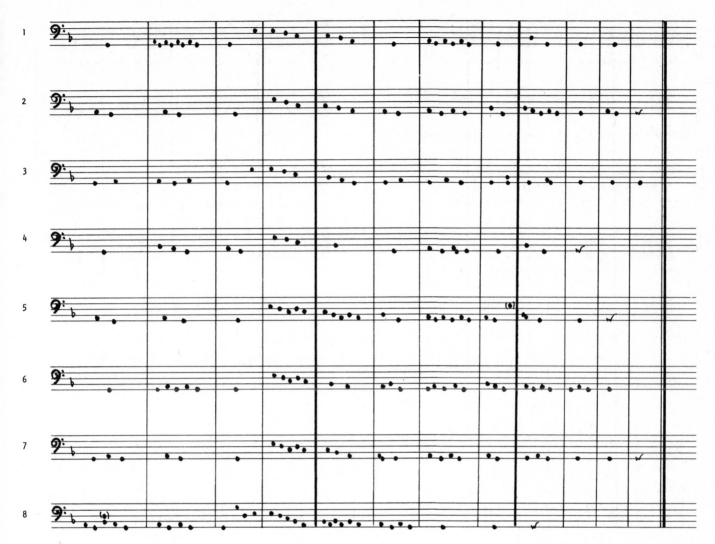

Example 31   Notated melodic outlines of eight *tingarri* songs with equal numbers of isorhythmic units in vertical alignment.

Example 32 Reversal of relationship between word group and melodic division in two songs from Restricted (a) series.

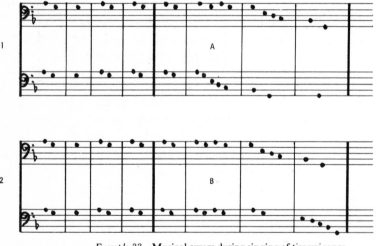

Example 33 Musical errors during singing of *tingarri* songs.

(otherwise they could not tell it was an error), and something which was fixed in position in the melody (otherwise they would all make such mistakes)—in other words, they were referring to a constant. Such a constant is embodied in the compartmentalisation of the melody as described earlier, and in this particular example the barlines indicate visually the parameters of the melodic contour. 'On the far side' thus refers to the premature singing of material belonging to a later division of the melody, and 'on the near side' refers to the continued use of melodic material from one division into the following division (where the two are not identical). 'Far side' and 'near side' describe relative proximity in terms of one particular dimension—physical distance—as a means of verbalising about an analogous relative proximity occurring in another dimension—melodic distance.[7]

Two questions raised earlier remain unanswered—having established that the word group as a whole, and the rhythmic divisions within it in particular serve to regulate the melodic movement, can we then isolate any one word as necessarily

---

7. This nomenclature was subsequently corroborated in both Balgo and Kungkayunti.

beginning the group, and can we talk of any one point as necessarily starting the rhythmic group? The two questions refer to different aspects of the same material, and a single positive answer will satisfy both.

In the analysis of the *tingarri* sample earlier, the rhythm of the word group was divided into four, regardless of explicit divisions into any other number. Further division for all the songs in the sample is impossible without splitting up individual words in the word group among two or more such divisions; at present however, each division comprises whole words only. The subject of song texts is a thorny one, not just in matters of translation but even, in some cases, to the point of identifying individual words. As mentioned earlier, song texts contain linguistic material which may or may not be identical to that of normal conversational speech; if it is not, then there is a likelihood that individuals who are unfamiliar with the particular song in which a specific word or word group appears will be unable to supply a meaning. Even in cases where the individuals *are* familiar with the song series and myth, there is still the real possibility of disagreement over specific meanings, despite agreement as to the general referent. The *form* of the words, too, may differ from that of normal speech. Strehlow (1971:67ff) gives examples of different kinds of phonetic changes found in Aranda songs, including both the alteration of speech sounds and also the addition of extra syllables. The situation for Pintupi songs appears to be similar (although, of course, only a linguist fluent in Pintupi and familiar with the musical material could hope to confirm this). However, one readily observable change which occurs often is for pronominal suffixes to be detached and prefixed to the following word in the word group, apparently in order to satisfy the content of the respective rhythmic units in which each word is found, e.g. the spoken form

mututju mututju manuya malaluwaniya kilurrluwaniya

takes the sung form

yamutu tjumututju manu yamalaluwani yakilurrluwani,

with the pronominal suffixes to the first, third, fourth and fifth words prefixed to the second, fourth, fifth and first words, respectively.[8]

This is in order to meet the dual requirements of a melodic contour conforming to that of the other songs in the series, and a rhythmic structure consisting of four divisions. (This is presumably what Strehlow (1971:96) is referring to when he speaks of

the Luridja practice of superimposing 'verse accents' on 'a prose line'.) Thus the rhythm of the former:

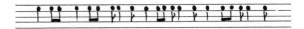

mututju mututju manuya malaluwaniya kilurrluwaniya

is organised to become:

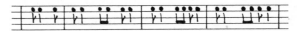

yamutu tjumututju manu yamalaluwani yakilurrluwani

(exemplifying the (x3) + 1 rhythmic structure). Basically, the reason why rhythmic divisions of the word group number no more than four in this particular series is that four is the greatest number possible in which a consistent relationship between rhythmic and linguistic units (in terms of whole words, with changes as described above, where necessary) can be maintained for all songs. Insofar as a concept may be defined as anything which permits people to make consistent and discrete judgements, the Pintupi concept of structural organisation appears to limit the divisions of the word group which may be made both consistently and discretely to four, in this case.

Having concluded that the individual songs in this *tingarri* series have word groups each with four divisions, it remains to be demonstrated that any one of these four can be considered the 'first'; putting it another way, the question of whether or not the word groups have such a thing as a 'first' word remains unanswered. (However, in the earlier transcriptions of the *tingarri* sample, the question had been begged to some extent, with thicker vertical barlines delineating the 'start' of each word group; justification of this step has been delayed until now in order to complete earlier parts of the analysis.) In this matter, we have a situation in which explicit verbalisation is absent; the evidence is limited to two corroborating pieces of information which relate specifically to the same one division, and the conclusion following this is that, in the absence of further evidence, this division may be assumed to be of more structural importance than the other three, and therefore to represent the 'start' of both the word group and the rhythmic groups.

The first piece of information concerns performance errors. It is founded on an assumption arising from the Pintupi's explicit verbalised preference for

---

8. *Tingarri* series, song 51 (field tape 58).

Example 34 Basic melodic contour for *tingarri* songs.

vocal unison at all times during singing (and, by examining the total recorded sample for this one song series). If certain stages in the melodic contour can be shown to be sung consistently in unison by all singers whereas at other stages the singers frequently sing more than one pitch simultaneously, then those in the former category are of more importance to the melodic structure than those in the latter category. Let us examine the incidence of errors involving the simultaneous singing of more than one pitch, dividing the stages into (a) those occurring at the start of an indicated rhythmic group, and (b) those occurring within such a rhythmic group.[9]

The results show that of a total of 103 errors, 15 (14.6%)[10] occurred at the start of an indicated rhythmic group, while 88 (85.4%) occurred within such a group.

Secondly, by reducing the contour of each individual song to a series of pitch changes and plotting these according to the rhythmic divisions of the word group (as, e.g., Example 31), and also by eliminating those pitches or pitch sequences which are not found in a majority of the songs, it is possible to produce a 'basic' melodic contour to which most of the songs will adhere, as in Example 34.

Two features of this contour require explanation. From the presentation of pitch changes for the *tingarri* sample (*see* Example 31), it will be noted that the first pitches of the third and sixth complete word groups as delineated, vary between a and g, and Bb and A, respectively; including the notes before, the following intervals result:

This variation occurs on two levels—between successive repetitions of the same individual songs, and between different songs—and the results appear to be emically identical. The basically undulating contours at the start and end of each *tingarri* song tend to have their upper pitches sung more forcefully, and often, individual singers will produce higher notes at such points (although these have not been included

in the earlier transcriptions); this is especially so in example B above where on occasion a singer may go as high as c or even e, and in most songs there tends to be a cluster of different pitches at this point. There is thus every indication that the upper pitches at this point, despite their variation among the singers or between repetitions of the same song or between different songs, are differences of etic degree only, but manifest the same tendency for a rise in pitch accompanied by vocal accentuation. To this extent, the various precise intervals function identically, and can be treated as being the same emically. In the 'basic' contour analysis, Bb and A appear together for this reason. A similar phenomenon occurs in example A where, on several occasions, a and g are heard sung simultaneously, at least for the first note of the rise from the lower octave; in more than 80% of the songs, this note is a, and the remainder use g (and in one case, bb). As in example B, the first note at this higher pitch tends to be sung more forcefully, and despite variation in the interval of the rise, the a and g (and the single bb) appear to be identical emically; a and g thus appear together in the 'basic' contour analysis.

Comparison of the 'basic' contour in Example 34 with the individual songs will indicate the particular points of pitch difference. To the extent that the pitches at such points may, in some songs, differ from those of the 'basic' contour, they may be considered as variations; and insofar as these pitches were sung by all the singers, they may be said to be acceptable. On the assumption that specific pitches which have little or no variation at all within the entire sample are of more structural importance than those with considerable variation, let us now plot the incidence of conformity to the 'basic' contour, *see* Example 35 and Fig. 14.

As the focus here is specifically with the four divisions of each word group, let us examine the rates of conformity of the initial pitches of these divisions; numbering from the thicker barlines in Example 35, the average rates are unit 1: 88.9%, unit 2: 80.5%, unit 3: 72.4%, unit 4: 86.9%. Taking each unit as a whole, the average conformity rates are: unit 1: 86.1%, unit

9. These errors comprise only those made by more than one singer, and clearly audible on the recording. Where the error continued for more than one consecutive pitch, only the point of commencement was noted, and included in the count. The sample consisted of 54 different songs.

10. The spread of these 15 errors in the former category over the four rhythmic divisions of the word group is relatively even—3, 2, 5, 5, respectively, counting the first division to be the one immediately following the thicker vertical barlines in the earlier transcriptions.

Pitch number	Per cent of conformity	Pitch number	Per cent of conformity
1	77.8	23	100.0
2	64.4	24	84.4
3	80.0	25	62.2
4	88.9	26	95.6
5	82.2	27	97.8
6	95.6	28	82.2
7	86.7	29	95.6
8	93.3	30	73.3
9	66.7	31	73.3
10	66.7	32	77.8
11	93.3	33	82.2
12	95.6	34	77.8
13	97.8	35	64.4
14	93.3	36	86.7
15	93.3	37	51.1
16	100.0	38	80.0
17	100.0	39	96.7
18	80.0	40	86.7
19	84.4	41	84.4
20	91.1	42	66.7
21	88.9	43	55.6
22	88.9		

Figure 14 Degree of conformity of recorded sample to basic *tingarri* melodic contour as shown in Example 35.

Note For the purposes of this analysis, pitches with less than 50% conformity do not appear. The lower ratings at the start and end are due to individual songs starting and ending at different points on the contour.

2: 82.4%, unit 3: 81.7%, unit 4: 85.9%. Thus unit 1 is shown to be sung with consistently (if only slightly) less melodic variation than the other units, and one concludes that this reflects a greater structural importance not inconsistent with the concept of a 'first' word in the word group, and the 'start' of an isorhythmic division. (A further observation tends to strengthen this particular case, especially at the unit beginning with note 17, above: it is generally here that the accompaniment starts, and also here that singers who have remained silent hitherto will commence singing.)

To summarise the findings for this particular *tingarri* series, it has been demonstrated that:

(a) each song has an underlying rhythmic structure which divides the word group into four units;

(b) these units function to regulate melodic movement;

(c) there appears to be a concept of a starting point for the word group and the rhythmic units, despite variety in the choice of the first word on which to actually commence singing.

Arising from this last feature is one noteworthy corollary: the 'text reversal' already mentioned. The 'first' word in the word group is determined by reference to the melodic contour, and to this extent

Example 35 Basic *tingarri* melodic contour with individual pitches numbered.

the relationship is constant during the singing of any song. However, this is not to imply that on all repetitions of any given song, the 'first' word is necessarily the same; in 16 of the 59 songs in this particular series, there is in fact change in this word. Relating the changes to the rhythmic structure of the word group, we find that they reflect the concept of a word group divisible into two parts (of equal overall duration in all cases except (x3) + 1), so that if, on one occasion, the order of the rhythmic units is 1234, then after the change in the word group order, the units will be 3412. Six of the eight types of rhythmic unit structure mentioned earlier are rearranged in this way in Fig. 15. There are thus different levels of structural organisation proceeding simultaneously; in terms of the order of the individual words, the word group is divisible into two parts, while the rhythmic structure divides each of this pair into two further parts.

Type of rhythmic organisation	Change from	To
x4	aaaa	aaaa
$\simeq$4	aaaa′	aa′aa
(x3) + 1	bbba	babb
x2	abab	abab
$\simeq$2	abab′	ab′ab
(x2) + (x2)	aabb	bbaa

Figure 15 Possible rearrangements of internal constituents of isorhythm.

The extent to which the findings for the analysis of this *tingarri* series are typical of Pintupi music as a whole will be tested over the remainder of the total sample. However, using that prescience which is every author's blessing, the results will be seen to show differences in degree rather than kind, suggesting an overall unified basis of structural organisation.

95

Musical notations

Tulku

Yikuluku

The songs in this *tulku* are almost equally divided between two melodic contours, the one having a three-unit isorhythmic structure (Example 36) and the other a four-unit structure (Example 37).

It has already been observed that contours which normally contain lower-octave repetition of melodic material may omit such material if the starting pitch of any given song is too low for the singers' voices, in which case level or near-level movement on the tonic, or repetition of the contour at the upper-octave will follow the first complete utterance of the melodic material (cf. *mungamunga* p. 99). In this particular *tulku*, which was recorded on two separate occasions, the total melodic contours vary according to the starting pitch, *see* Musical notation 1. (*Note:* All Musical notations have been grouped together starting on p. 108.)

At point A those songs whose original pitch was too low to allow lower octave repetition simply stopped. By contrast, those songs starting on a higher pitch tended to repeat the melodic material as indicated by repeat marks.

At point B those songs which were pitched high to begin with started lower octave repetition of the contour, while those starting lower repeated the contour without dropping an octave, or stopped after a moment or two of level movement on the tonic (not indicated on the above reduction).

It is this *tulku* which is said to have originated from Ulumbra Bore in the early '70s.

Tarrkalpa

The melodic contour is as follows:

Songs consist of the repetition two to four times of this contour (*see* Musical notation 2).

Yununtju

The recorded sample is relatively small (a total of 21 different songs) and was sung by only four people; for this reason, the analysis is not as secure as for other, larger samples (*see* Musical notation 3). In common with other recorded song series, the singing at the start is not as sure or loud or high pitched or long (in some cases) as for subsequent songs.[1]

The basic melodic outline (*see* Example 38) consists of level movement on an upper tonic, an octave descent (one or two isorhythmic units later) spread over two units duration (or three, in three cases) followed by undulating movement in series.

Wantjiwantji

In 17 of the 20 songs recorded from this series (Musical notation 4), the word group is divided into four isorhythmic units, thus:

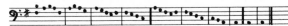

In the remaining three songs, there are only three isorhythmic units per word group. A similar situation was described earlier for the *kipara* and *wangata* series, and in those two cases it was suggested that individual songs whose structural organisation differed from that outlined in the Analytical Method section could be accounted for if they referred to mythological sites or activities occurring outside Pintupi territory. A similar explanation for these three *wantjiwantji* songs seems probable in the light of information given at the time of recording, as an immediate origin located in Pitjantjatjara country was claimed (*see* Categories of Song).

Yunpu

Of the entire analysed sample (Musical notation 5), this series has the most close-knit structure, e.g.

(a) the first nine songs have the same isorhythm;
(b) all songs have 18 syllables in the word group;
(c) all songs have a x3 isorhythmic form.

The melodic contour is shown in Example 39.

Of the 20 songs in the recorded sample, eight contain no repeat of section A above, ten contain a single repeat of this section, and three contain two repeats of it. It is noticeable that single and double repeats tend to occur the first time songs are sung in the course of the series, and from the recordings it is

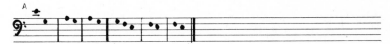

Example 36   First *yikuluku* basic contour.

Example 37   Second *yikuluku* basic contour.

Example 38   Basic contours for *yununtju* songs.

Example 39   Basic contour for *yunpu* songs.

apparent that some singers are unsure of texts and isorhythms—e.g. certain individuals identifiable by their loud voices do not sing, the accompaniment is very late in commencing or does not commence at all, and there are frequent deviations from vocal and instrumental unison. Such matters are usually rectified by the time the first or second repeat of this section is sung, and indeed it appears that this may be precisely the reason for such repeats. The corollary also holds true—in the second and subsequent performances of individual songs, fewer instances of repeats are found, the accompaniment starts closer in real time to the start of the singing, and the performance is louder and seems more confident.

---

1. The first occurrence of some of the early songs may start at the 4th or even the 5th unit, below.

Example 40 Basic contour for *marali* songs.

Example 41 Two of the three melodic contours for *kungka kutjarra*.

Example 42 Basic contour for *wangata* songs.

Yilpintji

Marali

Performance of this series was interrupted by the arrival in camp of a car, and was not continued at any later date. Because of this, the sample is scarcely adequate, and the following analysis should be seen in this light (Musical notation 6). The basic contour is shown in Example 40.

Kungka kutjarra

The only recorded performance of this *yilpintji* was interrupted after some 30 minutes of singing by the impending arrival of a vehicle in camp, and because

of this, it was not analysed as fully as other, more complete series. Three different melodic contours are used two of which are shown in Example 41. The third contour is that of the *tingarri* series (q.v.). The first contour (Musical notation 7) is associated with the Two Girls (*kungka kutjarra*), while the second (Musical notation 8), all examples of which are sung unaccompanied, is said to represent *tingarri*. The ideological distinction between these *tingarri* and those connected with the contour found in *tingarri* is not known.

Wangata

The basic contour for this series shown in Example 42 and Musical notation 9 consists of three sections, the third being a lower octave repetition of the first, and the second providing a link between the other two.

In this respect, the overall organisation of the contour is identical with that of the *kipara* series. As with the *kipara*, there are fairly evenly distributed numbers of songs having isorhythms comprising 3 and 4 parts. Only in those with 4-part isorhythms does the lower octave repetition of the melody commence with the same word as for the start of the upper octave section; on this stylistic basis, those songs of such a structure are considered Pintupi, while those with 3-part structures are considered non-Pintupi. Future research into the geographical sites associated with the songs of both structures will help determine whether these musical differences really reflect differences in ownership of the myth.

The *wangata* series as recorded at Kungkayunti, is said to start from Putarunkana, a site south of Jupiter Well (*see* Fig. 1); this may lie outside Pintupi territory, tending to strengthen the argument for independent local stylistic organisation of a melodic contour associated with a myth which moves across tribal boundaries.

Maanytja

The contour for this *yilpintji* is as follows:

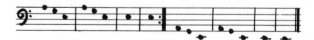

The contour is repeated once, sometimes twice at the upper level, before repetition an octave lower. The degree of conformity between the contours of the ten songs published (Musical notation 10) is less than for other series, and is indeed typical of the whole of the recorded *maanytja* sample.

Note To avoid inordinately long transcriptions, repeat marks have been used at the end of the first page; during these repeats, occasional pitch departures from those presented here do occur, but are considered of no great significance, and thus are not notated. *See* Analysis section for details of elimination processes applicable in such cases.

Yawulyu

Mungamunga

For the first nine songs, the melodic movement has the following outline (which may be repeated one or more times):

For analysis purposes, I have called this outline the nucleus of the melody. From the ninth song onward, the initial d of the second isorhythmic unit is omitted from some songs and replaced by g-f-d or f-e♭-d movement. This melodic nucleus, which occupies four isorhythmic units, is present in all songs in the recorded sample (Musical notation 11). Further material, occurring before and after the nucleus, is added in three ways:

(a) As in the *kungkayunti* series, the leader's line at the very beginning of some songs consists of level movement on a pitch an octave above the tonic, lasting here for up to one complete utterance of the word group, e.g.

In the sense that it tends to be sung solo by the leader—the others entering at the start of the nucleus—and contains little or no pitch change, this may be considered an introduction to that nucleus; this term is used in the analysis.

(b) The second extending device is virtually an inversion of the first. Immediately following the singing of the nucleus, the singers choose whether to repeat it (in which case the sole aural clue seems to be the continuation of a loud singing voice by

the leader), or to stop at once, or to continue on the tonic. Continuation on the tonic is not prolonged beyond two isorhythmic units, possibly owing to the difficulty encountered by some singers in maintaining the low pitch; there is also a noticeable quietening of the voices, as individual singers break off.

(c) There is another option available to singers immediately following the nucleus, and that is to repeat it an octave lower. This is possible only when the song has been pitched high enough initially to position such a drop still within the singers' vocal capacities. In the recorded sample, only on the second day of singing did this higher overall pitching occur.

Finally, although no one song contained all possible means of extending the nucleus—by the introductory level movement, repeat of the nucleus itself, a further repetition an octave lower, and a lengthening of the tonic—all songs contained more than a single statement of the nucleus, and several

Introductory level movement	Nucleus	Nucleus repeated	Lower octave repetition of nucleus	Lengthened tonic	Incidence
		•			47
		•		•	28
•		•			4
•		•		•	7
		•	•		7
	•		•		4
•	•			•	2
	•		•	•	2
•		•	•		3
	•	•	•	•	2
Total					106

Total recorded sample = 106

Figure 16 Melodic constituents of *mungamunga* songs.

99

embodied two or even three such devices. A breakdown of incidences and combinations is shown in Fig. 16.

Kungkayunti

Like the *tingarri* and initiation series, this *yawulyu* from Balgo has an associated myth extending beyond the boundaries of Pintupi territory. The section sung at Balgo, and forming the basis of analysis in this present work (Musical notation 12), starts north of Pintupi territory and proceeds south, touching on the creekbed called Kungkayunti, a kilometre or two away from the camp now called by the same name. As with the other series whose associated myth is shared among several groups, so do the Balgo people in this instance acknowledge that they are singing only part of the total Dreamtime story. It has already been observed that the music of such song series may contain individual items whose structural organisation differs from that of other Pintupi series, and the suggestion has been made that the division of the musical material reflects the division of the ownership of the mythological material. The *yawulyu* called *kungkayunti* is a further case in point.

The melodic contour for the series is as follows:

However, more than half the total number of songs in the recorded sample treated this same contour material in a different way *vis-à-vis* the word group. The word group in the above example is in three parts; those of the other songs have four-part word groups. The difference becomes noticeable where the melody uses a short section of the contour in series; as the sections comprise three isorhythmic units, the songs with four-part word groups do not start each successive statement of this section with the same word.

It is suggested that such four-part word groups are indicative of non-Pintupi items; their frequency of appearance is accounted for by the numbers of Gugadja women present during the performances—the myth is said to enter Pintupi territory from that of the Gugadja.

Restricted (a)

This series was sung in 1976 by the same women who sang the other women's series at Kungkayunti, and was recorded during their normal performances.

There is only one isorhythmic form in the whole recorded sample—(x2) + (x2), corresponding, in the texts, to two phrases each repeated. The melodic outline is as follows:

Unlike other series in which there is repetition of melodic material at the lower octave, there is a significant difference in the Restricted (a) series. The isorhythm of a given word group comprises four divisions, but the melody itself proceeds for six isorhythmic divisions before dropping to the lower octave. In other words, the duration of the word group does not equal that of the melody for each section which is subsequently duplicated an octave lower, thus:

This difference from the rest of the sample raises the question as to the authenticity of this series as an example of Pintupi music.

The melodic rhythm of the last two notes before the start of the lower octave repetition is of specific musical interest. These notes tend to halve the duration of the syllable concerned, resulting in the songs using a hemiola effect in a triplet configuration, thus:

The total incidence of text reversal, a far higher rate than for the other series in the recorded sample, is also an interesting phenomenon.

Documentation of stylistic stability or otherwise over a period of time in any given song series has not been made previously in Aboriginal music. The second recording of this particular series, a year after the first, reveals certain constantly recurring changes in the structure. In Musical notation 13, the second group of five songs is from this second performance, and features the same singers.

The average contours for the 1976 and 1977 performances, respectively, are shown in Example 43.

The chief points of difference occur in units 6 and 8. In 6, in the 1977 songs, the melody always moved to g and stayed there, whereas in the earlier recording it fell to f, or e, or even d. In unit 8, the rise d-e-f occurred in less than half the 1977 songs, whereas a year earlier it was found in virtually every item. In the second performance also, in those songs with the d-e-f rise, the hemiola figure was absent. Most of the 1977 songs were pitched lower than a year earlier, which possibly explains the repetition of part of the contour at the same, rather than the lower octave in the 1977 examples.

Common to both performances is the uneven ratio of melodic to textual repetition, described above.

The conditions of recording for the 1977 performance were such that it was not possible to elicit detailed explanations of the songs. The removal of the entire camp personnel to Haasts Bluff for extended trachoma treatment some minutes later effectively curtailed further investigation, as well as putting a premature end to fieldwork. The whole issue is left unresolved, due to lack of documentation of performances in the period between the two recordings, and lack of verbal comments on what, to a non-Pintupi researcher, appear as small musical changes. The differences indicated above may represent ongoing musical modification of a particular contour, or recurrent performance errors, or acceptable variations; on the other hand, they may not be regarded as differing in any way.

Restricted (b)

This is a women's series, performed over several days at Kungkayunṯi. As in the case of the *tingarri* contour, the same melodic material is treated in more than one way *vis-à-vis* the word group. In this particular case, three types of construction are used, as shown in Example 44. It has not been possible to ascertain the reasons for such changes, musical or otherwise.

Kutitji

The *kutitji* sample (Musical notation 15) illustrates the way in which performance characteristics influence the melodic content. It has already been noted that singing often commences in a middle register[2] and continues thus for several minutes before a marked rise in the overall pitch occurs, accompanied by an increase in intensity. In contours which involve the drop of an octave and subsequent

Example 43 Differences between performances of Restricted (a) series.

Example 44 Basic contour for Restricted (b) songs.

repetition of the word group at that lower pitch, it is apparent that this drop is beyond the normal singing range of some singers if the commencement point of the song is in the middle register. Consequently, while some may just be able to produce a sound, others have to stop singing altogether. On the other hand, following the marked rise in overall pitch and the correspondingly higher commencement of the song, the octave drop becomes attainable and the singers are able to continue the melody at this lower pitch.

In the *kutitji* songs performed for recording purposes at Kungkayunṯi the tonic for the first 17 songs is d, and only one of the singers is able to reach D; consequently, following the octave drop, the word group is sung only once in two songs, and stops short before it was sung completely in the other 15 songs. Following an overall pitch rise of one octave, however, lasting from the 18th to the 26th (and last) song, what had been the pitch *before* the drop now becomes the pitch *after* the drop, and can thus be sung by all the men. In all but two of these songs, two complete word groups are sung before the singing ends. (In one case, the men attempted yet another drop of an

---

2. The term 'register' is used here in a general sense, to refer to an approximate position within the voice-compass, rather than in the sense which denotes a type of voice-quality or voice-production.

octave at this stage, but gave up after only three notes—this, of course, was the same low pitch which had bothered them earlier.)

The contour is as follows:

(As indicated above, however, not all songs contain the two lower octave reduplications.)

Ngalungku

Malu

There are several myths associated with the initiation period, and most of those about which information was collected during fieldwork centre around the travels and exploits of the kangaroo (malu).

Example 45 Two melodic contours associated with *malu* series.

Note The series of pitches within brackets are indistinct, because of the heavily accentuated *ngutulmaninpa* style of singing at these points.

Example 46 Melodic outline of *wayuta* songs appearing within the *malu* series.

Sometimes alone, sometimes in the company of the euro (*kanyala*), possum (*wayuta*) or dogs (*papa*), the kangaroo is one of the key figures in men's mythology not only for the Pintupi but for virtually the whole of the Central and Western Desert area. The kangaroo has its own contours in song, but in the limited sample available for analysis, the possum is also distinguished musically (Musical notations 16 and 17).

Information concerning initiation series is less extensive than for other series. It is not clear whether the associations between contour and mythological character occurring in exclusively Pintupi music also occur in the same way in other series which are openly acknowledged as being of other than Pintupi origin. What is clear, however, is that multiple melodies occur in the kangaroo series as recorded by Gould in 1966; further, men at Balgo and Kungkayunti identified these melodies as pertaining to different characters in the myths, which suggests a situation similar to that for exclusively Pintupi items. However, not all the songs having these respective melodies were identified as pertaining to the same character; individual songs of the *malu* (i) contour (*see* Example 45) were claimed to pertain to the possum (*wayuta*), and indeed the particular texts also make direct reference to this animal. (There is a separate *ngalungku* series devoted to the *wayuta*, but this was not recorded.) Likewise, individual songs with the *malu* (ii) contour (*see* Example 45) were claimed to represent the emu and again the texts at this point offer corroborating evidence. The precise nature of the melody-character relationship is thus not yet clear, and although all the contours below have been assigned names, on the basis of the identity of the character claimed for most of the songs, these should be considered tentative for the moment.

A separate *wayuta* contour occurs only twice in the recorded *malu* sample (Musical notation 18), and is shown in Example 46. Because they occurred in the course of the *malu* ceremony, they are examined here together with the *malu* melodies themselves. There is, however, reason to doubt the exclusive Pintupi origin of the *wayuta* series, and indeed that of the *malu* series as a whole, on the grounds of the geographical location of the associated mythology. The present state of anthropological research is such that further comment is not possible at this stage. While there is no doubt that the Pintupi have fully incorporated the *malu* rituals and songs into their own repertoire, analysis later in this book indicates a stylistic difference between the scalic structure of the _wayuta_ songs and those in the rest of the recorded sample. It is suggested that such a difference may result from the possible non-Pintupi origin.

Kipara

The melodic contour for this series is shown in Example 47, and comprises a melodic unit lasting two utterances of the word group which is presented once, repeated a fifth lower, then again an octave lower. The overall structure is unique to the recorded sample, whether one treats this as essentially lower-octave duplication of an earlier section of the melody because the two sections are separated by a link also lasting two utterances of the word group, or alternatively as the presentation at three different pitches of the same melodic material.

There is some doubt whether the _kipara_ myth is of Pintupi origin, even though the ceremony is now an integrated part of their initiation complex. The doubt arises because the country in which the myth is localised appears to start somewhat south of Pintupi territory, then heads even further south (Mountford 1976:506). The nature of the structural organisation of the melodies adds to this doubt; the recorded sample is divided between songs with isorhythms having three and four units. However, only in those songs having three-unit isorhythms do the repetitions of the melodic material at lower pitches—as mentioned—begin with the same word as for the start of the upper octave statement of this same material. Such coinciding is found elsewhere in Pintupi music where the overall contour contains lower-octave repetition of previously sung material (e.g. _wanapa_ (iii), _yunpu, yikuluku_ (i) and (ii), etc.), and is assumed to represent an element of the indigenous style. The four-unit isorhythmic structure, on the other hand, does not allow organisation of the contour _vis-à-vis_ the word group on the same basis, and is therefore assumed to represent a non-Pintupi trait. Only examples with three-unit structures appear in Musical notation 19.

Ngintaka

Songs from this series were sung by a small group of men from Balgo; there are two melodic contours (_see_ Example 48). A feature of the second contour is the frequent alternation between notes a M2 apart, the upper of the two receiving a vocal accent. Indeed, at

Example 47   Basic melodic contour for _kipara_ series.

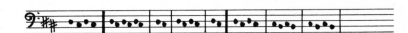

Example 48   Two melodic contours found in _ngintaka_ series.

points in the singing, the men are heard encouraging each other to sing in this style, with calls of _ngutult-jungkaman! ngutultjarra! ngutulmanin!_

Two further stylistic features are apparent in this second contour.

Accented vocables

During the periods of melodic alternation, the upper note is generally louder than the lower, and a few are decidedly accented; in the transcriptions, only this latter class are indicated. In such cases, and where a vowel occupies more than consecutive pitch, individual singers may precede the final note with violent aspiration.

ra-nga-ra becomes _ra-nga-ra_-[ha!]

pi-ki-tja-lu becomes _pi-ki-tja-lu_-[ha!]

A repeat of the 6th song in the series contains a considerable amount of this type of aspiration, as shown within brackets in the underpinning in Example 49. The phenomenon is similar to that found in the initiation and post-initiation series (_see_ Musical notation 20), and appears to be confined to male singing of a restricted nature.

103

-tja-lu-[hu] pi-ki-[hi]-tja-lu-[hu] kurr-kal-pa ya-wa-[ha]-rra-nu-[hu]

ka-lu-ki-tja-lu-[hu] pi-[hi]-ki-[hi]-tja-lu-[hu] kurr-kal-pa ya-wa-rra-nu

ka-lu-ki-tja-lu pi-ki-[hi]-tja-lu-[hu] kurr-ka-[hal]-pa ya-wa-ra-nu-[hu]

ka-lu-ki-[hi]-tja-lu-[hu] pi-[hi]-ki-[hi]-tja-lu

Example 49 Violent aspiration in *ngintaka* songs.

Example 50 Outline of first type of *yarritjiti* melody.

Example 51 Outline of second type of *yarritjiti* melody.

Example 52 Outline of *ngaturr* (or *ngaturrpa*) songs in *yarritjiti* series.

Syllabification of sonorants

There are occasions involving the liquids l and rr where they are syllabified and separated from the vowels following.

li-lya rra-ngu-ya   becomes *l-i-lya rr-a-ngu-ya*

Similarly, for the semi-vowel y:

ka-ltu ya-rra-ka-ltu   becomes *ka-ltu y-a-rra-ka-ltu*

Yarritjiti

Four melodic contours appear in the recording of this series of 35 songs. The first which is contained in the first eleven songs, is associated with the *yarritjiti*—the two young initiates. In some cases, the melody from point A to the end of the song is an octave lower than written in Example 50. The second contour, found in songs 12 to 14, is somewhat uneven in the direction of its melodic movement, and because of the smallness of the sample it is not clear which is the more correct. The associated mythological referent is not known. The melodic movement for the two songs in the published sample is shown in Example 51.

The third contour is associated with the *ngaturr*, or *ngaturrpa*, a species of bird figuring in the myth. The outline is contained in songs 15 to 21, and 25 to 35 and shown in Example 52.

The fourth outline is limited to songs 22 to 24; the precise referent here is unknown to me.

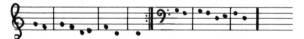

Eight of the *yarritjiti* songs are given in Musical notation 21 to illustrate the three melodies.

Tingarri

Tingarri series were sung at both Kungkayunti and Balgo, but, as mentioned earlier, it is not clear if each performance represented a discrete myth, or individual parts of longer stories. Whatever the situation, the melodic contour for all the recorded performances was identical, even though there were recurring differences in the way the contour related to the word group.

Ten *tingarri* songs are analysed in Musical notation 22.

Three contour-word group relationships were identified, from two performances each at Kungkayunti and Balgo. The first appears in Example 53; the second melodic descent (*see* Example 54) is more gradual.

The third (Example 55) takes 12 complete utterances of the same group of words to complete the whole contour. However, as indicated earlier, this may be considered a variant form of the second if one sees the word group as consisting of a group of words repeated once. This line of thought seems more correct. Elsewhere in the overall recorded sample the word group consists of as little as a single word repeated perhaps 40 times in the course of the song. To consider that single word as constituting the entire word group on the grounds that it was the smallest overt unit into which the text could be divided would be plainly ridiculous. In such a case, as indeed in this present case, the word group consists of a number of words which may or may not include repetition of individual words or groups of words; in any cases of doubt or ambiguity, reference to the melodic contour and to the isorhythmic structure reveals the underlying pattern, and thence the delineation of the word group.

Having come to the conclusion that the second and third contours are the same, comparison of the first and second contours shows that the only difference is the position within the isorhythmic units of the rise of M6 towards the end of the contour; in the first contour this rise occurs on the fourth isorhythmic unit, but on the first unit in the second contour. Instances of the contour as in the second, presented as a percentage of the total number of different songs in each of the recorded performances, are given in Fig. 17.

Date of recording		Per cent	Total number of songs
6.1.75	Kungkayunti 1	7.4	59
19.3.76	Kungkayunti 2	20.0	34
20.3.75	Balgo 1	55.4	79
24.3.75	Balgo 2	44.9	71

Figure 17 Incidence of the second type of textual treatment of *tingarri* contour.

On the basis of these four series it might be argued that the higher incidence of such melodies from Balgo reflects a regional variation of the same melodic material. However, a number of other

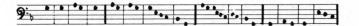
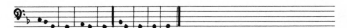

Example 53 First type of textual treatment of *tingarri* contour.

Example 54 Second type of textual treatment of *tingarri* contour.

Example 55 Third type of textual treatment of *tingarri* contour.

matters need consideration, e.g. the localising of the myths in each of the recorded series, the establishment of the geographical location of those considered owners, and possible musical or extra-musical reasons for the musical changes, should they be considered as such. Unfortunately, the present state of anthropological research in the area is such that these matters cannot be resolved, and the whole issue must stand as a possibility.[3]

Wanapa (kutatji)

Three melodic contours appear in this series; one of these however is used in two songs only, and there are numerous points of dissimilarity between them, consequently they are omitted from the analysis. The remaining two contours are shown in Example 56. On playback of each of these contours, men identified them simply as *wanapa* (sorcery), and subsequently I was unable to determine the particular referents within the associated myth.

Transcriptions of eight *wanapa* songs illustrating the two melodies are given in Musical notation 23.

3. The recordings of *tingarri* songs made at Lapilapi in 1957 by Donald Thomson show an incidence of the second type of textual treatment in more than half of the recorded sample; the practice is thus not confined to Kungkayunti and Balgo.

Example 56 Two melodic contours found in *waṉapa* series.

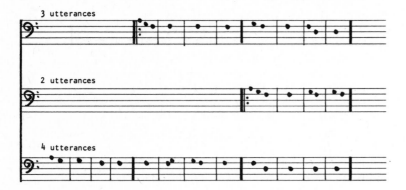

3 utterances

2 utterances

4 utterances

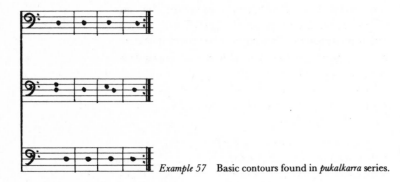

Example 57 Basic contours found in *pukalkarra* series.

Pukalkarra

The recorded sample is small, comprising only nine different songs sung specifically for recording purposes by three men from Kungkayunṯi; for this reason, the results of the analysis are rather tentative (*see* Musical notation 24).

The bulk of the melodic material comprises repetition of a number of utterances of the word group: three utterances in six songs, four in two songs, and two in one song. The basic contours for these are shown in Example 57.

Despite differences in overall duration, the structures of these three contours are identical, each comprising an equal number of rhythmic groups on an upper and lower pitch level. Thus, in the examples above, melodic movement on g and f proceeds for six, four and eight rhythmic groups respectively before dropping to d for an equal number of rhythmic groups. Such a structural organisation is unique in the recorded sample, while still using the word group as the unit of temporal and melodic duration. For this reason it is not possible to give a single basic contour for the whole series based on rhythmic groups alone.

Following the contours shown in Example 57 are the beginnings of what are assumed to be lower octave repetitions of the entire melodies; however the singing lasts only a few seconds at this lower pitch, possibly because it is too low for the singers.

During the upper octave repeat of the melodic material in some songs, the singers descend prematurely to the lower octave, that is, during the ultimate or penultimate rhythmic groups (e.g. nos. 4, 8 and 9). This is ascribed to unfamiliarity with the songs or the contour on the part of the one man who sings thus and who on occasion took the other singers with him.

Tuyuṯu

Yawarra

This series is sung to effect healing from a spear wound, *yawarra*, in the thigh, an injury which appears more common as a form of punishment than the result of fighting. All five songs sung are included in the analysis (Musical notation 25); the first three were sung together by three men, while the remaining two were recorded separately by one man, which may explain the several melodic differences in these last two songs. The man concerned was not regarded as a good singer.[4]

The melodic contour consists of the following pattern repeated once:

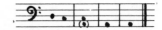

---

4. It was the criticism of the poor singing of this same man on another occasion which led to the discovery of the nomenclature for music structure (*see* p. 89).

In common with other healing items, but in contrast to the rest of the recorded sample, the *yawarra* songs do not constitute a whole series but rather are a section within the series, dealing with the mythological character's curing of a spear wound. It is not known whether the name of the series as a whole is *yawarra* or something else, nor is the category of the complete series known.

Paniya

The *paniya* is a series sung to cure disease of, or injury to the eye. The four different songs from this series, three of which are included in the analytical sample, (Musical notation 26) were sung by one man, who claimed them as his own personal property. The series was learnt from his classificatory father and brothers at a place called Karapilyilpa, said to be close to Yuendumu.[5]

The melodic contour consists of the following pattern, repeated once:

Tuyu̱tu (a)

Three melodic contours figure in this series, a short section of which was recorded at Kungkayu̱nti.

The first contour is that of the *tingarri* series (q.v.) and shown in Example 58.

The second contour is also associated with the *tingarri*, in particular with the *tingarri*'s metamorphosis in the course of the myth; further details are lacking. (In the Analysis section, this contour, and its derived scale, are referred to as *tuyu̱tu* (a), (i).)

The third contour appears in only two songs in the recorded series and there are enough points of difference in their melodies to render difficult any reduction to a unit by unit breakdown of their isorhythmic structures. The issue is further compounded by the fact that one song has a three-unit isorhythmic construction and the other only two. No conclusions as to the precise contour is thus possible at this stage; the individual melodies are shown in Example 59. (In the Analysis section, this contour, and its derived scale, are referred to as *tuyu̱tu* (a), (ii).)

Example 58   First basic contour in *tuyu̱tu* (a) series.

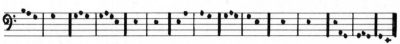

Example 59   Third basic contour in *tuyu̱tu* (a) series.

On playing back both songs to men at Balgo, as well as to the original singers, a year later, all agreed that they had the same melody, although no explanation of the types of differences indicated above was offered. The contour represents the two *kuniya* snakes which figure in the myth.

Ten of the *tuyu̱tu* (a) song transcriptions are given in Musical notation 27.

Tuyu̱tu (b)

Songs from this series were recorded at the same session the *tuyu̱tu* (a) items were performed, although the men singing were adamant the two represented discrete myths. As with the other *tuyu̱tu* series, three contours were also used, the first and second corresponding to the two *tingarri* melodies already presented in the *tuyu̱tu* series. The third, of unknown identity, is as follows:

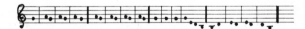

There is considerable variation in the way this contour is treated in the various songs. After completing the contour as represented above, some songs follow approximately the contour for the fourth complete utterance of the word group, while others appear to be repeating the third and fourth utterances an octave lower.

Seven *tuyu̱tu* (b) song transcriptions illustrating the three melodies are given in Musical notation 28.

---

5. The fourth song recorded is not included in this analysis as the singing on the original recording is indistinct.

♩ = 120
lana
kantunu yulununa
rawurrmintji wangkanu
tjinali palulana
sts: etc.
♩ = 124
nyakunyaku katima
warinkura wanana
puntukuli tjanampa
sts: etc.
♩ = 116
tjara yulpali nyangu
puli kaltjili lirri
kantunuli ngarala
sts: etc.
♩ = 128
-lu lanya
ngulultjingal katingu
sts: etc.
talalpalatju yanu
munu malulu
♩ = 120
palitju
wantantari tjunu kanyinu
pana minmiminmi kanyinu
mılanngulu
♩ = 110
tapawalmana tjarangka tjara
tapawalmana tjarangka tjara
munu wangkana kangingarama
munu wangkana kangingarama
♩. = 121
mitjimarila parrparrayana
mitjimarila parrparrayana
wayalpa lampaya witikatima
wayalpa lampaya wiyikatima
♩ = 125
walkamintila miilyinama
walkamintila miilyinama
wantarungula wamparararama
wantarungula wamparararama

Musical notation 1 Eight *yikuluku* songs illustrating the two melodies.

st/g: etc.
ngiilala ngiilya ngiilala
pungkula watuwatutjinu ngiilya
st/g: etc.
kararukararu
yunayuna tjanpingka tjanpingka
yunayuna
st/g: etc.
ratura--tula
ratura--tuni pilalka
st/g: etc.
kanyinu kanyinu
ngarangku yanuni pilalku
kanyinu
st/g: etc.
tatunanga tjalkurrumpana
pipunkuru wirulu
kumpana
parataparata
pipunpungu warinkatinyi pipitja
st/g: etc.
na tjanpa
st/g: etc.
pipirungkana
pipirunkana tjaralan tjaralan
st/g: etc.
kuntuna kurrpungu nyina
walu kurrpunganyi yintirri
st/g: etc.
wilatjarra tjipulupulu
tjawanatjunu tjawanatjunu malinypa
st/g: etc.
tjanpungkuntjana tjanpungkuntjana
kurrkurrku ralupungu yakurrkutju

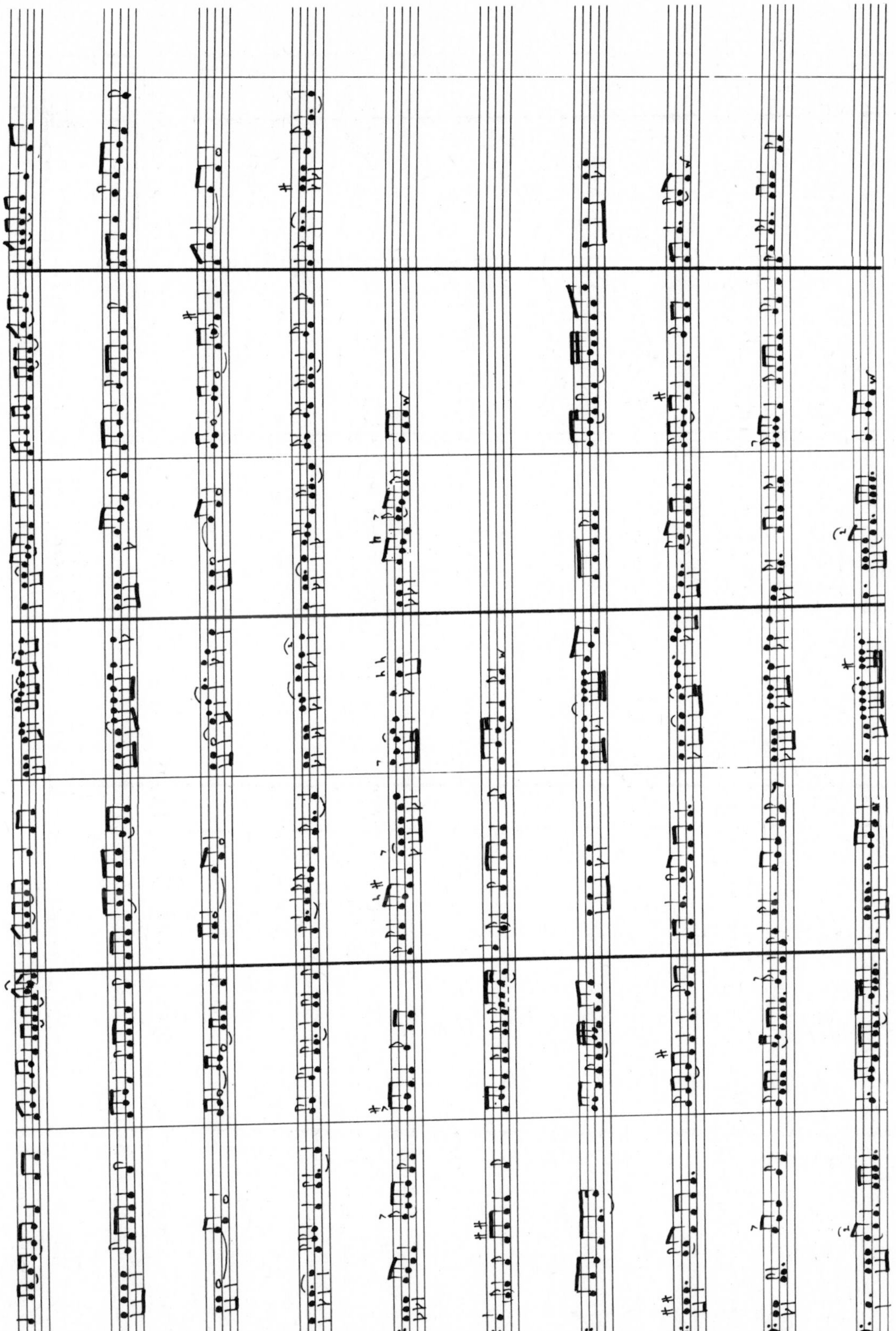
1
2
3
4
5
6
7
8
9
10

Musical notation 2   Ten *tarrkalpa* songs.

1 +8 ♩ = 116
wirunguruya kakarara nyawa
2 +5 ♪ = 124
yawatjiri latjanampa lululu ngaranpa
puntu nganalu lulumpu tjawalu
puntu nganalu lulumpu tjawalu
3 +12 ♪ = 186
wantirinama
nyumaya nyumatjunayi
nyumaya nyumatjunanyi
4 +10 ♩ = 100
ngarama
ngurra watjantupana ngarama
yununtjulangku kantunu
yununtjulangku kantunu
5 +8 ♩. = 77
ngululkatima
wampana turrurru ngululkatima
kirikingala tina kantunu
kirikingala tina kantunu
6 +8 ♪ = 171
timpitimpila wantikatingu
tarayi timpitimpila wantikatingu
kulayi pila wurrpungalunga
kulayi pila wurrpungalanga
7 +12 ♩. = 81
mukala tjalalu mintira wanaraninpa
warrurru ngayinpiringala piranganpala nyininpa
warrurru ngayinpiringala pirangampala nyininpa
mukala tjalalu mintira wanaraninpa
8 +8 ♪ = 162
tjurritjurri tjurra
palamantu palamantu tjurritjurri tjurra
matulaya palakutu mangari
matulaya palakutu mangari
9 +10 ♩ = 119
-tjingana
kilpin karangaranga
munu pilpantjingkana

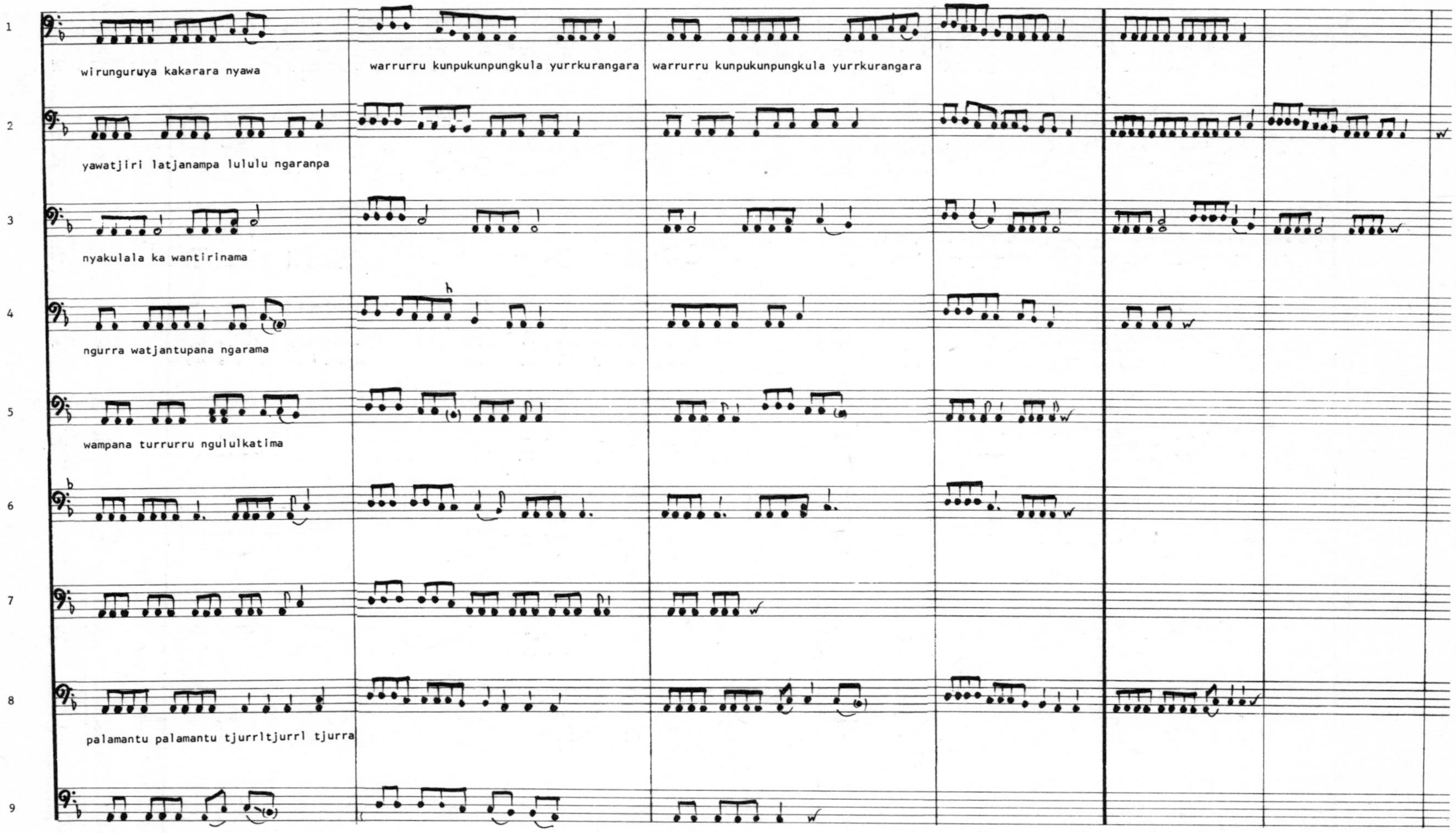

Musical notation 3 Nine *yununtju* songs.

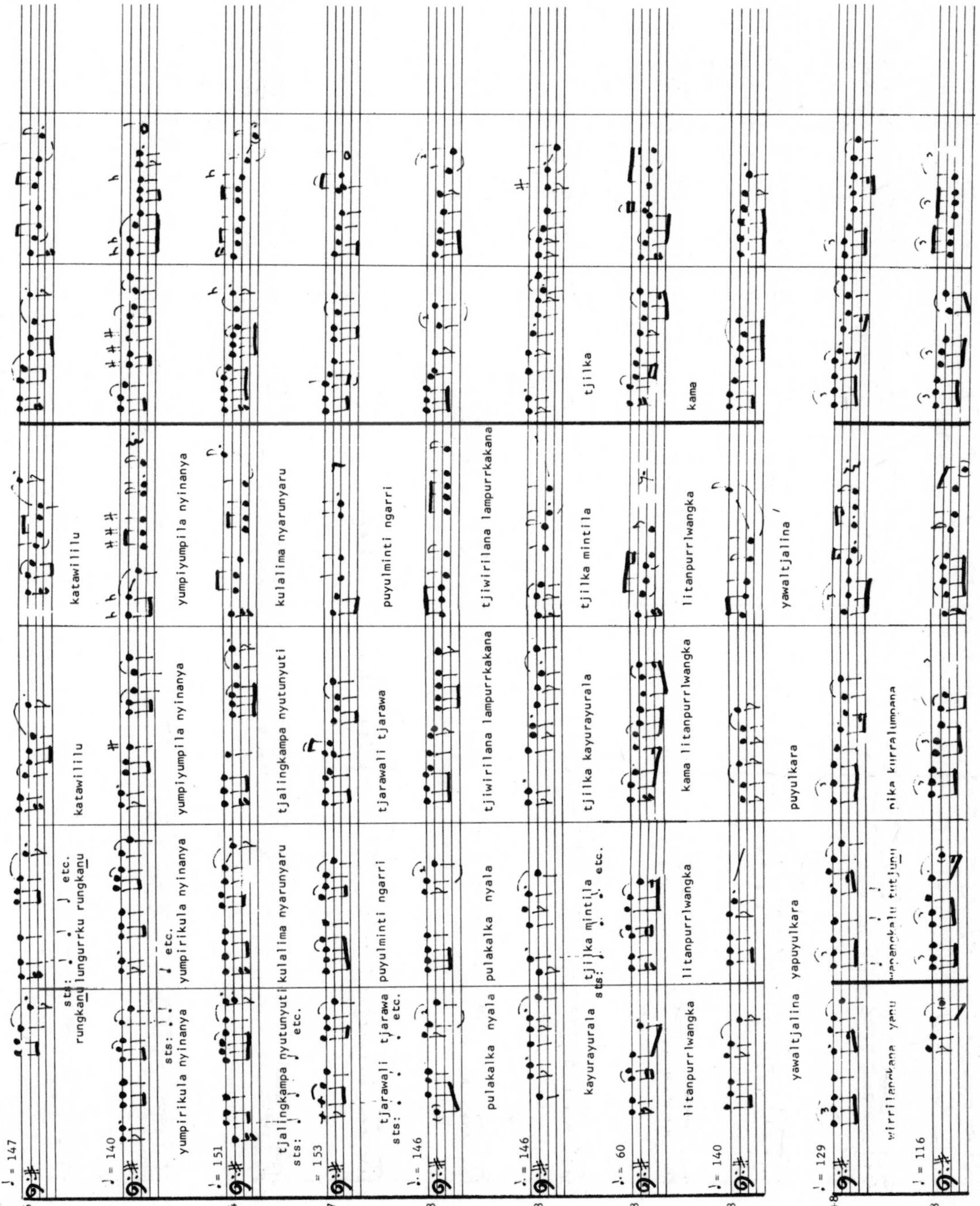

1　♩=147

rungkanu lungurrku rungkanu

2　♩=140

katawililu

3　♩=151

yumpirikula nyinanya　yumpiyumpila nyinanya

4

tjalingkampa nyutunyuti kulalima nyarunyaru

5　♩=146

tjarawali tjarawa　puyulminti ngarri

6　♩=146

pulakalka nyala

7

kayurayurala　tjilka kayurayurala

8　♩=140

litanpurrlwangka　kama litanpurrlwangka

9　♩=129

yawaltjalina yapuyulkara　puyulkara

10　♩=116

tjalkani tjapurutjapuru　tjapurutjapurula

115

116

Musical notation 4   Ten *wantjiwantji* songs.

Note: women double men an octave
higher than written, and
use hcl at same rate as bcl.

♩ = 152

-rungkana   tatira ngarala   kuwilan ngarringu   tjilu kurungkaṇa
bcl: ♪ etc.

♩ = 151

kantura ngarala   kuwilan ngarringu   tjilu kurungkan
bcl: ♪ ♪ ♪ etc.

♩ = 133

pungu tjaratjunu   tjarutjaru nyara   yunpu karatjana
bcl: ♪ ♪ ♪ etc.

♩ = 152

pungu tarrngintjunu   nginingini yanu   waralwaralpana   etc.
bcl:

♩ = 111

-nguru mirala wananu   pilpipilpilkati   yatayatanguru bcl: ♪ ♪ ♪ ♪ etc.
bcl: ♪ ♪ ♪ etc.

♩ = 112

ngunytjukumpa nyara wantiltira nyangama   mitjinkara nyangu   etc.
bcl: ♩. ♪ ♩. etc.

♩ = 73

-langa   yunpura wananyi   puṇtunya tjananya tjalilirrkalanga
bcl: ♫♫   etc.

♩ = 121

-natja   pilpitjurayana   tjurinpirilkati   ngayulumpanatja   etc.
bcl: ♪ ♪ ♪

♩ = 121

nyakitjurakati   mirimiriyanu   tjintu ṉalkunana
bcl: ♩. ♩. ♩. etc.

♩ = 73

-ratjunu   pukunpukuntjari   yiwalintji pana   manu ngaratjunu

1
2
3
4
5
6
7
8
9
10

-1
-2
-3
+1
+3

117

Musical notation 5 Ten *yunpu* songs.

Musical notation 6 Six marali songs.

Musical notation 7 Five *kungka kutjarra* songs illustrating first melodic contour.

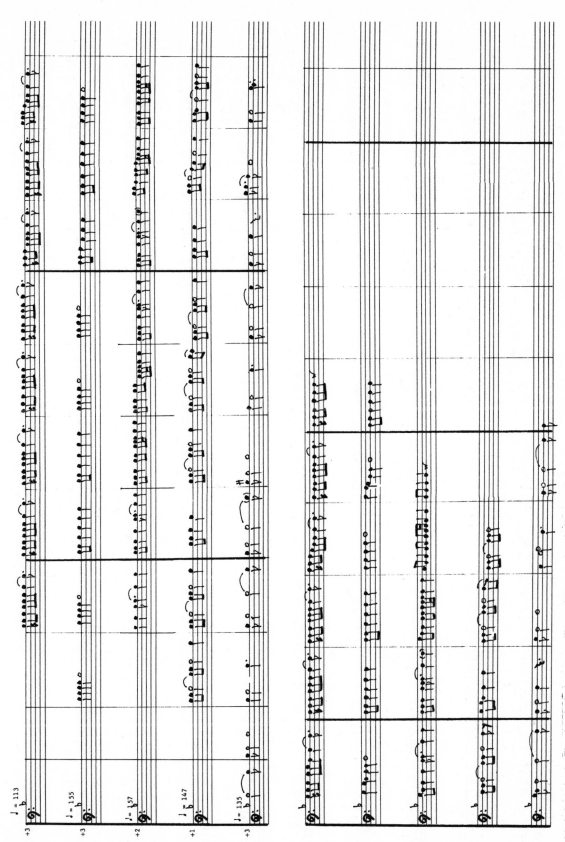

Musical notation 8 Five *kungka kutjarra* songs illustrating second melodic contour.

121

122

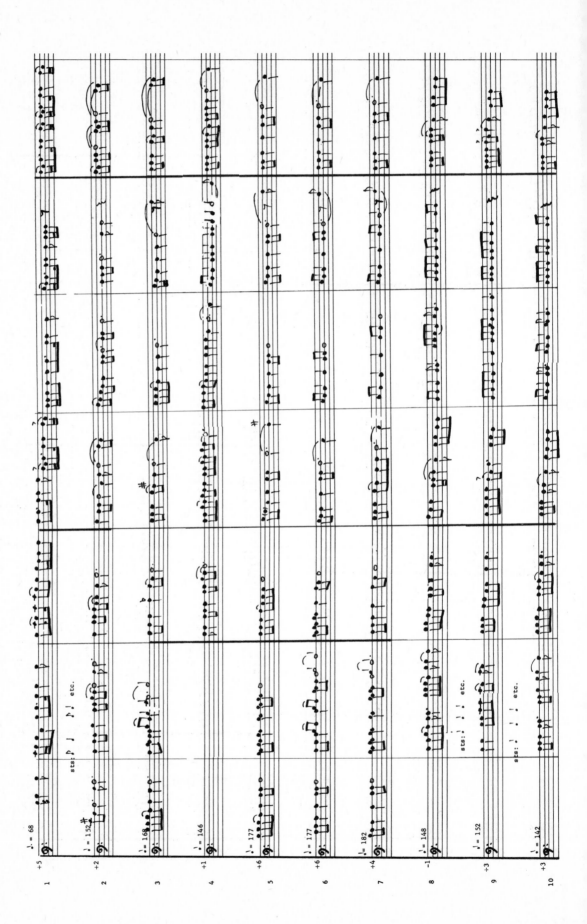

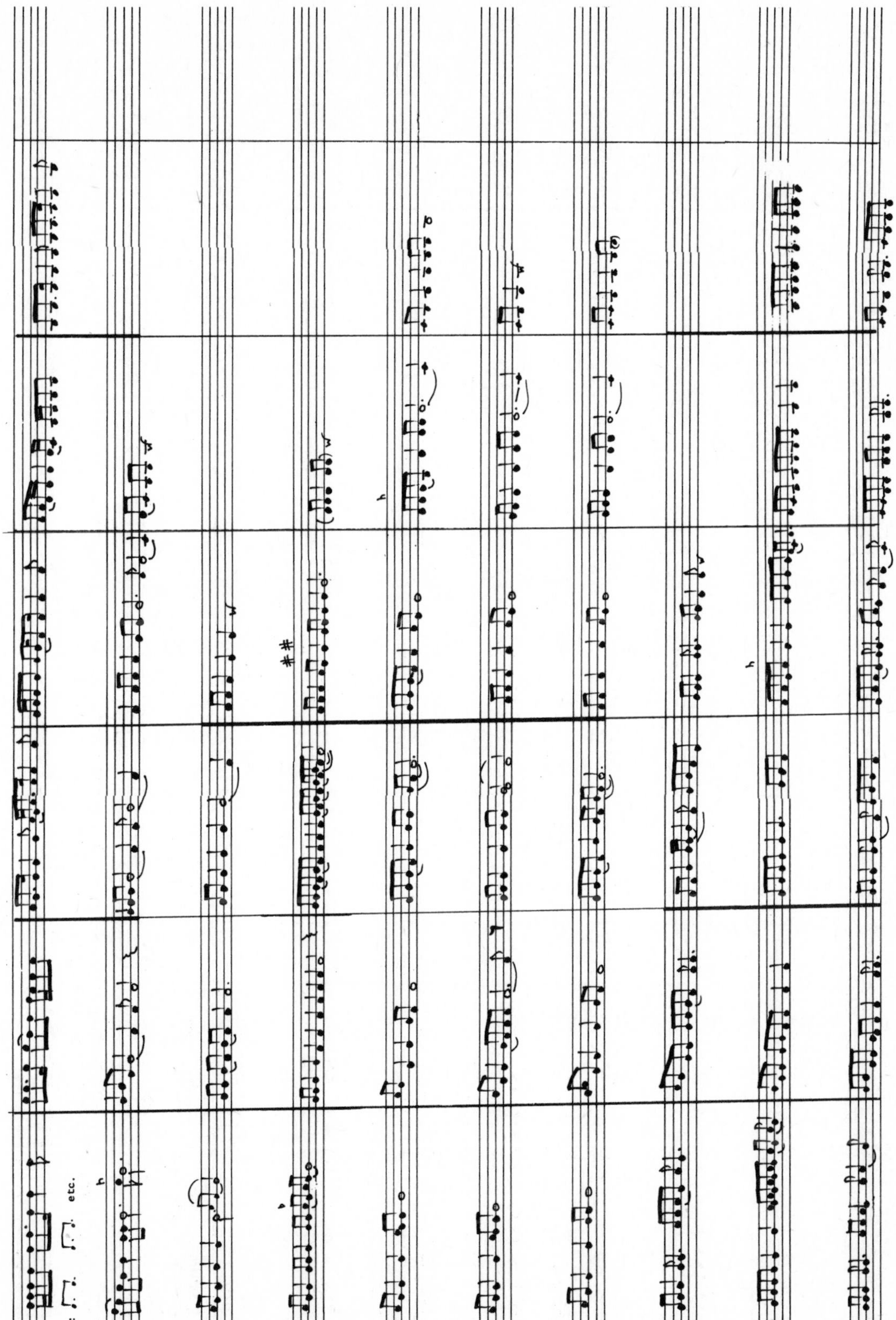

Musical notation 9   Ten *wangata* songs.

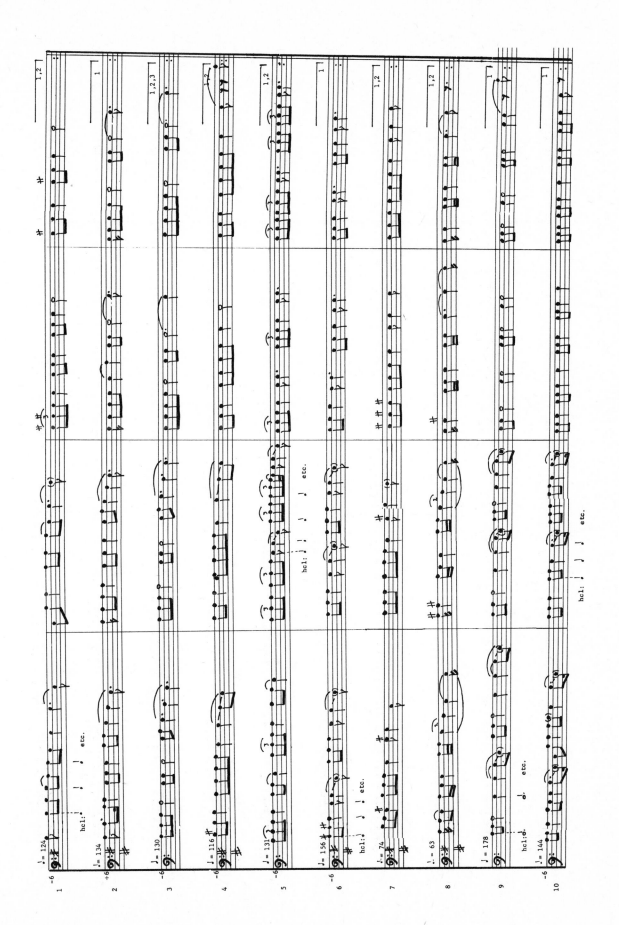

125

126

Musical notation 10 Ten *maanyitja* songs.

Musical notation 11   Ten *mungamunga* songs.

127

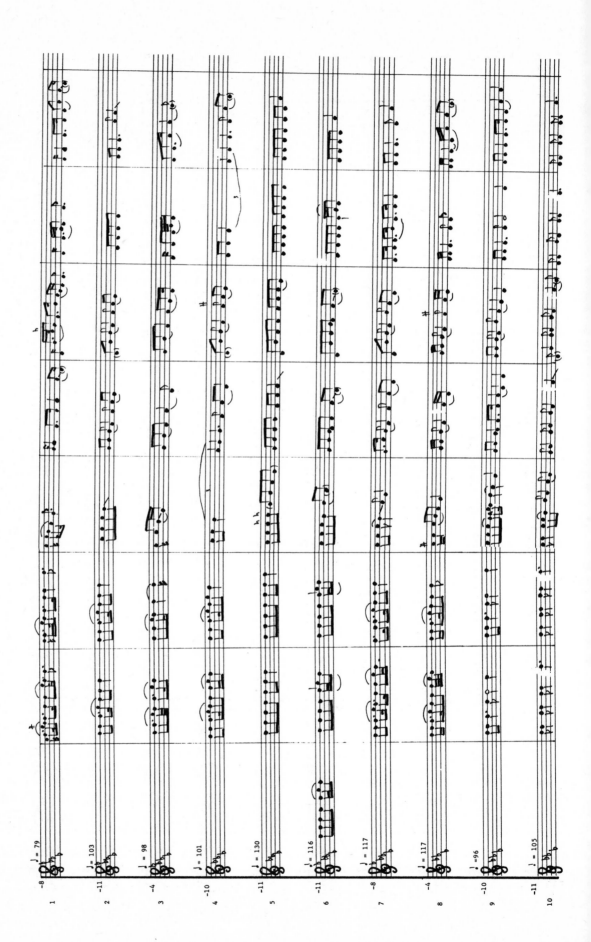

Musical notation 12 Ten *kungkayunti* songs.

129

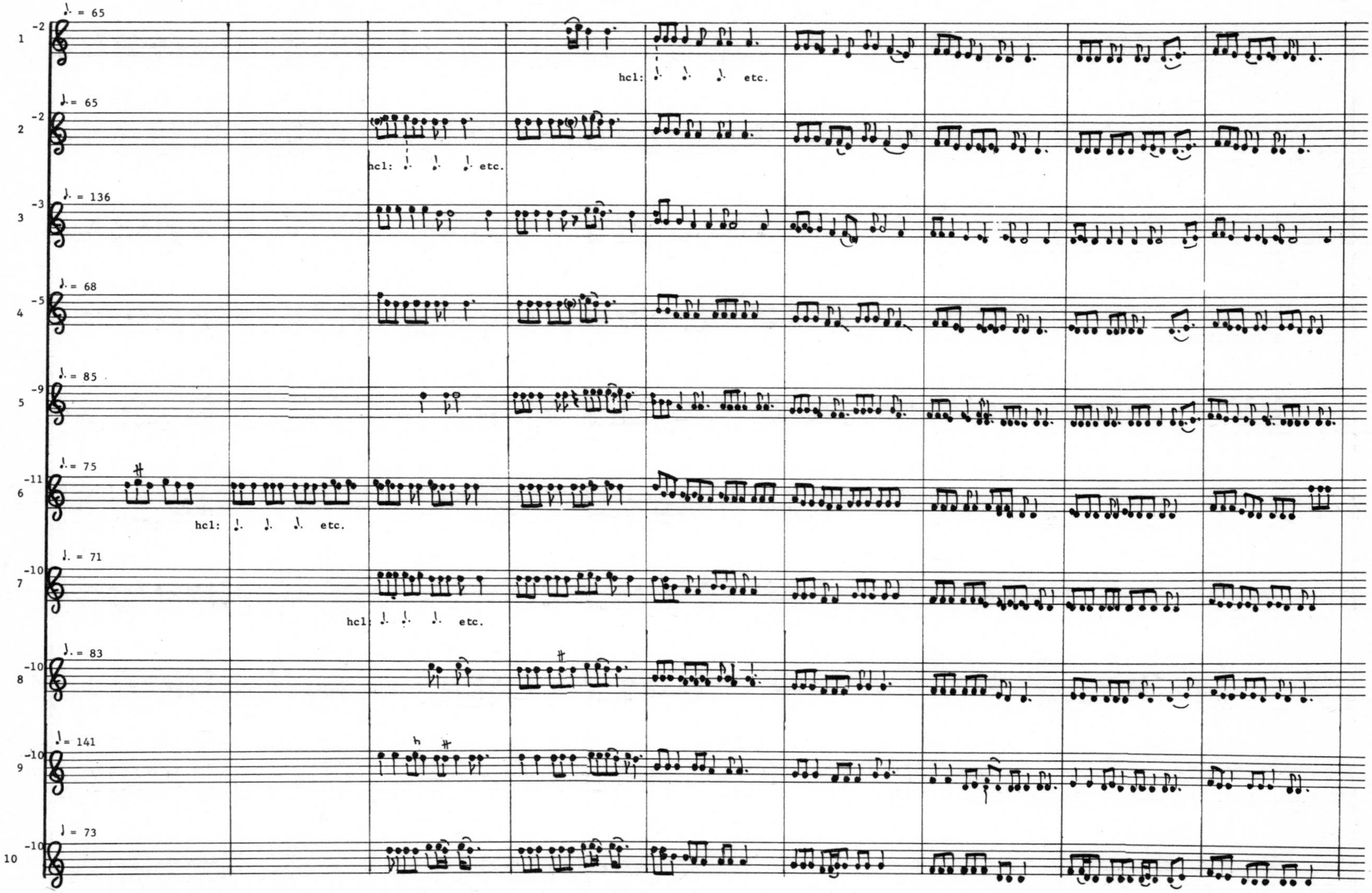
1
♪. = 65
-2
hcl: ♪. ♪. ♪. etc.
2
♪. = 65
-2
hcl: ♪. ♪. ♪. etc.
3
♪. = 136
-3
4
♪. = 68
-5
5
♪. = 85
-9
6
♪. = 75
-11
hcl: ♪. ♪. ♪. etc.
7
♪. = 71
-10
hcl: ♪. ♪. ♪. etc.
8
♪. = 83
-10
9
♪. = 141
-10
10
♩ = 73
-10

Musical notation 13 Ten Restricted (a) songs.

131

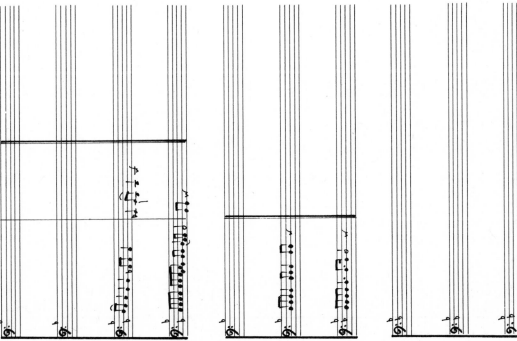

Musical notation 14 Nine Restricted (b) songs illustrating the three different treatments of the melody *vis-à-vis* the word group.

133

134

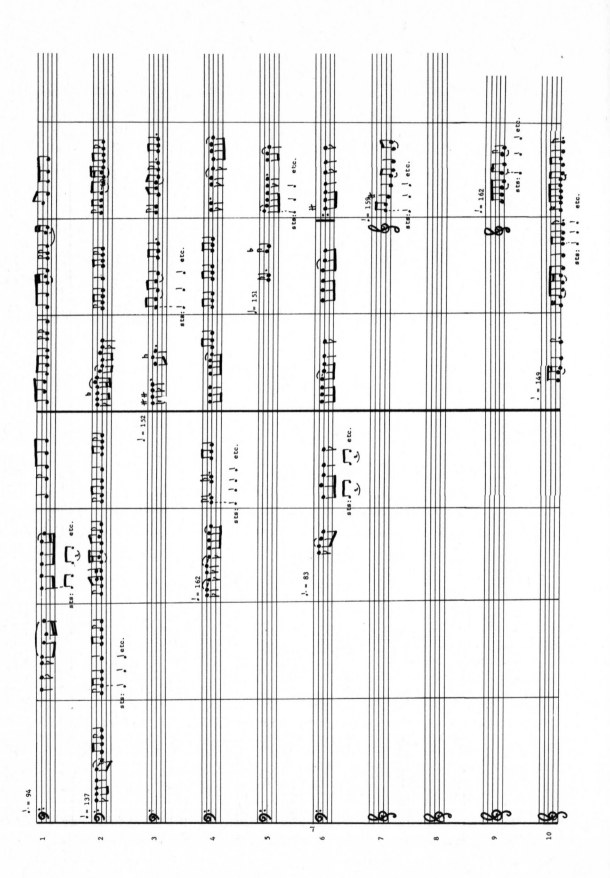

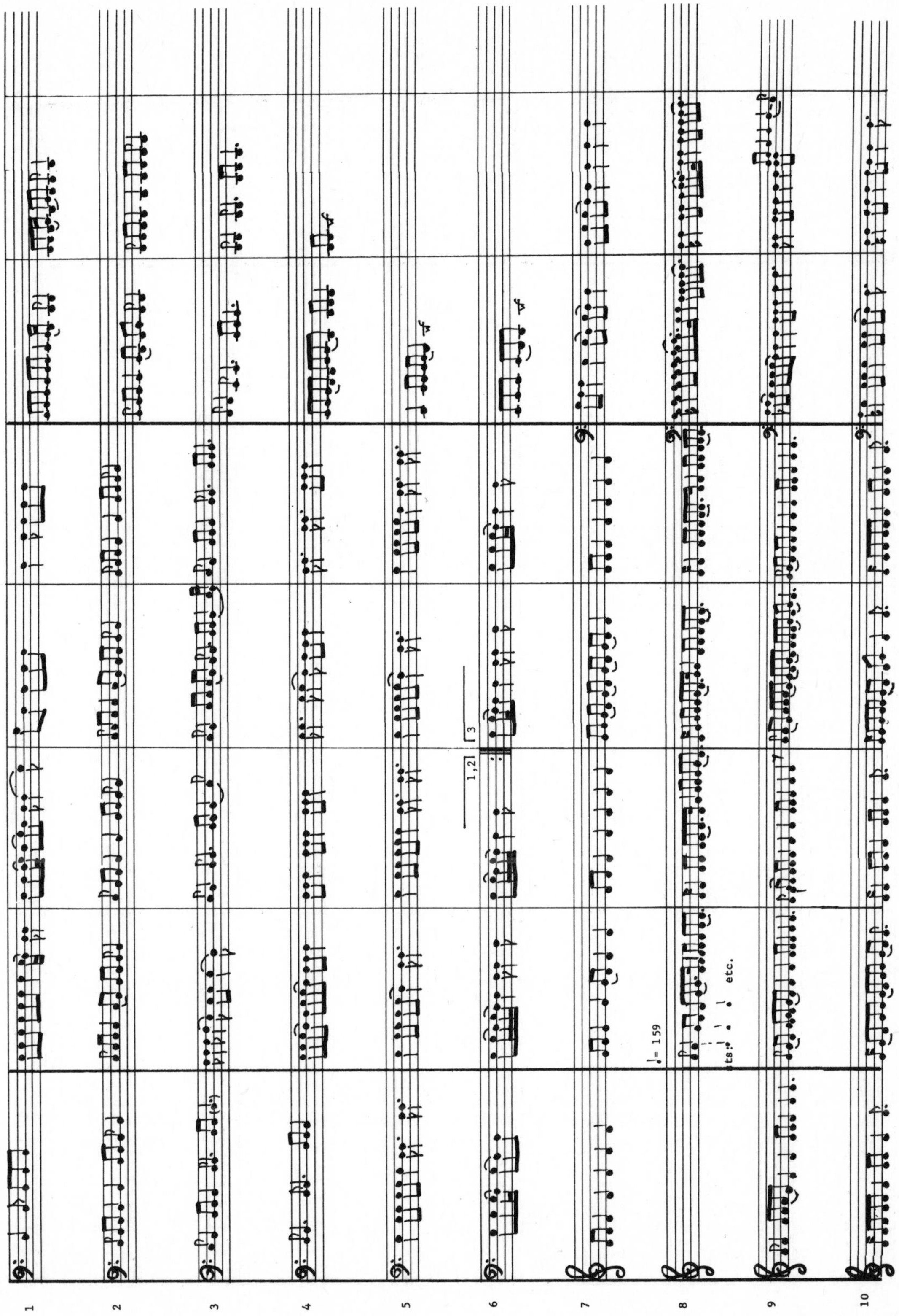
1
2
3
4
5
6
7
8
9
10
1,2
3
♩= 159
etc.

Musical notation 15 Ten *kutiji* songs.

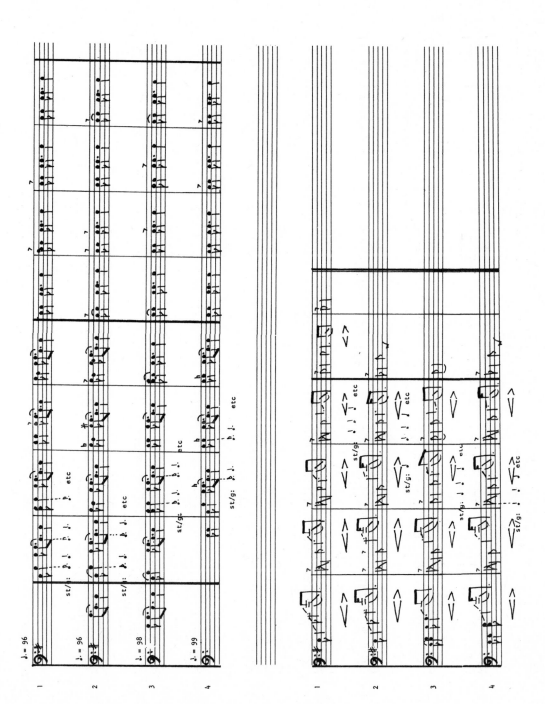

Musical notation 16 Four *malu* songs illustrating first contour.

137

Musical notation 17   Five *malu* songs illustrating second contour.

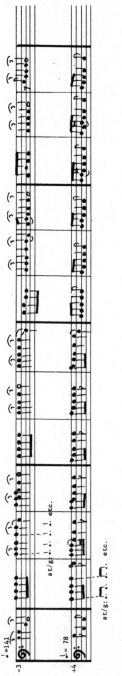

Musical notation 18   Two songs associated with the *wayuta*.

Musical notation 19   Five kipara songs.

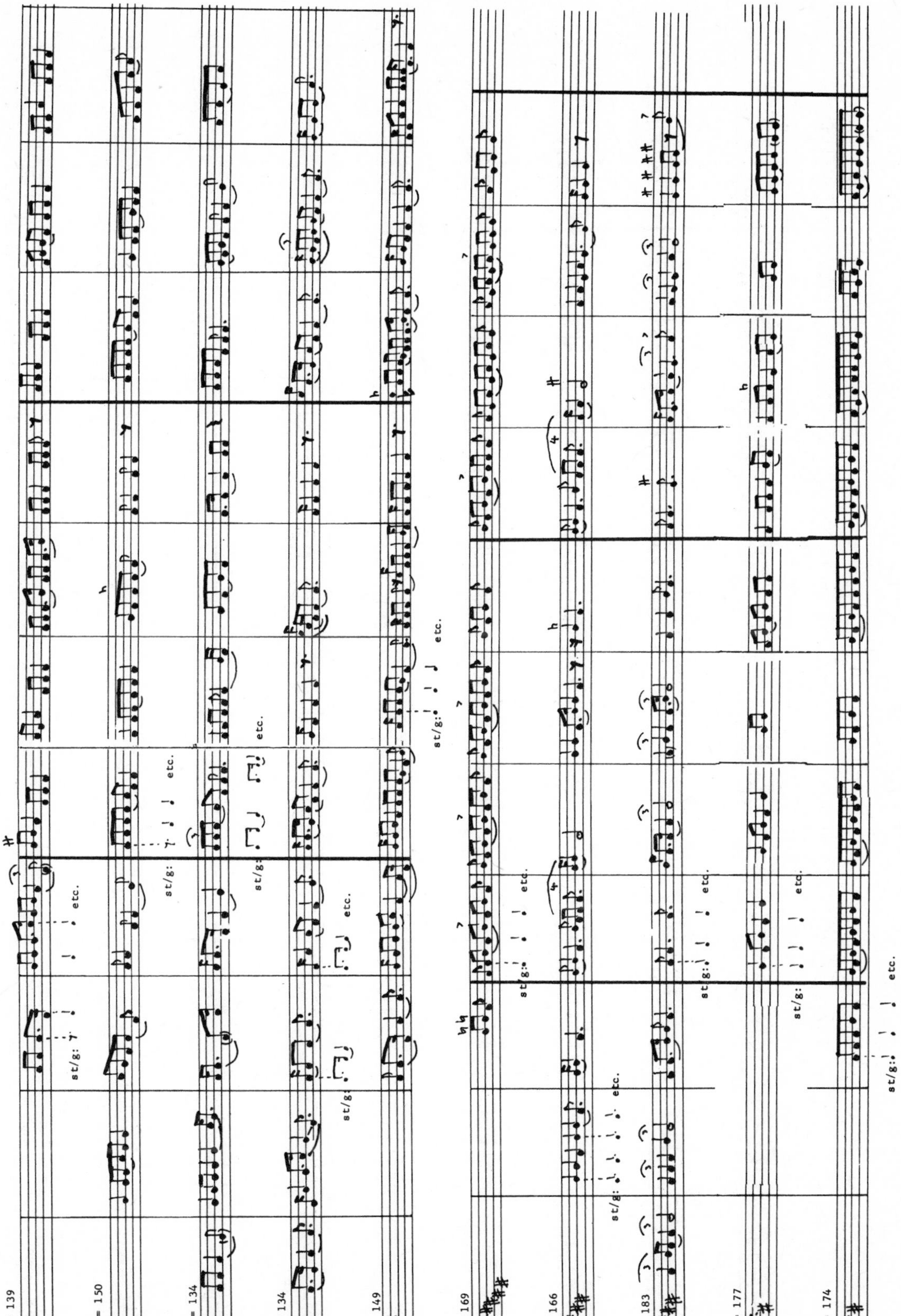
1 ♩ = 139
2 ♩ = 150
3 +3 ♩ = 134
4 +3 ♩ = 134
5 -1 ♩ = 149
6 +1 ♩ = 169
7 -1 ♩. = 166
8 -1 ♩. = 183
9 +5 ♩ = 177
10 ♩. = 174
st/g:
etc.

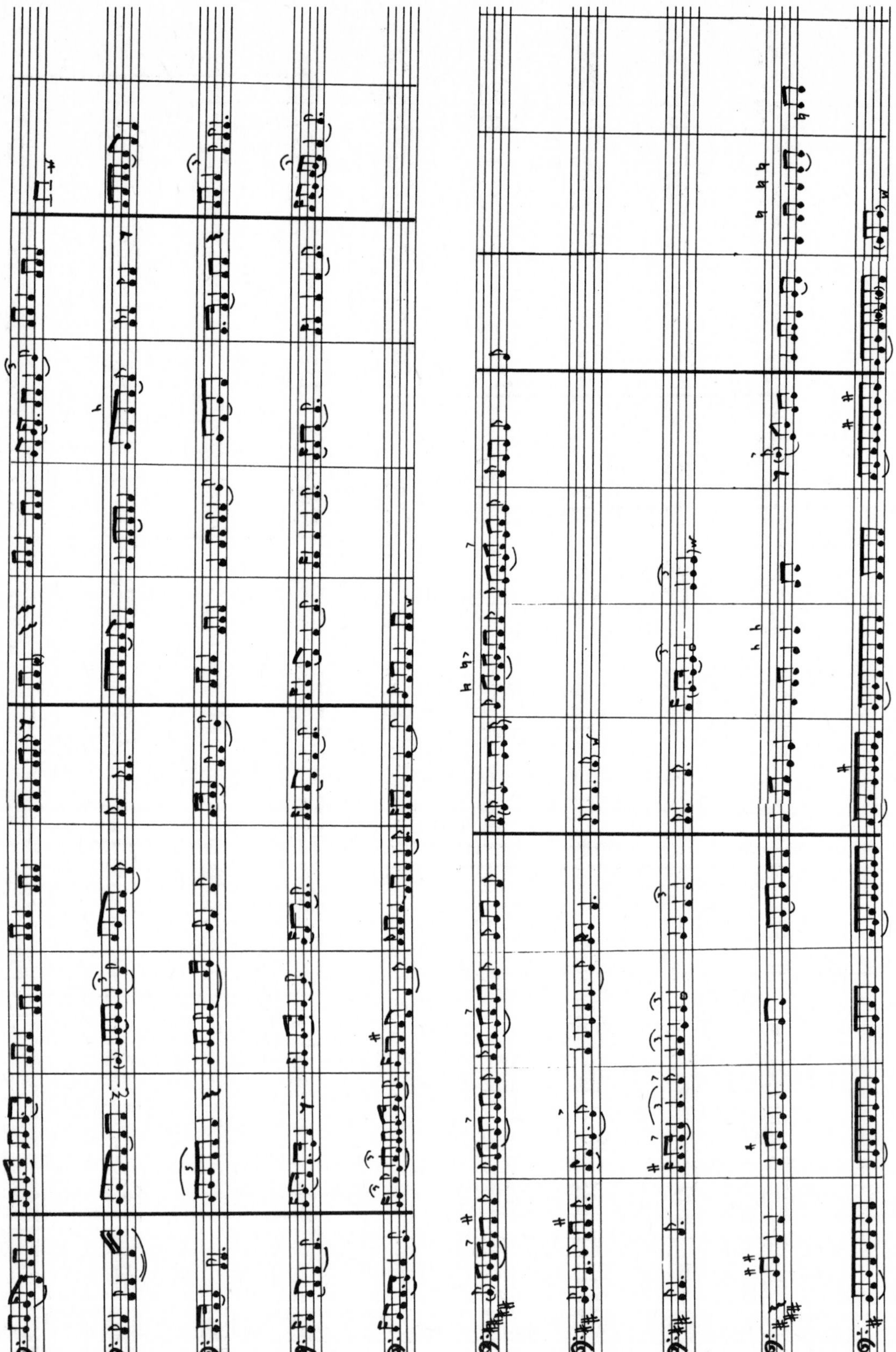

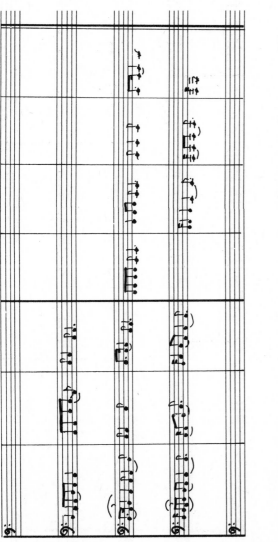
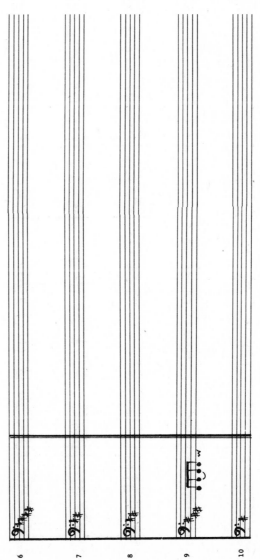

Musical notation 20 Ten *ngintaka* songs illustrating the two melodies.

144

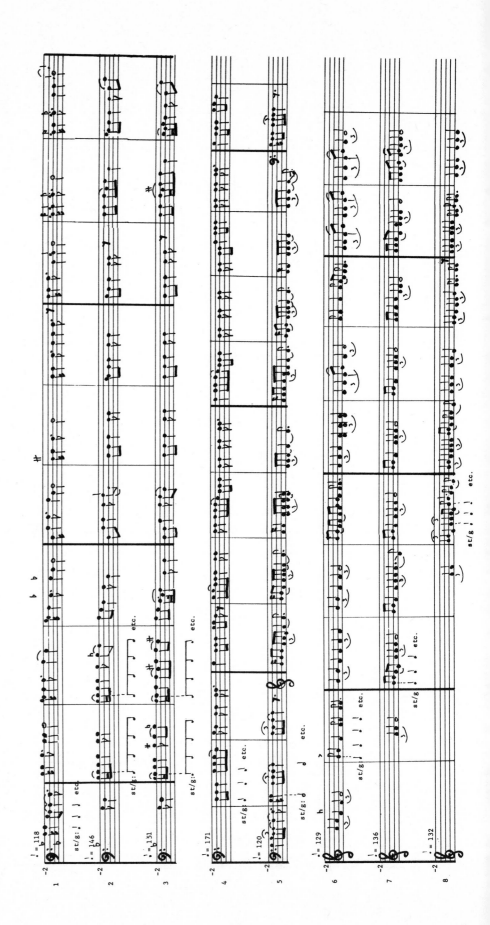

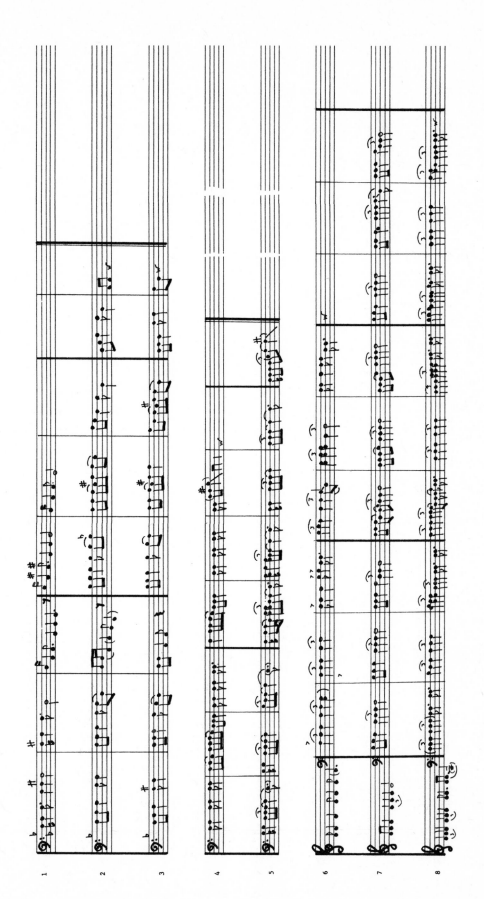

145

146

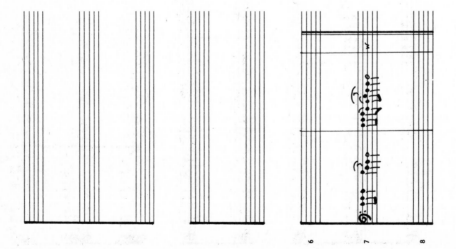

Musical notation 21   Eight *yarriɲjii* songs illustrating the three melodies.

147

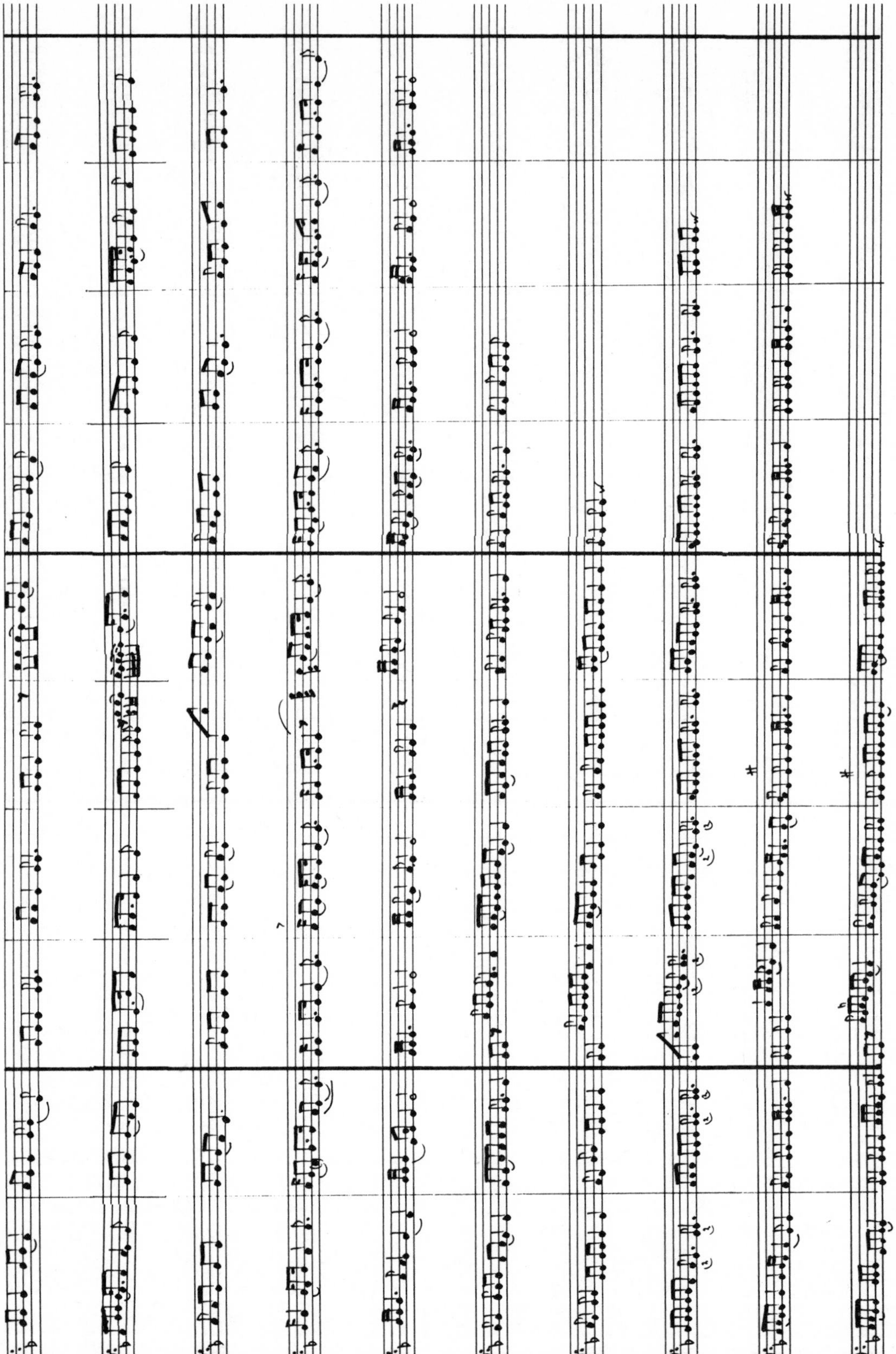
1
2
3
4
5
6
7
8
9
10

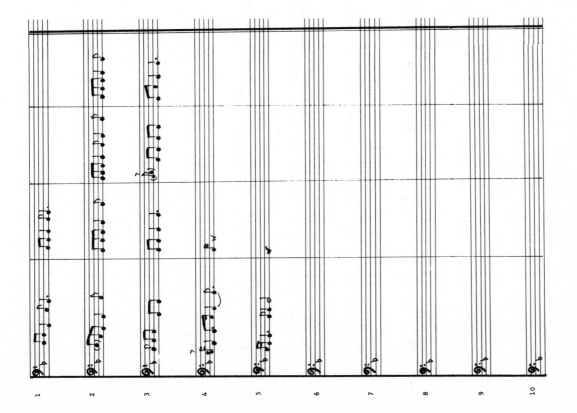

Musical notation 22 Ten *tingarri* songs.

149

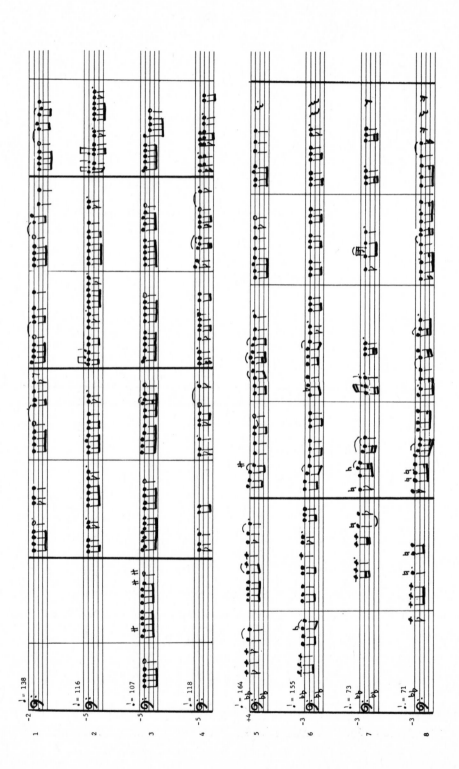

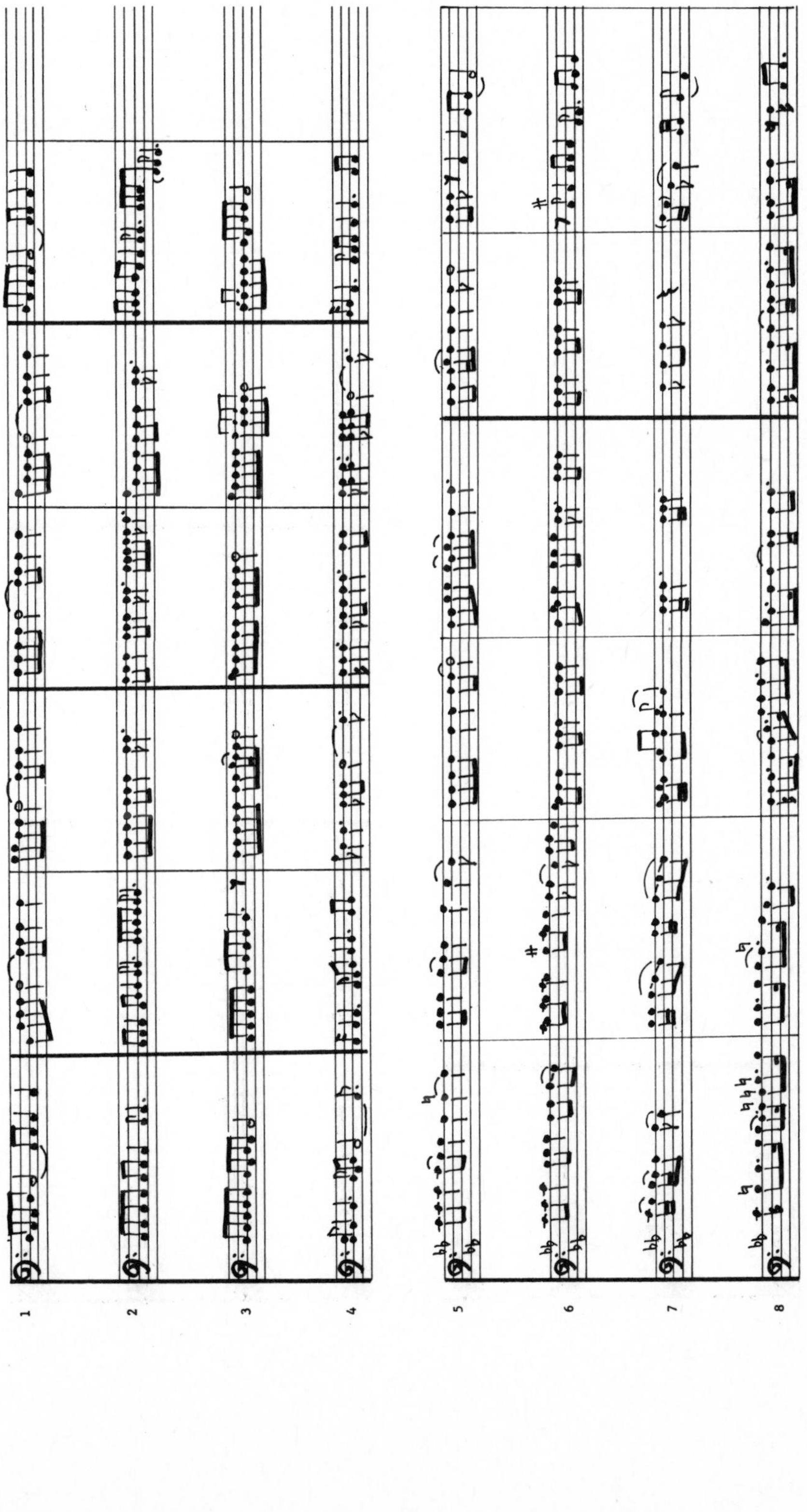

152

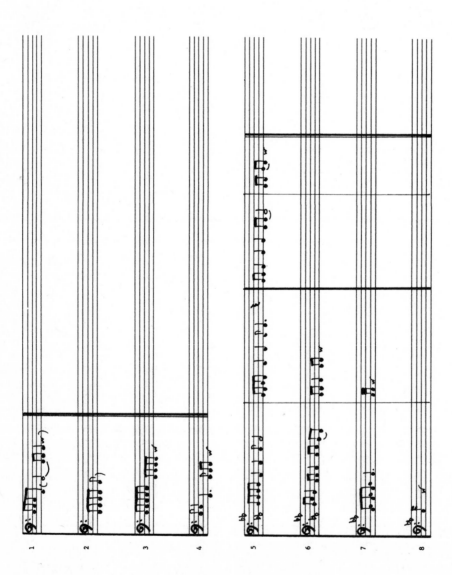

Musical notation 23 Eight *waŋápa* songs illustrating the two melodies.

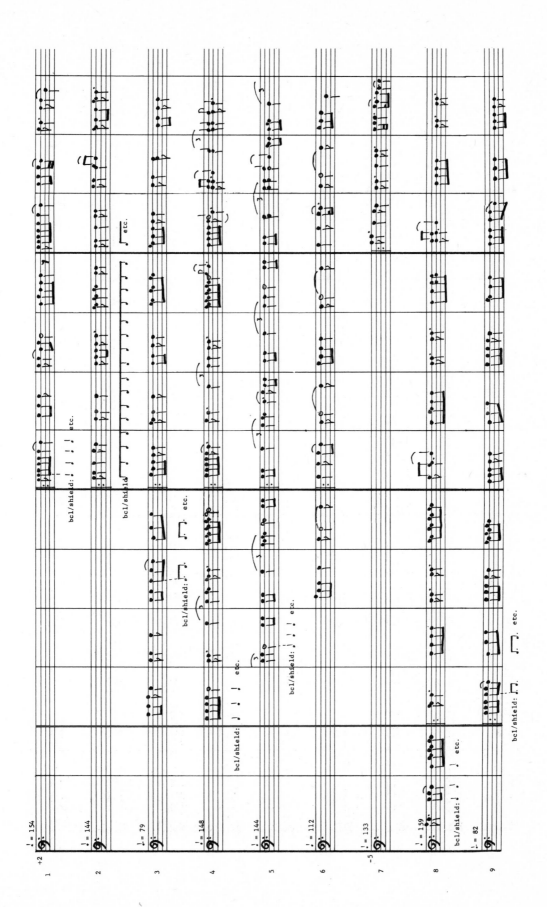

153

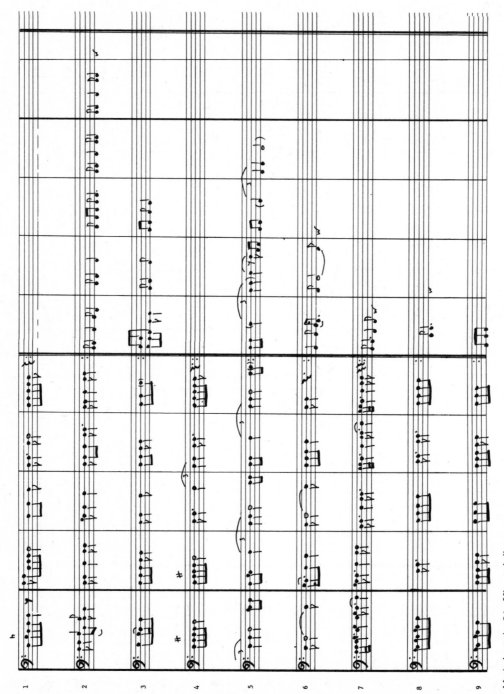

154

Musical notation 24   Nine pukalkarra songs.

Musical notation 25 Five yawarra songs.

155

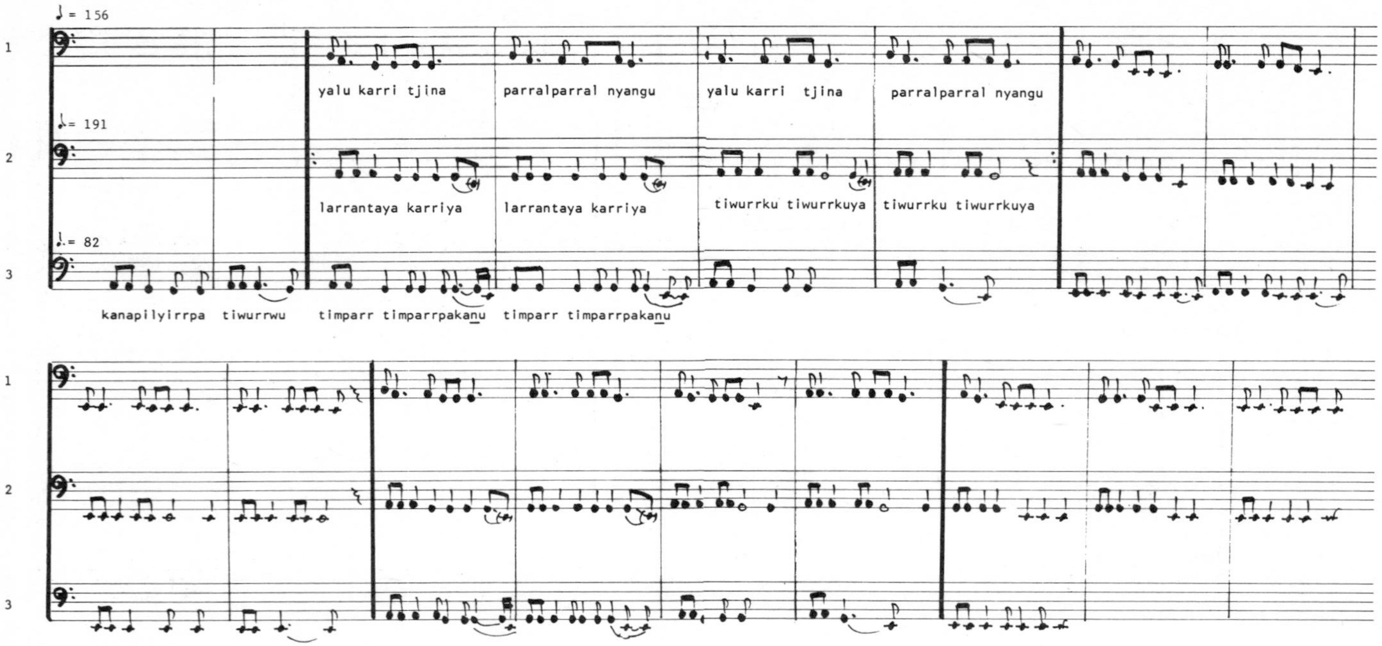

Musical notation 26 Three *paniya* songs.

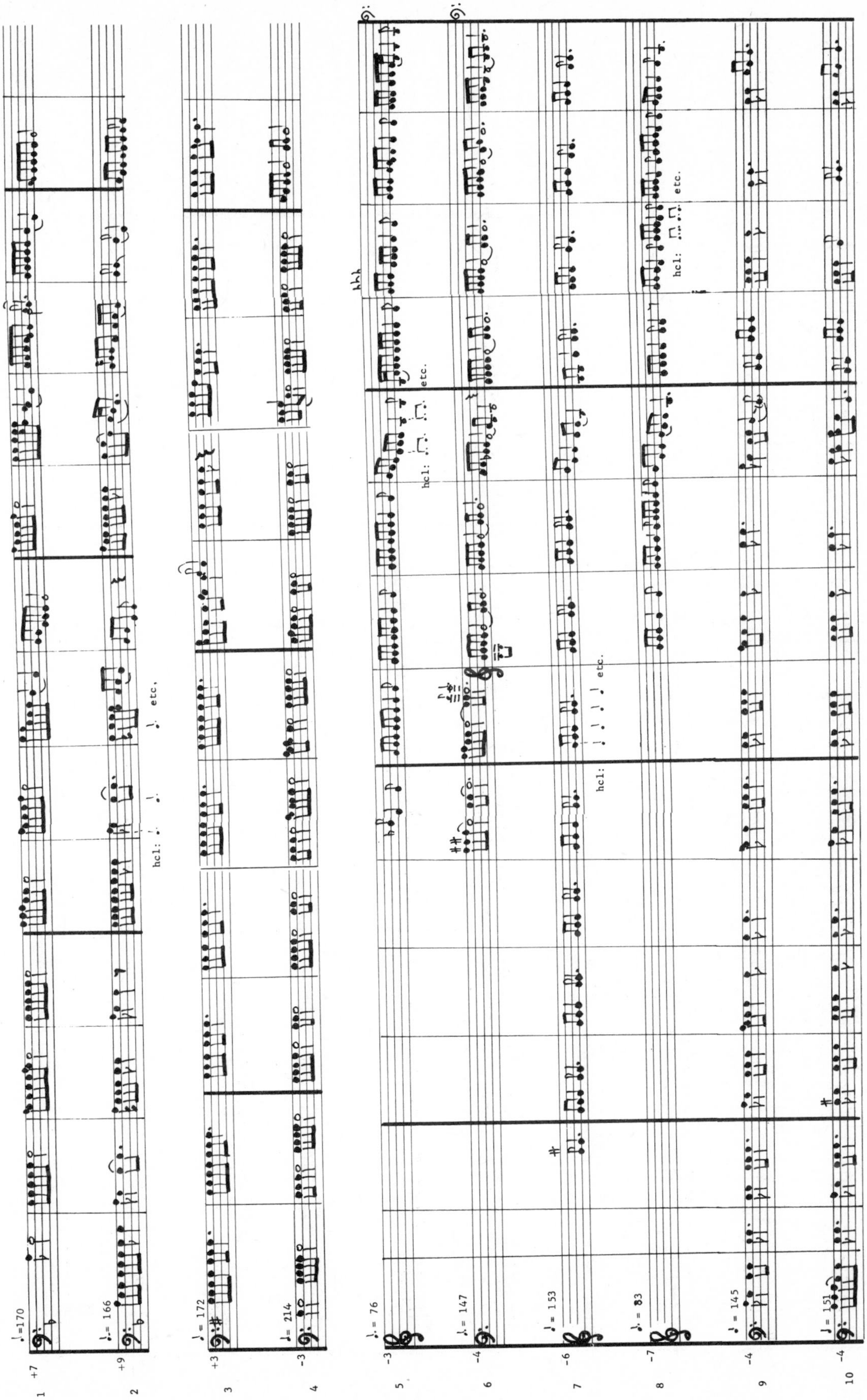
hcl:
etc.

Musical notation 27 Ten *tuyutu* (a) songs illustrating three melodies.

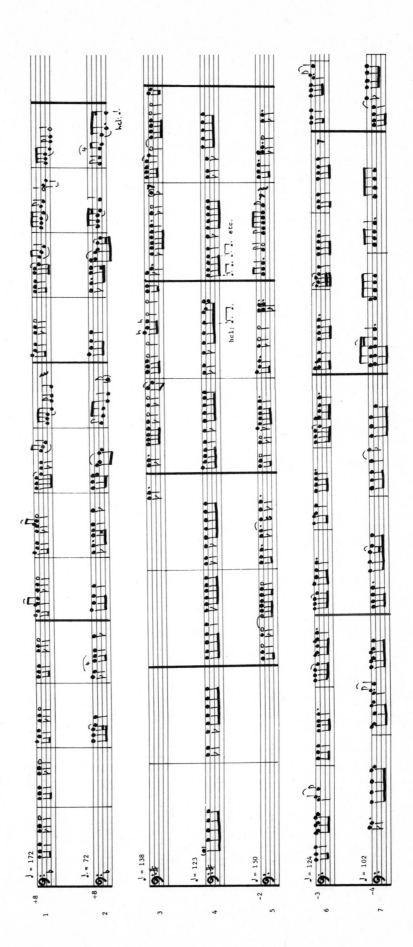

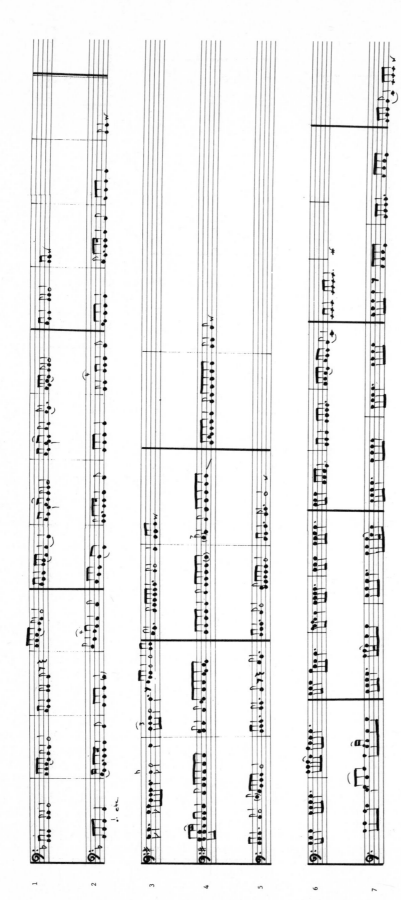

Musical notation 28   Seven *tuyutu* (b) songs illustrating three melodies.

Analysis

Rather than include in the derived scales the sum totals of the various different notes appearing in the published samples, a series of elimination processes was used to remove those individual notes considered structurally insignificant. The basis for differentiation in these processes was one of frequency of appearance, on the assumption that recurrence of a note implied deliberate choice and thus structural significance, whereas non-recurrence implied accidental error and thus no structural significance. The elimination processes occurred on four levels, three of which are similar and are discussed at this point and the fourth will be discussed later.

1. In totalling the frequency of use of notes in individual songs, those with a figure of less than 1% of the total were eliminated. While this did not account for the theoretical possibility of given notes appearing with less than 1% frequency and still being of structural importance, checking with other songs in the same series revealed no general recurrence of such notes, and although this 1% figure is somewhat arbitrary, the empirical evidence suggests that, if anything, it is too low, a situation remedied in the second elimination process.

2. The scale for each individual song was arranged in percentage form, and then the results for the songs in the published sample totalled and averaged; again, a cut-off figure of 1% was used to eliminate any notes considered of no structural significance to the contour as a whole. There were occasional instances where, mostly because of the smallness of the published sample, a particular note could appear frequently in only a few songs and yet emerge with a figure greater than 1% in the second elimination process above. In such cases, a check was made with the remainder of the transcribed sample, and, depending on its occurrence there, the note was either included in or excluded from the final averaged total.

Note: All tonics transposed to d, where tonic = lowest note; all tonics transposed to D where tonic other than lowest note. Melodic significance is in direct proportion to durational values, with tonic = semibreve. Proportions of less important notes approximate only.

Example 60   Weighted scales derived from 34 basic contours.

3. There were also occasions where individuals who happened to be singing most loudly at certain points in specific songs—and whose efforts were thus transcribed—used notes which, in comparison with the same points in other songs where they did not dominate the singing, differed by up to a semitone. For example, in a published sample of, say, ten songs, five might have a scale of b-a-g-f-e-d (where d is the tonic), while five have a scale of b-a-ab-f-e-d. The second elimination process above might well remove both the g and ab, whereas it could be seen clearly that all songs had either one or the other note, and thus *something* ought to be represented in the final scale. In these cases, comparison was again made with the transcribed sample, sometimes also with the whole recorded sample, to determine which of the two occurred more frequently. This note was then considered more correct; the percentage frequencies for both this note and the other were combined, and that figure entered in the final scale.

The derived, weighted scales for the 34 contours in the analysed sample are given in Example 60.

The durational values indicated in Example 60 reflect the degree of melodic importance of each note in the respective scales, as determined by a weighting process in which

(a) each occurrence of a given note received a rating of one;
(b) a common denominator of, say, a quaver was established and given a rating of one; the duration of each occurrence of a specific pitch was totalled relative to this denominator and the total duration of the pitch within the melody then computed;
(c) the initial note in each word group received a rating of two.

Having claimed that certain notes may be classified as 'more correct' in some circumstances, what then of those other notes which by implication must now be 'less correct'? Within individual songs, there are often points at which not all of the singers are in perfect unison, e.g.

At such points, the blending of the voices or the position of the microphone, or both, can make it virtually impossible to tell which pitch most of the singers are singing, consequently both notes appear in the transcriptions. Such singing, more often than not, consists of movement approaching, or on, the tonic, with the two groups of voices separated by not more than M2. Examination of these points, in other songs where there *is* melodic unison, reveals no apparent consistency of melodic movement based on numbers of syllables, accompaniment beats, or note durations, which, when applied to the songs containing brief heterophony, could indicate the 'correct' pitch or pitches for each syllable. Since repetitions of the same song do not always contain an exact repetition of this, the duration of the heterophony appears optional, and since not all songs have this feature anyway, the phenomenon itself would not seem integral to the melodic contour. As already observed, the phenomenon is restricted to notes m2 or M2 apart, the lower of which, if not the tonic itself, is usually a note of melodic importance, with a ranking of a minim or better in the above inventories. It follows that if such heterophony is indeed optional, then the phenomenon cannot be considered a performance error, a view confirmed by informants who described it as *kutju* (the same) or *palya* (good). Several said it was a sign of a happy (*pukulpa*) singer.

In Example 61, the (a) versions represent the melodic lines which, when compared to those of the other songs in the series, appear the more strictly correct; the (b) versions indicate heterophonic variations of these lines.

A further case of departure from strict vocal unison, differing from the above in that it appears to result from unfamiliarity with the melody or text, or possibly both—and thus constitutes an error—occurs often at points of pitch change in the melodic contour. As Example 62 shows, singers of the upper, incorrect melodic line quickly return to that of the lower, correct line. Such errors seem to occur in virtually every recorded song, though not necessarily by a greater proportion of singers; indeed, most are by individual men or women, and receive no apparent attention or overt criticism from the others.

Insofar as they are confined within individual isorhythmic groups, such errors do not appear to be classified as 'singing on the other side' or 'singing on the near side', and possibly for this reason are tolerated.

The order of the scales in Example 60 has been

Example 61   Cases of heterophony.

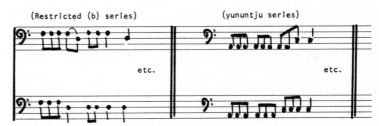

Example 62   Cases of apparent melodic error.

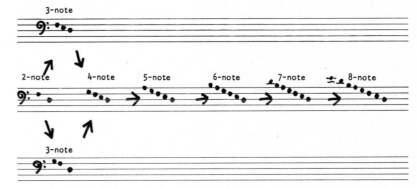

Example 63   Scalic hierarchy growing by acretion.

arranged to illustrate similarities between the various contours. Comparison of these scales reveals that an arrangement of the material in this way separates four groupings:

1. From *malu(i)* in the first column to *yununtju* in the second column. The derived scales here are found to be capable of arrangement into a hierarchy growing by accretion from a two-note kernel f-d, where the tonic is d. For example, to this two-note kernel is added a third note, either e or g; in the former case, *kutitji* and *malu (ii)* contours use this scale, and in the latter case, the scale is used in the *tuyutu* (a), (i), *yawarra* and *maanytja* series. Combination of the pitches in these two three-note scales produces a four-note series g-f-e-d, which is used in the *pukalkarra*, and *yarritjiti* (ii), (iii) and (iv) contours. By similar accretion, five-, six- and eight-note systems are built. In notational form, the process is as shown in Example 63.

163

The hierarchy is not perfect; the four-note *wayuta* 'lacks' an f, the five-note *wangata* 'lacks' a g, the five-note *kungka kutjarra* (ii) 'lacks' an e, the eight-note *wantjiwantji* alone has a c ♭, and the seven-note *yununtju* 'lacks' a ♭ b. However, the fact that the hierarchy does hold for 15 out of the 21 contours represented in this part of the sample would appear to rule out a purely accidental arrangement.

2. From Restricted (b) in the second column to *paniya* in the third column. The chief differentiating feature of these five scales is the presence of the e ♭; a similar hierarchical process is evident, starting from the four-note kernel g-f-e♭-d, where d is the tonic. It is also noteworthy that three of the five are from women's series.

3. The remainder of the third column as far as *ngintaka* (ii). These scales are distinguished by all occurring together with other contours in their respective series rather than on their own, but, more to the point, they each have their tonic at the upper end of the scale. There are indications of a similar accretive process in those remaining scales whose tonic is at or near the top of the pitch inventory, starting from a d-b-a kernel and adding notes above, within and below. However, because only five scales are of this type (and another is apparently an exception), any conclusion cannot be as firm as for the remainder of the sample.

4. By reason of its f ♭ the *tarrkalpa* scale stands alone.

Thus far, then, we have what appears to be four discrete scale categories. However, the elimination process described earlier may be taken to a fourth stage. If, in comparing versions of the same song, or different songs using the same contour—all of which are considered by the singers to have been performed acceptably—we find, for example, melodic movement f-e-d in some cases and f-d in others, at the same point in the contour, we may reasonably conclude that the e is not essential to the contour, but rather that it is a passing note between pitches of greater structural importance. If subsequent checking shows that the e occurs only when preceded or followed by either f or d, and is not approached by leap from any non-adjacent scale note, then its exclusion from a scale of structurally significant notes can be justified. To generalise from this particular case: a scale note is considered structurally insignificant if

(a) it does not occur within the same isorhythmic division in the contour for all repeats of the same song, and in all songs having the same contour, and if,

(b) where it does occur, it is always by stepwise movement to and from adjacent scale notes, and if,

(c) when it does not occur, melodic movement is between these same adjacent scale notes.

When this definition is applied to the scales in Example 60, it has the effect of removing all es and e♭s from the scales having the tonic as their lowest pitch, with the exception of the *kipara, wayuta, yarritjiti* (iv) and *wangata* (which are possibly non-Pintupi) and the *yunpu*, Restricted (a) and *yikuluku* series (which are of known recent composition). The derived scales for the remainder of the sample now read as follows:

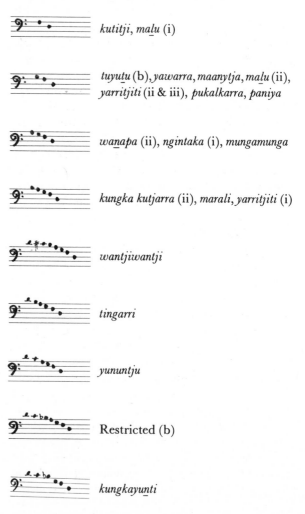

kutitji, malu (i)

tuyutu (b), *yawarra, maanytja, malu* (ii), *yarritjiti* (ii & iii), *pukalkarra, paniya*

wanapa (ii), *ngintaka* (i), *mungamunga*

kungka kutjarra (ii), *marali, yarritjiti* (i)

wantjiwantji

tingarri

yununtju

Restricted (b)

kungkayunti

Example 64 Derived scales after processing.

To sum up the situation: the evidence is that

(a) At the same points in repeats of the same songs, and in different songs, movement consisting of either d-e-d or ♭-d occurs. (For all occurrences of e in this and the next paragraph, read also 'or ♭-d'.)

(b) In other songs in the same series, movement is level on d at these same points.

(c) All three types of movement are considered by the singers as constituting acceptable performance procedure.

We conclude that e is not essential to the contour at these points; in the various songs, differences in the precise points at, and durations for which it occurs are considered optional. This is of course not to deny the existence of the e; rather, one may say that on the basis of the recorded sample, if the e appears in any individual songs, it will be used either as a descending passing-note between f and d, or in undulating fashion to and from d. It will not be approached by leap from any other scale note or, with the sole exceptions of Restricted (a) and *yarritjiti* (iv) figure in upward stepwise movement d-e-f. Thus, while e as a separate and consistently pitched note occurs in many scales, it is integrally related to the tonic in such a way that at any point where it occurs, it may be replaced by a d; that is, it may be considered an acceptable substitute for d.

This final elimination process applies only to the first, second and fourth scalic groupings mentioned earlier. A similar phenomenon does not occur in those scales having their tonic at the top of the pitch inventory. In the case of the *tarrkalpa* contour, the e is eliminated, giving a scale a-g-f ♭-d.

Thus the surface groupings of the scales as shown in Example 60 become modified and, despite differences in the notes higher in the various scales, each retains the lower kernel of f-d. Melodic differences between the contours are generally confined to movement above this kernel.

Of the exceptions to the fourth elimination process described above, that is, of those contours where the e (or e♭) appears to be of structural importance, *yunpu*, Restricted (a) and *yikuluku* present a tantalising possibility, as all three are known to be of recent origin. The possibility is that there is a connection here, and that despite surface stylistic similarity with the rest of the recorded sample, in terms of overall structural organisation, this one intervallic feature is indicative of a recent change in the style of Pintupi

music. I offer this suggestion with only such support as three contours can provide, and obviously each new Pintupi series must be measured against it; however, should future research confirm this situation, then we will have evidence of that rarely documented phenomenon in ethnomusicology—stylistic change of an apparently non-acculturative nature within the music of a non-literate people.[1]

---

1. The word 'apparently' is used advisedly, in anticipation of base studies of the music of other Central and Western Desert Aborigines.

Conclusions

Writings on Australian Aboriginal music may be grouped according to their focus. Firstly there are those whose titles, at least, purport to deal with the continent as a whole; some mention the music of the Central Desert area, but do not include the Pintupi. Among such writings are Kennedy (1933), Tate (1951), Strehlow (1955), Waterman (1958), Jones (1962, 1965, 1968) and Ellis (1969). And then there are those which deal with particular sections of the continent; limiting our attention to those pertaining to the Central and Western Desert areas, these include Davies (1927), Ellis (1963, 1964a, 1965, 1968) and Strehlow (1971). Finally there are the anthropological accounts dealing with specific communities within the Western Desert, for example de Graaf (1968) and Tonkinson (1974). With the exception of Strehlow (1971), none deals specifically with the Pintupi, and indeed Strehlow's comments relate to peripheral matters. The only published example of Pintupi music consists of one song appearing in Ellis (1964a:341-42), the song having been recorded in 1957 by Tindale. Although Ellis does not identify the song, the melody is identical to that of the *tingarri* series.

Largely because of the vagueness of the geographical referents in the above publications (of which the terms 'Central Desert' and 'Western Desert' are the chief culprits), but also because several articles have generalised titles whose use does not appear justified by the contents (*see* especially Ellis 1968 and 1969a), it is hardly worthwhile comparing the findings contained there with my own. Instead, I have turned to the only attempt to classify Aboriginal music in terms of music areas; Alice Moyle's Tribal Area marked 'CA' (1966: Map 1) lies neatly inside the more easterly of the two areas delineated in Fig. 1. The vocal features associated with this area are said to include:

(a) 'Correspondence between verbal units and rhythm formulae' (1966: xvii). If this is taken to mean that repetition of the word groups use the same syllabic rhythms, then the statement holds true for the Pintupi.

(b) 'Regular verbal repetition' (*ibid.*). If this is taken to mean repetition of the word groups in a consistent manner in the various songs and song series, then it too holds true for the present sample, as does Moyle's additional comment, 'verbal repetition (per song-item) exceeds melodic repetition' (*ibid.*).

Moyle's listing of types of musical instruments—paired sticks, boomerangs, single sticks beaten on the ground, and 'stick beating on sundry weapons' is consistent with some of those used by the Pintupi. In sum, as far as it goes, this taxonomy of characteristics does not conflict with those features of Pintupi music contained in the recorded sample.

Attention is now given to specific elements of the recorded sample.

Melody

With the sole exception of healing items, the musical unit is the series rather than the individual song. Typical performance consists of singing in their correct sequential order all the songs associated with a particular myth; however, certain songs may be omitted if they are considered to contain direct or indirect references to a recently deceased person. In the case of *tingarri, mungamunga, wantjiwantji* and *ngalungku* series, the Pintupi acknowledge that the myth extends over the period before and after that sung by them; in these cases it is not possible to say whether or not any linguistic changes occur at the changeover points—the Pintupi themselves claim not to know, and the similarities between Pintupi and neighbouring languages coupled with the practice of using little-known or restricted words in the texts hinder further investigation. Certain songs in such series show stylistic characteristics different from those of exclusively Pintupi series, particularly in their manner of structural organisation; it is considered a distinct possibility that such characteristics are non-Pintupi, and that those songs exhibiting them are, or were at some time in the past, non-Pintupi, in terms of the geographical territory referred to in their texts or in the associated sections of the myths. More definite conclusions await localising of these myths.

Healing songs consist of individual items taken from longer series; in the course of treatment only those specific items are performed, thus providing the exception to the norm wherein complete series are sung in their entirety.

The structural organisation of Pintupi music centres around the division of the word group of each song into isorhythmic units, usually three or four. The melodic contour is apportioned to these units in such a way that movement may not proceed from one unit to the next until all of the text encompassed therein has been sung. Differences in the numbers of words and syllables in the various songs in any given series are accommodated by appropriate changes in the constituents of the isorhythmic units; melodic movement within such units is respectively identical in each song. There is a possibility that procedural rules exist determining precise moments of pitch change within isorhythmic units; however, such rules have yet to be discovered. Although the notion of accompaniment of some sort appears integral to Pintupi singing, it is not organised rhythmically in tremolo- or bullroarer-accompanied items. However, in those same items featuring an instrumental tremolo or bullroarer, the isorhythm is not always exact, especially in longer durations, suggesting that the function of rhythmic accompaniment in the other items is to synchronise the syllabic rhythm.

In the course of any given song, the word group is repeated several times; although there is some flexibility about which individual word or syllable commences the song, in most series repetition of individual songs involves identical apportioning of word group divisions to melodic contour divisions. In several series, however, and especially in the Restricted (b) series, text reversal occurs.

With the exception of *yikuluku*, unrestricted series (*tulku*) have only one melodic contour for all their songs, while the others may have more than one, each outline associated with a particular principal character in the associated myth; details of the nature of these associations have yet to be examined. The immutability of myth generally, as suggested in the strict ordering of individual songs in any series, the close attention to ceremonial detail, and the ready criticism of any deviations from accepted performance procedures, appears to be an ideology which at least some Pintupi recognise as such. The particular explanation for the phenomenon of multiple melodies which ascribes melodies additional to those known by all Pintupi to the activities of individuals in the historical past is clearly a

167

departure from such an ideology. Investigation of the resolution of this apparent contradiction would have required greater linguistic fluency and time than I had available, and as such a musical situation is not reported from other Desert groups, little more can be said at this stage. For the remainder of the recorded sample, origins can be divided neatly into those ascribed to the Dreamtime, and those held to have been the results of the relatively recent nocturnal activities of human spirits.

For most men's ceremonies and song series, ownership is on the basis of the 'sun'—'shade' moiety division; the only exceptions are the *tingarri* (which is owned by the local *nintipuka*) and the *maanytja* (which belongs to the Tjapangaṯi subsection). By contrast, women's ceremonies are owned by particular subsections. *Tulku* appear to be the only type of series owned by individuals. According to the type of ceremonies and song series, ownership is either transferable to a younger sibling at death, or inherited at birth by all new members of particular subsections, or widened through trading.

Teaching song series is a formal activity concentrating in the first instance on accurate performance of melody, rhythm, accompaniment and texts. It is but one part of the process of progressive revelation, later stages of which include explanations of the associated myths, texts, ceremonial objects and accompanying rituals. Teaching is by the owner, or a member of the owner subsection or moiety. By contrast, learning is not confined to formal sessions as, for example, when an individual attends a performance for the first time. In both formal and informal settings, the learning process is by progressive participation—from silent observation, to accompanying, to adding visible lip movement, to audible singing and accompaniment.

Terminology for, and analysis of melodic contour is a problematic area in ethnomusicology, and analogous difficulties are presented in three-dimensional form as regards musical instruments. The significance of the problem lies in the general belief that the shape of both musical sounds and the devices which produce those sounds are an integral part of musical style; appropriate nomenclature is considered necessary not so much for purely analytical as comparative purposes. Solutions range from, on the one hand, a retreat into broad generalisations (e.g. Nettl 1956: 51ff), to the creation of a complex system of re-notation and supportive vocabulary (e.g. Kolinski 1964), on the other. In this present work no

attempt is made to analyse melodic contour, principally because of the overall similarity of most of the material, which consists of descending movement. In this respect, Nettl (1956:52) notes:

> Various theories have been promulgated about the scarcity of ascending melodic movement. One is that breath control is the basic factor, that as a singer loses breath he finds it easiest to sing down. High singing is facilitated by full lungs, so the high pitches are apt to come at the beginning of a song. This theory, however plausible, could only have been applicable to very remote times when singers had not grasped the technique of catching a breath during a song . . . The theory of breath control is also refuted by the fact that towards the end of many songs we find the phenomenon known as 'final lengthening', that is, the rhythmic units have increased in size. If singers regularly ran short of breath at the end of a song, this could not take place—the final notes would be hurried.

Several points need examination here:

(a) '. . . high pitches are apt to come at the beginning of a song.' This is true of Pintupi songs, but more important, also true for pitches immediately following breath-breaks during songs.

(b) '. . . applicable to very remote times when singers had not grasped the technique of catching a breath during a song . . . ' Pintupi singers generally take their breaths together and at the same points in the contour in each successive song. Nettl's objection is thus inapplicable.

(c) '. . . final lengthening . . . ' This situation does not occur in Pintupi music.

It is also noticeable that where an individual singer takes a breath-break at a moment different from those of the other singers, he or she will recommence singing at a pitch higher than that of the others; after a syllable or two, unison is restored. In short, Nettl's evidence strengthens rather than weakens any argument in favour of overall contour direction in Pintupi music deriving from breath control. The subject is a difficult one on which to elicit specific comments from the Pintupi, and the whole issue must, for the time being at least, remain in the realm of probability; what can be stated at this stage, however, is that there seems to be no objection to the proposition on theoretical grounds.

Almost a third of the total number of contours in the analysed sample include lower octave repetition of material previously sung an octave higher; according to the starting pitch of the song, and the singers' vocal capabilities, this lower octave section may or may not be sung in its entirety. On a few occasions, singing commences on such a high pitch that a further repetition of material an additional octave lower is attempted, suggesting that there is no concept of a fixed two-octave structure for such melodies. Two series whose authenticity as exclusively Pintupi is dubious—the *kipara* and *wangata*—each have a short melodic section between the upper and lower octave portions; such a contour arrangement may well be a characteristic of Pitjantjatjara music, whence both series seem most likely to have originated. The remaining contours fall into two broad classes: those whose tonic is also the song final—in which case prolonged melodic movement on that final is common; and those whose tonic is at or near the top of the scale—in which case there may be little level movement on the final.

Despite an explicit verbalised preference for unison singing, heterophony sometimes occurs, particularly in the form of simultaneous sounding of the tonic and a pitch m2 or M2 above it, the phenomenon often continuing for several syllables before the upper part drops to join the lower. The evidence suggests that performance in this manner is entirely acceptable to the singers and is not categorised as an error, that its use is optional, and that it is conceptualised as no different from level movement on the tonic.

Especially in mixed groups of singers, but also in segregated choirs where younger and older voices are present together, octave doubling occurs.

Vocal ranges for the Pintupi vary from individual to individual; most songs in the recorded sample go no higher than d″ and b′, or lower than e and E for women and men respectively. There are a few people who can exceed these limits, but because singing is typically a group activity, very little takes place at pitches unobtainable by the majority of the participants. For women, a change in voice register is apparent at around g′; although it is assumed to be present, no such change is apparent from recordings of male singing. The highest pitches in any given series are not reached until round 10-20 minutes after singing has commenced; at such a point there is generally an overall rise in the pitch, sometimes by as much as one octave. Thereafter, overall pitch tends to drop gradually until it is again raised by the song leader; in most cases, the process of gradual lowering

and sudden raising of pitch which continues throughout the performance takes place within the ambit of P4. The lowest pitches occur in those periods immediately prior to such sudden raisings.

Tempo

The method of tempo analysis developed by Kolinski (1959), which is based on the number of notes, rather than on note durations per minute, has been used here to compare the various series in the transcribed sample with each other. Ranking the averages for the different series from highest to lowest, the following results shown in Fig. 18 are obtained. Several aspects are noteworthy:

Series	Average tempo figure	
tjatiwanpa	277	
ngintaka	261*	
yikuluku	234	mixed singing
yununtju	228	
tarrkalpa	219	
tingarri	213	
yarritjiti	212	
wantjiwantji	209*	
kungka kutjarra	200	
kutitji	199	
wayuta	199	
kipara	197	men's singing
pukalkarra	197	
malu	194	
yunpu	193*	
wangata	193	
marali	193	
wanapa	189	
mungamunga	186	
kungkayunti	180	
maanytja	173*	women's singing
Restricted (a)	169	
tuyutu	168*	
Restricted (b)	150	

* = exception

Figure 18 Range of tempi in analysed sample.

Note For the purpose of this listing, all the *tingarri* series have been grouped together (and even when taken separately their figures varied only little, from 215 to 210), and a composite figure appears for all series having multiple melodies.

(a) The series with the highest reading is of non-Pintupi origin.
(b) There seems to be a tendency for series sung by the same kinds of musical forces to have similar tempo figures. For example, with two exceptions, the *tulku*, which are sung by men and women

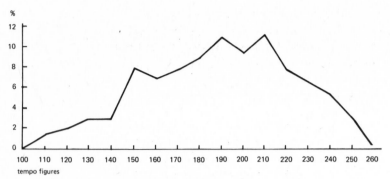

Figure 19 Tempo profile for analysed sample.

Note The figures have been grouped by tens, e.g. all examples from 110 to 119 appear in the 110 listing. The actual figures for each such grouping are 110: 1.7%; 120: 2.0%; 130: 3.0%; 140: 3.0%; 150: 7.9%; 160: 6.9%; 170: 7.9%; 180: 8.9%; 190: 10.9%; 200: 9.6%; 210: 11.2%; 220: 7.9%; 230: 6.3%; 240: 5.6%; 250: 3.3%. A cut-off figure of 1% frequency was applied to the original sample.

together, are grouped consecutively on the above readings, from 234 to 219. With two exceptions, the series from 213 to 189 are all sung by men, and with two exceptions, series with a reading of 186 and less are sung by women. The exceptions are asterisked.

(c) There is a tendency in all the series which feature them for individual songs either unaccompanied or sung to an instrumental tremolo to have significantly lower figures than those songs whose accompaniment consists of a regular rhythmic pattern. The greater frequency of songs of the former category within women's rather than men's series is considered directly responsible for the lower women's ratings.

Although not indicated in the above list, the highest tempo figure, 336, occurred in the *ngintaka* series, and the lowest, 113 in the *wangata* series.

The essentially comparative nature of these tempo indications is useful not only for contrasting various Pintupi song series, but also, by reorganisation of the original data, for presenting tempo information on the entire transcribed sample. Fig. 19 is based on tempo figures for the 607 different songs in the transcribed sample, and within the limitation of scope of this study, represents a tempo profile of Pintupi music.

Accompaniment

The opinion cited earlier in which one man claimed that songs could not be sung if there was no means of accompaniment is more than a simple ideology. For individual songs which normally are accompanied, singers lacking the usual implements will use virtually anything at hand to beat, and failing this will even move their empty hands in the actions of accompanying; to this extent the accompaniment may be considered integral to the singing. However, especially in the women's series but also elsewhere, unaccompanied singing occurs, and although vocal unison is sometimes impaired as a result, the performances do not break down. Similarly in some men's series, individual songs are accompanied by instrumental tremolo in informal performances, and the swinging of bullroarers in formal presentations; here too, while the singers do not stay together as well as for rhythmically accompanied items, they appear to consider their efforts satisfactory. It is not certain, in the case of tremolo-accompanied women's songs, which particular ceremonial objects would be used in formal performances.

In general, men's series contain the most variety of accompaniment rhythms, while women's and mixed singing tend to use only two. Men's singing also includes types of rhythm not found elsewhere in the recorded sample. Within the limitations of scope of this study, it can be said that men's singing therefore involves more complex rhythmic accompaniment than that found in the women's and mixed repertoires.

Scales

It is in the nature of the musical style of an area or people that, despite surface variety in the different genres, and perhaps also the distinguishing of particular genres on musical grounds, there are common structural elements of a deeper nature which serve to give internal cohesion to the body of material as a whole. These two elements—variety and unity—are entirely complementary, the one allowing the creativity and individuality integral to any living art, and the other providing the underlying consistency necessary to sustain the sense of a single geographic or ethnic identity. Such a consistency in Pintupi music is perhaps best evinced in the derived scales for the 34 contours analysed in this study. Limiting discussion to those notes considered of structural importance in the respective scales, and listing the scales according to their number of notes, it is possible, in all but seven cases, to form a hierarchy growing by accretion from a two-note kernel (as already demonstrated in the Analysis section). However, such a hierarchy is but a symptom of a more significant reality: it represents the type of underlying consistency described earlier, in the form of a common scalic stock from which the melodies of four-fifths of the analysed sample are drawn.

Foreign influences

Foreign musical influences on the Pintupi today are undoubtedly stronger and more varied than in traditional times. Because of increased mobility on the one hand, and the establishment, on the other, of settlement areas containing a greater variety of peoples than might otherwise be found in any one location, there has been a compression of the time-scale during which contact with foreign ceremonial and musical idioms is made. Balgo Mission is perhaps an outstanding example of such a cosmopolitan settlement, where, with musical activity of some kind or other occurring almost daily, the permanent residents are at least exposed to, if not intimately familiar with, more musical styles and genres in a single lifetime than those of their parents' generation.

Attempts to discover the stylistic basis of Pintupi music as such have been aided by the presence of a relatively large body of material acknowledged as belonging to the Pintupi; further, the Pintupi's use of material which they consider to be either a 'mix-up' of more than one tribal origin, or of foreign origin, provides a convenient opportunity for comparison with any characteristics or patterning evident in the indigenous sample. The results of the analyses presented in the preceding sections of this volume indicate that identification of Pintupi music on stylistic grounds is a definite possibility; structural organisation on the basis of isorhythm is consistent in song series of known Pintupi origin, and inconsistent in series of mixed or suspected foreign origin. The word 'possibility' is used advisedly, since, in the virtual absence of other musical studies from the Central or Western Desert areas, the uniqueness of such a situation to the Pintupi, and thereby the reliability of the phenomenon as a positive identifier of Pintupi music, have yet to be confirmed.

Summary

The principal aim of the research behind this volume, and of the volume itself, was to establish the nature and variety of Pintupi music in its various cultural settings; the degree to which this may have been achieved will be for the individual reader to assess. While there have been a number of limitations on this research from within (in the form of time, geographical scope and linguistic ability), there have also been limitations of a more frustrating and serious nature imposed from without. Chief among these has been the dearth of base studies of the other Desert groups. It is apparent that the Central and Western Desert areas comprise an interlocking complex with not only common cultural, social and political features, but also a number of distinct groups who are shareholders in the same myths, and thus in the ceremonies and song series associated with those myths. To examine any one of these groups in isolation is therefore useful only insofar as that group is concerned. How the group relates to its neighbours will not be fully known until the neighbours too have been examined. If this volume sought to achieve any forward-looking purpose, it was to demonstrate the need for further base studies in the Aboriginal music of the Desert area.

Glossary of Pintupi terms

kalatjiti	The name of one *yilpintji* (q.v.) of Walbiri origin known by men at Kungkayunti.
kalaya	emu; also the name of one *yilpintji* (q.v.) of Walbiri origin known by men at Kungkayunti.
kali	boomerang.
kaltji	white ochre.
kipara	turkey; also the name of one initiation ceremony and song series.
kuna	anus; also the hand-grip of a boomerang.
kungkaku	literally, 'For a girl'; also the name of one *yilpintji* (q.v.) of Walbiri origin known by men at Kungkayunti.
kungka kutjarra	'two girls'; also the name of a *yilpintji* (q.v.).
kungkayunti	the name of a *yawulyu* and a specific place (q.v.).
kuniya	a type of snake; also a song series associated with healing.
kutatji	a sorcerer; the song series associated with sorcery is called *wanapa*.
kutitji	a shield; also the name of the ceremony signalling the start of the initiation period.
kutungulu	the so-called 'workers' or 'managers'; a moietal division whose counterpart is the *mayutju* (q.v.).
maanytja	the moon; also the name of a *yilpintji* (q.v.).
malu	kangaroo; also the name of one complex of initiation ceremonies and song series.
mama	father; also the name given to the principal owners of the *tjatiwanpa* ceremony (q.v.).
mangaya	'big one'; also the name given to the individual in charge of proceedings in the *tjatiwanpa* ceremony (q.v.).
marali	the name of a *yilpintji* (q.v.).
mayu	scent; melody.
mayutju	the so-called 'owners' of ceremonies and song series; a moietal division whose counterpart is the *kutungulu* (q.v.).
mungamunga	a woman's name and the name of a *yawulyu* (q.v.).
nintipuka	'learned one'; a tribal elder who has discovered a new song series and teaches it.
ngalungku	the collective term for the complex of secret initiation ceremonies and song series.
ngintaka	the perentie, a large type of lizard; also the name of one initiation ceremony and song series.
ngutulmaninpa	'ejaculating'; the term used for the style of rising accentuated glissands found in some initiation song series. The forms *ngutultjarra* and *ngutultjungkaman* are also found.
nyampinyi	the general term for female dancing.
pangaltjuninpa	the term used for the heavily accentuated enunciation associated with some initiation song series.
paniya	the name of a healing ceremony and song series associated with eye ailments.

papunpa	the generic term for song accompaniment devices using the hand or hands—hand-clapping and slapping the chest or crotch.	*warrmala*	an alternative name for the revenge expedition and its ceremony and song series; *see* also *pukalkarra*.
pukalkarra	a revenge expedition; also the associated ceremony and song series and for which *warrmala* is a synonym.	*wangata*	echidna; also the name of a *yilpintji* (q.v.).
		wantanturu	the name of one Walbiri *pulapa* (q.v.) known by men at Kungkayunti.
pulapa	the Walbiri equivalent of the Pintupi *tulku* (q.v.) genre.	*wantapi*	the generic name for ceremonies and song series at which men sing while women crotch-slap; at certain times, women are not allowed to observe the associated activities.
tarrkalpa	a song series claimed to originate outside Pintupi territory; it shares some characteristics of the *tulku* genre (q.v.).		
timpilpa	the beating together of boomerangs as song accompaniment.	*wantjiwantji*	the name of a *tulku* (q.v.).
		wayuta	possum; also the name of one initiation ceremony and song series.
tingarri	a specific type of Dreamtime being; ceremonies and song series relating their exploits are for men only.	*winparrku*	an alternative name for the *tjatiwanpa* (q.v.) ceremony; also the name for Blanche Tower, the starting point of the associated dreaming.
tulku	the generic name for song series and dancing open to all members of a community.		
tuyutu	the generic name for healing ceremonies and their song series.	*yarritjiti*	the name of the ceremony and song series occurring at the end of the initiation period.
tjatiwanpa	the name of a ceremony of probable Walbiri origin; it was traded to the Balgo community by the people of Yuendumu in exchange for one of Balgo's own ceremonies.	*yawarra*	a spear wound; also the name of the song series sung to aid healing such a wound.
		yawulyu	the generic name for exclusively female ceremonies and song series associated with love-magic.
tjiwiri	rain; also the name of a *tulku* (q.v.).		
tjukurrpa	the Dreamtime.	*yikuluku*	the eaglehawk; also the name of a *tulku* (q.v.).
wami	the name of one *yilpintji* (q.v.) of Yanmatjirri origin known by men at Kungkayunti.	*yilpintji*	the generic name for exclusively male ceremonies and song series associated with love-magic.
wanapa	a sorcerer; also the name of the ceremony and song series associated with ensorcelling; a synonym for *kutatji* (q.v.).	*yukurukuru*	the name of a healing ceremony and song series of Walbiri origin known by men at Kungkayunti.
		yunpu	a man's name; also the name of a *tulku* (q.v.).
wankara	the name of one *tulku* (q.v.) of Aranda origin known by men at Kungkayunti.	*yununtju*	the name of a *tulku* (q.v.).

Bibliography

Abbie, A. A. 1958 The Aborigines of South Australia. In *Introducing South Australia*, (ed.) R. J. Best, pp. 21-31. Melbourne: Melbourne University Press.
—— 1969. *The original Australians*. London: Muller.

Apel, W. (ed.) 1965 *The Harvard dictionary of music*. London: Heinemann.

Barrett, M. J. 1964 Walbiri customs and beliefs concerning teeth. *Mankind*, 6(3): 95-100.

Bates, D. 1938 *The passing of the Aborigines*. London: John Murray.

Berndt, C. H. 1965 Women and the 'secret life'. In *Aboriginal man in Australia*, (ed.) R. M. and C. H. Berndt, pp. 238-82. Sydney: Angus and Robertson.

Berndt, R. M. 1959 The concept of 'the tribe' in the Western Desert of Australia. *Oceania*, 30: 81-107.
—— 1970 Traditional morality as expressed through the medium of an Australian Aboriginal religion. In *Australian Aboriginal anthropology*, (ed.) R. M. Berndt, pp. 216-47. Nedlands: University of Western Australia Press.
—— 1974 *Australian Aboriginal religion*. Leiden: E. J. Brill.
—— 1976 Territoriality and the problem of demarcating sociocultural space. In *Tribes and boundaries in Australia*, (ed.) N. Peterson, pp. 133-61. Canberra: Australian Institute of Aboriginal Studies.

Berndt, R. M. and C. H. Berndt. 1943 A preliminary report on field work in the Ooldea region, western South Australia. *Oceania*, 14: 124-58.
—— and —— 1964 *The world of the first Australians: an introduction to the traditional life of the Australian Aborigines*. Sydney: Ure Smith.
—— and —— (eds) 1965. *Aboriginal man in Australia*. Sydney: Angus and Robertson.

Birdsell, J. B. 1970 Local group composition among the Australian Aborigines: a critique of the evidence from fieldwork conducted since 1930. *Current Anthropology*, 11(2): 115-42.

Central Reserves Committee ?1965 *The Central Australian Aboriginal Reserves*. Perth: Government Printer.

Christensen, D. 1964 *Die Musik der Ellice Inseln*. Berlin: Museum für Völkerkunde.

Clune, F. P. 1942 *Last of the Australian explorers; the story of David MacKay*. Sydney: Angus and Robertson.

Davies, E. H. 1927 Aboriginal songs. *Journal of the Royal Society of South Australia*, 51: 81-92.

Dean, B. and V. Carell 1955 *Dust for the dancers*. Sydney: Ure Smith.

de Graaf, M. 1968 *The Ngadadara of the Warburton Ranges*. Unpublished B.A. thesis, University of Western Australia.

Densmore, F. 1918 *Teton Sioux music*. Washington: Government Printing Office.

Elkin, A. P. 1964 *The Australian Aborigines*. Natural History Library edition.

Ellis, C. J. 1963 Ornamentation in Australian vocal music. *Journal of the Society for Ethnomusicology* 7(2): 88-95.

—— 1964a *Aboriginal music making: a study of central Australian music*. Adelaide: Libraries Board of South Australia.

—— 1964b Ethnomusicology and its application in Australia. *Journal of the Anthropological Society of South Australia*, 2(7): 2-12.

—— 1966. Central and South Australian song styles. *Anthropological Society of South Australia*, Journal, 4(7): 2-11.

—— 1967 Folk song migration in Aboriginal South Australia. *Journal of the International Folk Music Council*, 19:11-16.

—— 1968. Rhythmic analysis of Aboriginal syllabic songs. *Miscellanea musicologica*, 3: 21-49.

—— 1969a Structure and significance in Aboriginal song. *Mankind*, 7(1): 3-14.

—— 1969b Non-specialist music teaching in Aboriginal schools. *South Australian Education*, 3: 9-22.

Ellis, C. J., A. M. Ellis, M. Tur and A. McCardell 1978 Classification of sounds in Pitjantjatjara-speaking areas. In *Australian Aboriginal concepts*, (ed.) L. R. Hiatt, pp. 68-80. Canberra: Australian Institute of Aboriginal Studies.

Ellis, C. J. and M. Tur 1975 The song is the message. In *Cultures in collision*, (ed.) I. Pilowsky, pp. 30-35. Adelaide: Australian National Association for Mental Health.

Ernabella Mission 1976 *Pitjantjatjara intensive course*. Alice Springs: Institute for Aboriginal Development.

Evans, E. C. 1960a A Northern Territory patrol. *Dawn*, 9(12): 16-22.

—— 1960b Report on overland patrol to Lake Mackay and Kintore Ranges. Northern Territory Administration, Welfare Branch.

Evans, E. C. and J. P. M. Long 1965 The Aborigines of Western Central Australia. *Geographical Journal*, September: 318-29.

Hansen, K. C. and L. E. Hansen 1969 Pintupi phonology. *Oceania Linguistics*, 8(2): 153-70.

—— and —— 1974 *Pintupi dictionary*. Darwin: Summer Institute of Linguistics.

—— and —— 1978 *The core of Pintupi grammar*. Alice Springs: Institute for Aboriginal Development.

Hiatt, L. R. 1965 *Kinship and conflict: a study of an Aboriginal community in Northern Arnhem Land*. Canberra: Australian National University Press.

Johnson, J. E. 1963 Observations and some Aboriginal campsites in South Australia and adjoining States. *Mankind*, 6(2): 64-79; 6(4): 154-81.

Jones, T. A. 1962 A brief survey of ethnomusicological research in the music of Aboriginal Australia. In *Australian Aboriginal studies*, (ed.) H. M. Shields, pp. 281-304. London: Oxford University Press.

—— 1965 Australian Aboriginal music: The Elkin Collection's contribution toward an overall picture. In *Aboriginal man in Australia*, (eds) R. M. Berndt and C. H. Berndt, pp. 285-374. Sydney: Angus and Robertson.

—— 1968 The nature of Australian Aboriginal music. *The Australian Journal of Music Education*, 2: 9-13.

Kennedy, K. 1933 Instruments of music used by the Australian Aborigines. *Mankind*, 1(7): 147-57.

Kolinski, M. 1959 The evaluation of tempo. *Ethnomusicology*, 3: 45-57.

—— 1964 The structure of melodic movement, a new method of analysis. *Studies in Ethnomusicology*, 2: 95-120.

Lockwood, D. 1964 *The lizard eaters*. Melbourne: Cassell.

Long, J. P. M. 1962 (Report on) Fieldwork West of Papunya June-July. Typescript, Australian Institute of Aboriginal Studies, Canberra.

—— 1963a Preliminary work in planning welfare development in the Petermann Ranges. *Australian Territories*, 3(2): 4-12.

—— 1963b Report on first patrol west of Papunya. Typescript, Australian Institute of Aboriginal Studies, Canberra.

—— 1963c Report on patrols west of Papunya. Typescript, Australian Institute of Aboriginal Studies.

—— 1964a Papunya: westernization in an Aboriginal community. In *Aborigines now: new perspective in the study of Aboriginal communities*, (ed.) M. Reay, pp. 72-82. Sydney: Angus and Robertson.

—— 1964b Report on patrols west of Papunya. Typescript, Australian Institute of Aboriginal Studies, Canberra.

—— 1964c The Pintubi patrols: welfare work with desert Aborigines. *Australian Territories*, 4(5): 43-48.

—— 1964d The Pintubi patrols: welfare work with desert Aborigines—the later phases. *Australian Territories*, 4(6):24-35.

—— 1969 Interim report on fieldwork in Central Australia, April-May. Typescript, Australian Institute of Aboriginal Studies, Canberra.

—— 1970 Change in an Aboriginal community in central Australia. In *Diprotodon to detribalization: studies of change among Australian Aborigines*, (eds) A. R. Pilling and R. A. Waterman, pp. 318-32. East Lansing: Michigan State University Press.

—— 1971 Arid region Aborigines: the Pintubi. In *Aboriginal man and environment*, (eds) D. J. Mulvaney and J. Golson, pp. 262-70. Canberra: Australian National University Press.

McCarthy, F. 1939 'Trade' in Aboriginal Australia, and 'trade' relationships with Torres Strait, New Guinea and Malaya. *Oceania*, 10(1): 80-104.

MacKay, D. 1929 The MacKay exploring expedition; Central Australia 1926. *Geographical Journal*, 73: 258-64.

Meggitt, M. J. 1962 *Desert People: a study of the Walbiri Aborigines of central Australia*. Chicago: University of Chicago Press.

Merriam, A. P. 1967 *Ethnomusicology of the Flathead Indians*. Chicago: Aldine (Viking Fund. Publ. 44).

Micha, F. J. 1970 Trade and change in Australian Aboriginal cultures: Australian Aboriginal trade as an expression of close culture contact and as a mediator of culture change. In *Diprotodon to detribalization: studies of change among Australian Aborigines*, (eds) A. R. Pilling and R. A. Waterman, pp. 285-313. East Lansing: Michigan State University Press.

Milliken, E. P. 1976 Aboriginal language distribution in the Northern Territory. In *Tribes and boundaries in Australia*, (ed.) N. Peterson, pp. 239-42. Canberra: Australian Institute of Aboriginal Studies.

Morice, R. D. 1976 Woman dancing dreaming: psychosocial benefits of the Aboriginal outstation movement. *The Medical Journal of Australia*, 2: 939-42.

Mountford, C. P. 1968 *Winbaraku and the myth of Jarapiri*. Adelaide: Rigby.

—— 1976 *Nomads of the Australian desert*. Adelaide: Rigby.

Moyle, A. M. 1966 *A handlist of field collections of recorded music in Australia and Torres Strait*. Canberra: Australian Institute of Aboriginal Studies.

—— 1973 AM Card Index: Copy Sheets. Listings of tape-recorded Aboriginal music collected in the field by Alice M. Moyle AIAS Library. Canberra: Australian Institute of Aboriginal Studies.

—— 1974 *North Australian music*. Unpublished Ph.D. thesis, Monash University.

Munn, N. D. 1973 *Walbiri iconography: graphic representation and cultural symbolism in a central Australian society*. Ithaca: Cornell University Press.

Nettl, B. 1956 Music in primitive culture. Cambridge (Mass.): Harvard University Press.

Oates, L. F. 1975 *The 1973 supplement to a revised linguistic survey of Australia*, 2 vols. Armidale: Armidale Christian Book Centre.

Oates, W. J. and L. F. Oates 1970 *A revised linguistic survey of Australia*. Canberra: Australian Institute of Aboriginal Studies.

O'Grady, G. N., C. F. Voegelin and F. M. Voegelin 1966 Languages of the world: Indo-Pacific fasicle. *Anthropological Linguistics*, 8(2): 1-197.

Rose, F. G. G. 1965 *The wind of change in central Australia: the Aborigines at Angas Downs*, 1962. Berlin: Akademie-Verlag.

Sachs, C. 1953 *Rhythm and tempo. A study in music history*. New York: Norton.

Scholes, P. A. 1955 (ed.) *The concise Oxford dictionary of music*. London: Oxford University Press.

Spencer, W. B. and F. J. Gillen 1899 *The native tribes of Central Australia*. London: Macmillan.

Strehlow, T. G. H. 1933 Ankotarinja, an Aranda myth. *Oceania*, 4(2): 187-200.
—— 1955 Australian Aboriginal songs. *Journal of the International Folk Music Council*, 7: 37-40.
—— 1965 Culture, social structure, and environment in Aboriginal central Australia. In *Aboriginal man in Australia*, (eds) R. M. Berndt and C. H. Berndt, pp. 121-45. Sydney: Angus and Robertson.
—— 1969 Mythology of the centralian Aborigine. *Inland Review*, 3(11): 11-17.
—— 1970 Geography and the totemic landscape in Aboriginal central Australia: a functional study. In *Australian Aboriginal Anthropology*, (ed.) R. M. Berndt, pp. 92-140. Nedlands: University of Western Australia Press.
—— 1971 *Songs of central Australia*. Sydney: Angus and Robertson.

Tate, H. 1951 Australian Aboriginal music. *Canon*, 5: 249-52.

Terry, M. 1974 *War of the Warramullas*. Adelaide: Rigby.

Thomson, D. F. 1962 The Bindibu expedition. *Geographical Journal*, 128(2): 143-57.
—— 1964 Some wood and stone implements of the Bindibu tribe of Central Western Australia. *Proceedings of the Prehistoric Society*, 30(17): 400-22.
—— 1975 *Bindibu country*. Melbourne: Nelson.

Tindale, N. B. 1974 *Aboriginal tribes of Australia*. California: University of California Press.

Tindale, N. B. and H. A. Lindsay 1963 *Aboriginal Australians*. Brisbane: The Jacaranda Press.

Tonkinson, R. 1974 *The Jigalong mob: Aboriginal victors of the desert crusade*. Henlo Park (California): Cummings.

Waterman, R. A. 1958 Music in Australian Aboriginal culture—some sociological and psychological implications. *American Anthropologist*, 60(3): 518-32.

Index

Page numbers in italic denote a major entry on a particular topic.

3830.—

19.95 A. $ / 8506/8

19.95 A. $ / 8506/8